Houston, Is There
A Problem?

LEADING WITH HEART

LEADING
WITH
HEART

Five Conversations that
Unlock Creativity, Purpose,
and Results

JOHN BAIRD AND EDWARD SULLIVAN

HARPER
BUSINESS
An Imprint of HarperCollins*Publishers*

HarperCollins books may be purchased for educational, business, or sales promotional use. For information, please email the Special Markets Department at SPsales@harpercollins.com.

FIRST EDITION

Library of Congress Cataloging-in-Publication Data has been applied for.

ISBN 978-0-06-305293-2

22 23 24 25 26   LSC   10 9 8 7 6 5 4 3 2 1

This book is dedicated to the brave souls who began showing up at work as they really are, with authenticity, curiosity, and open hearts, long before it was on trend or even safe to do so. You made the conversations we humbly attempt to capture in these pages possible.

And to our clients who have allowed us to witness their genius, courage, and growth over the last twenty-plus years. You are the leaders of our today and the builders of our tomorrow.

CONTENTS

LEADING WITH HEART

INTRODUCTION

It is only with the heart that one can see rightly; what is
essential is invisible to the eye.

—ANTOINE DE SAINT-EXUPÉRY, *THE LITTLE PRINCE*

Tucked between the Old Town Bar and ABC Kitchen in New York's Flatiron District is a nondescript white door marked with the number 37. When you ring the bell, the door buzzes open, and a waiting elevator takes you up to the fourth floor. You're now inside the Hive—a stunning loft office space with soaring ceilings, soothing pastel colors, dozens of plants, and roughly a hundred humans buzzing around, ranging in age from twenty-two to sixty-two.

Some employees clack away at their computers. Others laugh and chat loudly—the Hive can get pretty noisy. Just outside the kitchen a few people attend to a huge jigsaw puzzle. And beside the floor-to-ceiling windows still other members of the Hive perch at one of the drafting tables surrounded by stacks of clothing samples—socks, underwear, T-shirts.

Plush fabrics. Happy people. Cold brew and kombucha on tap. You probably have a life outside the Hive, but you could just as easily set up shop here forever.

In New York, it's often the most unassuming doors that lead to the most spectacular interiors, and the guy you're here to meet falls into that category, as well. Judging by his loose-fitting sweat-shirt, khaki pants, and comfy sneakers, you might mistake Dave Heath for a coder or a designer. Anything but the CEO of a multimillion-dollar apparel brand.

Dave's company, Bombas, started out selling socks online al-most ten years ago. Today, along with socks, they have a boom-ing business in T-shirts and underwear. You might be thinking, Millions of dollars? That's a lot of socks. Yes, it is. But Dave puts it another way: "We are cornering the market on comfort." And if that weren't enough, Bombas gives away one item to a homeless shelter for every one they sell.

Watching Dave move through the Hive is a little bit like watch-ing a dedicated gardener navigating a greenhouse full of roses. A gardener sees and studies every flower, taking in and appreciating their unique qualities. This damask rose might need more water, that Juliet rose more light, and the batch of Black Beauties a touch more fertilizer. Just as a gardener makes sure every flower has exactly what it needs to thrive, Dave does the same with each and every team member so that they can bloom more fully.

Everyone he encounters seems genuinely thrilled to stop and chat. No one looks intimidated. No one gathers in a tense semi-circle, competing for his attention. More importantly, Dave ap-pears genuinely interested in all of them. As he glides through the room, he seems to trail some kind of CEO pixie dust that leaves the people in his wake feeling validated, motivated, and, if possible, even more committed to the company than they were before.

Dave pauses to sprinkle some of that pixie dust on his head of marketing, Kate Huyett. Kate is a former Goldman Sachs invest-ment banker turned digital advertising guru. Years earlier, when she left Wall Street to put her quantitative mind to work on marketing analytics, Dave saw something special in her. Kate is reserved, but deeply insightful. When she speaks, everyone leans in to hear what's on her mind.

"What's the best way to handle a situation with an employee who has an increasingly negative attitude?" she asks Dave.

He fields her question with some of his own. "Well, what does that employee really need right now? What's behind their negative attitude? Are they not feeling heard? Do you think they're in the right role?"

It's typical Dave. Instead of jumping in with the answers, he always looks to uncover the subtext. He's eternally curious about what is going unsaid and responds with a series of targeted, insightful questions. Questions that invite conversation.

- What need isn't being met?
- What fear holds that person back?
- What is really driving that person?
- What gift is going unexpressed?
- What is that person's real purpose?

It's this supernatural curiosity and empathy that his team responds to, and it's at least partly responsible for the loyalty and commitment Bombas employees feel. Not only does Dave do this for his own team, but he also coaches his executives to use the same methods with their direct reports.

In a short period Bombas has become a breakout success in the direct-to-consumer category, while many of its peers have made big splashes, only to dry up later. Bombas has done it while winning numerous Best Place to Work accolades and chalking up some of the lowest employee turnover in the industry.

We believe this is because CEO Dave Heath *leads with heart*.

Let's contrast Dave with another of our clients. Since it's not the most flattering story, we'll call him Joe, out of respect and confidentiality.

When we met him, Joe ran a small public health-care company. Looking at Joe, talking to Joe, spending time with Joe, you'd think this guy had all the trappings of a successful CEO.

Stanford degree. Professional presentation. Deep domain expertise. Superconnected network. Process-oriented mindset. The determination and grit of a Scottish border collie.

Name a classic skill or trait of a successful leader that you'd find in all the business books—Joe had it. And operationally, Joe had implemented many of the latest best practices for organizing the team and their time. They had stand-ups and sprints. They had values that included words like *candor*, *empower*, and *celebrate*. They even had kombucha on tap.

But after some early success bringing a few new treatments for cancer and Parkinson's to market, Joe's company was going through a rough patch. Morale was at an all-time low, turnover was hovering at 50 percent, and most employees who did stick around were just calling it in.

Employees felt frustrated. Few felt "seen" or "empowered," in their words. Instead of working collaboratively, most sat alone quietly at their desks, writing long emails or swapping rapid-fire Slack messages with colleagues, some of whom were sitting three feet away. Meetings often ended without clear decisions or to-dos. Checked-out team members took two-hour lunches. And as a result, sales continued to dwindle.

Joe called us in to help with the "morale and performance issue." He was frustrated by "having to do everything." According to Joe, no one saw the business the way he did. No one had an eye for quality like he did. No matter how much time his team put into a press release, Joe had to rewrite it. Basically, no matter what happened, Joe found a flaw in it.

When we talked to his team, it was clear how dedicated they were to the company's vision and to their patients. Many of them got emotional when they talked about their sense of service and purpose. Some had family members who had died of cancer. Others had parents or grandparents with Parkinson's.

They also shared that Joe was one of the smartest and most charismatic people they'd ever met (literally, he was!), but he also made sure everyone knew it. Instead of showing any curiosity about his team—what they were good at, what motivated them, what they needed to flourish—and showing that he cared about them as people, Joe simply went around thinking big thoughts and barking orders.

And when members of his team quietly recused themselves, stopped putting forth great ideas, or left the company altogether, Joe still had no idea that he was part of the problem.

By our humble estimation, Joe did not lead with heart.

Dave's company is one of the great success stories in the very difficult direct-to-consumer category. Joe's company is languishing in a market with high margins and nearly limitless demand. Dave's company has had record low voluntary turnover, compared to peers. Employee turnover at Joe's company hovers around 50 percent. Dave finds himself less and less at the center of important decisions, giving him more and more time to think strategically about the long term. Joe is mired in the details because no one feels empowered to make any decisions without him.

What makes one person with no formal training or experience such an exemplary leader, while another with all the classic leadership skills and traits turns out to be such a poor one?

Answering that question is the crux of this book. And it has never come at a more important time.

Today's Growing Leadership Crisis

There is no arguing that we are in the middle of a leadership crisis. And not just in politics but in the business world, as well. We know this first and foremost because people aren't excited about their work. According to Gallup, two in three Americans are not "involved in and enthusiastic about their work and workplace," and 50 percent are actively looking for a new job. A separate report by the Society for Human Resource Management indicates that 25 percent of American workers actually "dread going to work" because they "don't feel safe voicing their opinions about work-related issues and don't feel respected and valued at work." In the same report, 84 percent of employees say that bad managers create unnecessary stress for them.

And while it's hard to quantify exactly how much these feelings of dread and disengagement cost, Gallup estimates that voluntary turnover (people quitting) costs the economy in aggregate $1 trillion every year—and this data was from *before* "The Great Resignation" of 2021. What's more, disengaged employees who do stay put another 10 percent drag on business through low productivity.

When we investigate why so many people feel anxious, disengaged, and disrespected, the problem is clear: too many people work for leaders like Joe—leaders who are disempowering, lacking curiosity, and simply unwilling or unable to establish real emotional connections with their teams.

Employees want to feel seen and appreciated for who they are and for the unique things they can contribute. Yet far too many leaders treat their teams as little more than cogs in a machine.

As coaches who have been working on the front lines of business and politics for decades, we decided it was time to figure out exactly why some leaders are able to make that heart connection, and why others can't.

About Us and Our Work

But before going much further, it might be a good idea to introduce ourselves. We're John and Edward. John was recruited into coaching more than thirty years ago when he left his business school professorship at San Jose State to help Apple University develop a leadership curriculum. His first coaching firm was born out of this Apple experience. He's a photography buff who values time with his family and grandchildren.

Edward entered leadership coaching nearly fifteen years ago, first advising political candidates domestically and around the world alongside James Carville, the Ragin' Cajun, and then spending close to a decade working with start-up founders and Fortune 500 executives in Silicon Valley and New York.

John is the data-driven academic, Edward the instincts-driven operator. And despite our differences, the two of us have at least one important thing in common: we're both passionate about unlocking the potential and creativity of leaders. Though we would never claim to know everything about leadership, we have been fortunate enough to spend most of our careers working alongside some truly exceptional leaders, from giants like Tim Cook, Steve Jobs, and Phil Knight to soon-to-be household names like Valerie Ashby, Justin McLeod, and Tony Xu.

Our book journey began, like many journeys do, with a question: What separates truly transformational leaders from the rest?

Every year literally thousands of books, articles, and blogs are published espousing the proven technique for everything from leading companies and parenting children to swinging a golf club and roasting chicken. We've been led to believe by legions of self-proclaimed experts that there's a right and wrong way to do nearly everything. Yet, as author and former Harvard professor Phil Rosenzweig put it, "for all the secrets and formulas, for all the self-proclaimed thought leadership, success in business is as elusive as ever . . . probably *more* elusive than ever."

With so much advice out there, why is great leadership so scarce?

Driven by that question, we decided to pressure-test some of those leadership how-to guides and listicles of simple leadership hacks. We looked deeply into the volumes of notes and data we've collected over our combined forty years working with many of the world's top leaders in business and politics to look for trends. If there were commonalities in behavior and habits among our most successful clients, we would surely find them.

But after poring over the data, we observed that the leaders with the best bottom-line business and organizational outcomes (i.e., in terms of growth, exits, retention, and employee satisfaction) were all over the map in what we think of as normal leadership behaviors or habits. Take a dozen great leaders, and you'll find they lead in a wide variety of ways.

- Some are extroverted inspirational speakers, and others are introverts who are more comfortable communicating via written memos or private conversations.
- Some set crystal-clear visions for the future and chart a bold path forward, while others make general observations about a problem area or customer profile and let their teams figure out the innovative solutions.
- Some have fixed morning routines, waking up at 5:00 a.m. to meditate, jump on their Pelotons, or do sun salutations. Others roll out of bed when they feel like it and show up at the office overcaffeinated and frazzled.

Everywhere we looked in the data for common traits or behaviors among our clients—the traditional dos and don'ts of leadership and executive presence—we encountered more variance than anything else.

What were we not *seeing*?

Redoubling our efforts, we delved even more deeply into our coaching archives—more files, more paper—but this time we asked a different question: What do the *teams* of great leaders— that is, the people closest to them, the people inspired by them every day—have to say about these leaders?

The answer, we realized, was right in front of us the whole time, hidden in plain sight:

- "He's incredibly self-aware and isn't afraid to take a hard look at himself."
- "She saw a potential in me I didn't see in myself."
- "He always knows exactly what I need to hear to get motivated again."
- "She helped me overcome my self-doubt and begin to believe in myself."
- "He's able to ask me questions and give me feedback in a way that helps me grow as a person and a professional."

It didn't matter whether these leaders were compelling public speakers, took a different employee to lunch every day, or placed their desk in the middle of the office to show how accessible they were. It wasn't in their tactics, habits, and hacks.

Instead, our data showed us that great leaders have five core characteristics that help them *connect at an authentic human level with their people*:

1. **They are aware of their people's needs.** They get curious about what they and their teams need to feel creative and resourceful. Getting our needs met is the foundation of all higher-order thinking and working. When you aren't taking care of yourself

or don't feel safe, you can't show up with your A game. You're not going to ask the hard questions or make the risky suggestions.

2. **They confront their people's fears.** They directly address the fears that are holding people back. Fear keeps us from taking risks and compels us to do hurtful things and make bad decisions. If your team members don't feel safe saying something when they smell smoke, you will always be putting out fires.

3. **They understand their own desires and what drives their people.** They get very honest about what their core desires and drivers are, as well as those of their team. What's more, they make sure to keep those desires in check, lest they or their team be derailed by them.

4. **They leverage their gifts.** They search deeply inside themselves and their teams for unrealized gifts. World-class skill and talent is often wasted because it goes undiscovered. Leading with heart requires giving up the idea of what you are good at to unearth what you might be great at.

5. **They connect with purpose.** Finally, they connect with their own core sense of purpose, and help their teams connect with theirs. The greatest work is done by teams who believe they are serving some greater good. The easiest mistake to make is to assume all your team cares about is money or prestige.

Armed with this unique array of abilities, the great leaders we've worked with make people feel seen, inspire creative thinking, unlock purpose, and ultimately drive bottom-line business results. There was the tech CEO with the incredible penchant for seeing talents and gifts in her people that they weren't aware of in themselves, often placing people in new positions and unlocking a new and powerful potential. Or the dating app CEO who, seeing that his top-down approach was killing morale and creativity, began pushing all product and design questions down into his team, giving them much-needed agency and authority. Or the social network founder who realized that his fear of failure was preventing him and his team from taking risks, making bold hires, and learning from customer feedback.

There were literally hundreds of examples.

What we learned is that much more than following formulas or playbooks, the greatest leaders of our time are simply the most relentlessly curious, caring, and insightful about themselves and their people. They have the courage and inquisitiveness to engage in conversations that are often considered taboo in the workplace. Conversations about what we really need to feel safe and creative, what we're afraid of, what we most deeply desire, what we're best at, and what our highest purpose is. Conversations that enable them to transform themselves, their teams, and their organizations.

That is what we mean by leading with heart.

A Little Heart Makes a Big Difference

Leading with heart isn't just about being chummy or making people feel good. It's about creating an environment of safety and connection versus fear and isolation. And lest you think this is all fluff, let's look at what a difference leading with heart makes in company culture and bottom-line business outcomes compared to fear-led companies.

CHARACTERISTICS AND OUTCOMES

HEART-LED COMPANIES	FEAR-LED COMPANIES
Lower turnover	Higher turnover
Decentralized decision-making	Inefficient overreliance on authority
Employees feel empowered to take smart risks and experiment	Risk avoidance and little experimentation and innovation
Healthy and constructive creative conflict	Absence of conflict and/or toxic backstabbing and secrecy
Rigorous debate and truth-seeking in meetings	Awkward silence and approval-seeking in meetings
Strategic alignment	Competing priorities
Sharing of resources to support company goals	Hoarding of resources to support departmental goals
Seamless flow of crucial information leading to early problem detection	Withholding of crucial information leading to unnecessary crises

As you see, leading with heart is not about creating an environment of permissiveness, navel-gazing, or low performance. It's about taking off the blinders of fear, scarcity, and ego and connecting as people. It's about creating breakthroughs for ourselves and our organizations. It's about putting aside all the meetings and to-do lists for a few minutes to connect at a deeper level—a more real and authentic level. Which, ironically, makes the process of completing all the tasks on those to-do lists that much easier.

The Conversations that Unlock Creativity, Purpose, and Results

When faced with a crisis, most of us want to know what to do. We want answers. But as coaches, our job is not to give answers. Our job is to hold up a mirror, ask the right questions, and help our clients find the answers in themselves through the power of conversation. So, in those moments when you just want an easy answer or a simple hack, our response to you will always be the same one we give to our clients: What is it you're not seeing right now? What are the conversations you need to have to lead with more heart?

Think of this book as a private coaching session. Over the next few chapters, we will walk you through the exact same process we ask the leaders we coach to undergo. We'll be inviting you to join conversations designed to help you gain valuable insights both about yourself and your teams.

While there are an infinite number of conversations we could have to help you get curious and achieve new insights about yourself and your teams, we've found there are five that go the furthest in unlocking new ways of seeing ourselves and others. These conversations correspond directly with the five core characteristics of the most successful leaders we've worked with.

Perhaps some people were born with a natural ability to gain insight into themselves and others, but we haven't met them yet. The rest of us need a process of inquiry to reach these insights—and the conversations we've outlined below and explore in great detail throughout this book are that process.

The *Five Conversations that Unlock Creativity, Purpose, and Results* all begin with deceptively simple questions, but don't be fooled—each question is designed to pierce the surface and go a few layers deep. Each question will likely lead to another, and then another, unfolding into a rich conversation that will help you see yourself and your teams in a more authentic and honest light. As you delve deeper into each area, we hope you gain greater and greater insights that unlock new potential for you and your teams and remove the barriers that may have kept you from leading with heart.

WHAT DO YOU NEED TO BE AT YOUR BEST?

When a houseplant wilts, we don't yell at it, offer it more money, or put it on a performance improvement plan. We give it more water, move it closer to the sun, and make sure it's getting the nutrients it needs until the leaves perk up and regain their color.

The same goes for us as people. Leading with heart is hard work. It takes a lot of energy to be courageous, curious, and vulnerable—to have the tough conversations. For this reason, we need to be very mindful that we are getting our physical, emotional, and environmental needs met, lest we descend into unproductive behavior.

When faced with difficulty with a colleague, instead of playing the blame game, what if we got curious to see if each of us was getting our needs met? What if we asked ourselves on a regular basis what we and our teams really need to succeed? To thrive?

Are we eating and sleeping well? When's the last time we exercised? Do we need more unstructured time together? How about fewer Zoom calls? Longer lunches? Less Slack? More direction? Hour-long walks in the afternoon? Twenty minutes of meditation? Kombucha and cold brew on tap?

To help you contemplate the question "What do you need to succeed?" we'll offer various tools designed to help you discern your deepest needs and those of your colleagues. And more importantly, we'll spend some time exploring why we don't get our needs met even when we know what to do. What are the competing commitments we have that sabotage our best efforts to get more rest, surround ourselves with supportive people, or live in a place that inspires us?

Having honest conversations about what we really need sets us up to have even richer conversations about our fears, desires, gifts, and purpose.

WHAT FEARS ARE HOLDING YOU BACK?

Now and then, fear holds *all* of us back. We create negative or self-limiting stories about ourselves. By uncovering what frightens us and by getting radically curious about the fears of our teams, we can begin ridding ourselves of blocks, untruths, and old defeatist stories that weigh on us, as well as all the unhelpful behaviors we engage in when we are triggered in response to our fears.

At an organizational level, the unacknowledged fears of executives often lead to conflict aversion, perfectionism, self-righteousness, not asking for help, and impostor syndrome. These often show up in an organization's cultural norms and lead to widespread risk avoidance, inability to give and receive feedback, and lack of constructive debates.

In this chapter, we explore the three fundamental fear responses and their distinctive tells. (In poker, a tell is a visual signal that indicates when another player is bluffing.) By exploring the stories of how some of our clients have dealt with fear through coaching, you'll discover the differences between leaders who are derailed by fear and those who learn to cope with and even overcome their fears.

We'll be asking you to ponder a few hard questions too: What fears are holding you back? In what ways are you afraid of being judged by others? What stories do you tell about yourself that you're scared to let go of? What are the coping mechanisms you rely on that could be good signals to you or to others that you're triggered?

We'll also discuss how to recognize when someone else is being triggered by fear, and how you might cope with that. What are the telltale signs? How do we talk someone down and connect with them again from a place of curiosity and openness?

WHAT DESIRES DRIVE YOU, AND WHICH ONES MIGHT DERAIL YOU?

Our deepest desires can be incredible sources of motivation. Feeling like we are winning, like we are contributing, like we have influence—these can get us out of bed in the morning. But if we let our desires get out of hand, we can get derailed.

In this chapter, we'll explore the five core desires that motivate much of our behavior. These include the desire to belong, to have influence, to win, to grow and learn, and to be of service. By having conversations about your desires and those of your team, you'll tap into a much deeper fount of inspiration. And by understanding the line between healthy and unhealthy expressions of your desires, you'll learn how to have boundaries and avoid falling into unhealthy patterns.

This chapter wouldn't be complete if we didn't bring in a few cautionary tales from Silicon Valley that show how fanning the flames of desire—to be liked, to be right, to take crazy risks, to dominate other people—can lead to self-sabotage.

WHAT ARE YOUR GREATEST GIFTS?

The greatest leaders we've worked with have had an uncanny ability to find the unrecognized gifts in their people. They see past what people think they are good at and find something instead that they are *great* at. And when self-limiting beliefs and the voice of doubt come up for their people, these leaders help them overcome those fears of failure and gain the courage to make the leap.

Our gifts sometimes come from curious places. From our

grief, our flaws, and even our darkest moments. We'll learn why we often discount the value of our own gifts, and we will explore how to take off the blinders and see ourselves and our colleagues more clearly.

Having conversations about our gifts can feel boastful. Naming the gifts in others can seem like flattery. Which is often why we shy away from these conversations. In this chapter, we will give you tools to have rich conversations that go beyond boasting and flattery and help us get real and own our gifts and those of others without ego.

WHAT IS YOUR PURPOSE?

People who experience a greater sense of "meaning and purpose" in their work are generally more committed and satisfied with their jobs. They also live longer, happier lives. The question is, what creates that sense of meaning and purpose in the first place?

Conversations around purpose are really about what impact we seek to have on the world. *What am I (or are we) here to do? Who am I (or are we) here to serve?*

In this chapter, you will meet the CEOs of companies that seek to create an impact in one underserved community, and others whose mission is the betterment of all of humanity. We'll also explore how a wide range of people—artists, actors, hedge fund managers, computer scientists, and others—uncover meaning in their work, and how they reignite that spark when it goes out.

Together, these five deceivingly simple conversations are designed to give you and your team insight into what makes both *you* and *them* tick. By looking deeply inside yourself and your people, uncovering your higher purpose, gifts, core desires, fears, and needs, you will be equipped with a new set of tools to help you refocus your perspective, your energy, and even your career.

We will end the book with an exploration around what it takes to lead the entire company with heart—the organizational-level applications of our five essential conversations. You will learn from our clients how they use this framework to manage and resolve conflict, improve diversity and inclusion, drive higher performance, and elevate morale in times of crisis, stress, and ambiguity. This chapter will center around a number of powerful exercises that will help you apply the Leading with Heart principles to your entire company.

Why Leading with Heart Is Hard

Leading with heart doesn't come naturally to most people for two main reasons: (1) The Work/Life Myth, and (2) Blindsets.

THE WORK/LIFE MYTH

First, leading with heart goes against what most of us have been taught about what we like to call the "work/life myth." We've all been led to believe that we should have a work self and a home self, and never the twain shall meet.

For well over a century, there has been a very clear distinction between our work life and our real life. Around the dinner table or on vacation, our real life might be interrupted by the dreaded "work call." Or if a family member or friend calls you at the office with a nonemergency, you might whisper into the phone, "I told you not to call me at work."

Similarly, until a few decades ago nearly all workers would suit up in some way before going to work, men and women alike donning specific uniforms to show that they were in work mode. In the 1950s we saw the advent of the business suit. In the 1980s we dialed it back to business casual. Lately in Silicon Valley, the cashmere hoodie, black jeans, and $200 sneakers have become the work outfit du jour.

While these psychological divisions between work and home can create an atmosphere of focus, discipline, and productivity—which is one reason why the military has uniforms—they also send one overarching message: It's not okay to be yourself at work. As a result, most of us psychologically suit up before going to work too.

Clients tell us this all the time: "I feel like I need to put on a coat of armor before going into work." "Walking into that office, I have to get into wartime mode." Or simply, "I'm doing all I can to stay professional given how much turmoil I'm going through at home." No matter what clothes we're wearing, we are all still psychologically suiting up.

The global pandemic of 2020 accelerated the dissolution of the work/life myth for many. For the first time, we began to see the insides of each other's homes on Zoom. CEOs did shareholder updates from their bedrooms. TV anchors had kids and cats climb into their laps on live television. Many of us didn't change out of our sweats for months at a time.

Yet although many of us enjoy hybrid work models now, that emotional division remains. There are still topics we are not supposed to talk about at work, fears and insecurities we are not supposed to share, needs we are not supposed to express.

Given this complex set of rules we've imposed on ourselves, it's no wonder leading with heart is hard. Our hope is that this book will give you and your colleagues a language to explore dismantling those rules and inviting each other to more heart-led conversations.

BLINDSETS

Even if we try to dissolve this imaginary separation between our work selves and our true selves, most of us have what we call "blindsets," default settings that keep us from seeing ourselves and others clearly. In our coaching lexicon, a blindset is any belief system or mindset that makes it difficult for us to clearly see the answers to the Leading with Heart questions outlined above.

Sometimes leaders have a *fantasy blindset*—they are overly optimistic and see what they want to see. A leader living in a fantasy world may think he has great relationships with everyone on this team, when in reality the team can't stand him and never tells him the truth. Every entrepreneur needs to be a little overoptimistic to do something as irrational as start a business, given that 90 percent of new businesses fail, but fantasy can be ruinous when we fundamentally ignore reality.

Other leaders have a *paranoid blindset*—they are pessimistic and fearful and see threats where none exist. A leader living with paranoia does not trust data or reports from her teams. She is worried that the competition is always gaining on them, or she thinks her board is always on the verge of firing her. A little bit of paranoia is good; it makes us cautious. But too much paranoia can be paralyzing.

When leaders fail to see or accept some painful truth, they have a *denial blindset*. Leaders living in denial cannot see the writing on the wall that the world is passing them by, that they need to innovate. Denial in management can keep a leader from seeing that she has lost the confidence of her team, or that she or her team are not up to the challenge of scaling the company.

Finally, some leaders have a *skeptical blindset*—they are pessimistic and don't see how good things really are. A leader who is too skeptical often micromanages. He tries to control how people do their work and does not get curious about what he might be able to learn from his team.

Throughout the book we will explore stories of leaders who were beset with one blindset or another, and we will take you into our coaching sessions with them as we tried to lift off their blinders and help them lead with heart. Our hope is that you will see yourself in these stories and get curious—and honest—about the blindsets you have.

How to Get the Most Out of this Book

The best way to read this book is slowly and thoughtfully. This is not a book you flip through to extract frameworks and ideas. It's a book you use to ask yourself and others some hard questions—more of a process you experience than a product you consume.

To make it easier for you to extract practical insights for yourself and your teams, we have highlighted several key principles and takeaways at the end of every chapter. We've also provided several "conversation starters" in each chapter, designed to help you take the insights a few layers deeper. The final chapter provides team exercises for you to explore with your colleagues.

In our online community, you'll also find various self-assessments—the same ones we use with our coaching clients every day. These can help you discover where you are today, and how primed and ready you are to uncover insights about yourself and others. You will find additional resources, tools, and success stories from other members of the Leading with Heart community on our website, www.LeadingWithHeartBook.com.

This is a book about developing your own authentic brand of leadership by looking through the lens of your own experiences and preferences. No matter where you are in your career, whether you are a CEO or a student, going through this process of introspection can transform you in ways that go well beyond any memoir, success story, or list of "leadership hacks."

Our coaching process is about having conversations that help us get curious and clear. Conversations that are honest and real. It's about opening up. And while it may feel challenging and confronting at times, we promise it will also feel rewarding and inspiring.

Thank you for trusting us to be your coaches on this journey.

1

WHAT DO YOU NEED TO BE AT YOUR BEST?

When a flower doesn't bloom, you fix the environment in which it grows, not the flower.

—ALEXANDER DEN HEIJER

Ernest Hemingway and Virginia Woolf did it standing up. Mark Twain and Truman Capote preferred to do it lying down. Ben Franklin and Victor Hugo liked to do it naked, and it's been said Thomas Edison did it best after a power nap. Maya Angelou enjoyed doing it first thing in the morning, and Barack Obama says he does it best between 10:00 p.m. and 2:00 a.m. Keith Richards of the Rolling Stones does it only after eating some shepherd's pie, and Eddie Van Halen liked having a bowl of M&Ms on hand while doing it—once all the brown ones were removed.

Throughout history, the most prolific artists, thinkers, and entrepreneurs have discovered they get their best creative and innovative work done under specific conditions. It's something unique to each individual—something most of us only figure out through experimentation and observation. If we ever figure it out at all.

You and your teams most likely have your own preferences or requirements for feeling maximally creative, effective, and resilient, whether or not you've ever sat down to think about it. Some of your needs may feel unique and quirky, others more typical. But no matter what, taking a good hard look and getting very honest with yourself about what you *really* need to feel your best—and learning why you often don't get your needs met—is the foundation of exceptional performance. And learning how to help your teams get their needs met so they can flourish is the cornerstone of exceptional leadership.

According to Abraham Maslow, the grandfather of all needs research, our needs fall largely into two categories: deficiency needs and growth needs. Deficiency needs are those things without which we tend to suffer—food, sleep, water, shelter, basic human connection. Growth needs are those things that we need to feel like we are living to our full potential—belonging, affirmation, intellectual challenge, access to the outdoors, and so on.

Leading with heart is hard emotional labor. We can't begin the process of learning how to show up emotionally for ourselves and our teams while we are feeling hangry, unrested, unsafe, or uninspired. As coaches, we tend to focus first on helping our clients understand and calibrate their own needs. Once they have optimized their own needs profile, they are in a better place to get curious about their team's needs and help them flourish, as well.

Our goal in this first chapter is to help you see more clearly the practices, conditions, and environmental factors that you and your team need to feel your most energized, resourceful, and resilient. Also, we hope you will gain awareness around what things sap your energy, kill your creative juices, or make you more risk-averse.

Even more important than gaining that awareness, however,

is having conversations around what stands in the way of getting your own needs met, and how you can help your teams get theirs met. Through a series of stories and exercises, we will seek to help you better understand what these unconscious or unexpressed needs really are and give you some baseline language to begin to have conversations about your needs.

The Needs System: Building upon Maslow

As coaches, we think about needs as an integrated system. In contrast to the hierarchy of needs that Maslow first developed in 1943 that included food, water, shelter, love, belonging, esteem, and self-actualization, our Needs System model has three main components: physical needs, emotional needs, and environmental needs.

We noticed in our work with clients that our needs are not necessarily met in the linear hierarchy first proposed by Maslow, in which physical needs must be met before emotional needs, and so on. We've found that we can actually have some higher needs met while not getting other lower needs met. Later in his life, Maslow came to the same conclusion, and recent research supports this theory.

We see this phenomenon at play both in companies where we coach and in our travels. In some parts of the developing world, we've met people who barely had their basic food and shelter needs met, yet they seemed to be filled with joy and laughter because their emotional needs of connection and community had been met in spades. Additionally, different people have different requirements for various types of needs. Deciphering that unique "needs map" for ourselves and others unlocks our ability to dive deeper into the Leading with Heart model.

As outlined above, we think about needs at three levels. First, we've found that high-performing leaders have *physical needs* far beyond the basics required to survive; they want to thrive. Thus they often have additional needs, such as diets and sleep schedules calibrated to their unique bodies, tailored exercise routines, and mindfulness practices. We'll get more into the specifics later, but let's just say for now that you are not crazy for saying things like "I really need to work out today." We believe you. That is an actual need.

Second, high performers are at their best when their *emotional needs* to belong, be safe, and have autonomy are met, although we all require different levels of each. Some people are lone wolves, while others require constant interaction and feedback. Some people thrive with lots of autonomy, while others like daily direction. The one thing we all require, however, is psychological safety, and we will explore how to create that.

Finally, in addition to these physical and emotional needs, the Needs System includes an important component we hinted at previously: *environmental needs.* Maslow's talks and writing from the 1970s include mentions of his increasing awareness of "aesthetic needs," but our model takes it a bit further than that, based largely on recent research and our own experience.

Physical Needs

We're going to operate under the assumption that if you are holding this book in your hand, you likely have most of your baseline needs met. You have access to food and shelter, you get decent sleep from time to time, and you got enough human connection as an infant to avoid withering away.

Given that, the big questions in our minds around physical needs are: What beyond your baseline deficiency needs do you need to thrive and to flourish? And more importantly, if you are not getting your needs met at that level, why not, and what can we do about it?

There are four key components to your physical needs: what you put in your body, how you rest your body, how you move your body, and how you train your brain. Let's take a quick look at each of these questions through the experiences of a few clients. Our hope is that through learning about their journeys, you will be able to get honest with yourself about what you really need. We'll then spend more time digging into why we might not be getting our needs met.

DIET: THE TRULY RANDOM VARIABLE

Legend has it that Elvis once took his private jet from Memphis to Denver to have what he said was the best sandwich in the country: the Fool's Gold Loaf, a messy pile of peanut butter, bacon, and banana on sourdough grilled to perfection.

In general, the clients we work with have more than quirky or capricious preferences around food. They've learned through trial and error that some foods and diets give them energy, while others lay them flat on their backs. The ideal diet should make you feel energized and healthy while still giving you freedom and options. Extremely restrictive diets that feel like a full-time job unto themselves can become time saps for busy executives.

We're not nutritionists, and we will not begin to tell you or any client what to eat. What we will do is encourage you to engage in a process of radical curiosity to discern what foods work for you and what foods don't. Let's take a look at one client who made a surprising discovery about his diet.

Brian was a senior executive we worked with at a Fortune 500 company. For decades he suffered from near-paralyzing migraines, and they were impacting his performance at the office. Not one of the litany of doctors and specialists he hired could figure out what was ailing him. They thought it must be the result of stress and sent him to numerous psychiatrists and therapists. All the experts found was that aside from the migraines, Brian was very healthy both mentally and physically.

During a coaching session, Edward suggested that perhaps it was something Brian was eating and recommended he consult an allergist (Edward has had his own decades-long battle with allergies). After a laborious process, Brian soon learned he was allergic to gluten. Instead of his migraines being caused by some horrible neurological condition, it was his love of pizza and pasta that ailed him. But even armed with this knowledge, he still had the hardest time giving up gluten.

Another client, Amanda, the general counsel at a top-ten tech firm, complained to John in one of her coaching sessions that she felt sluggish and foggy-brained all the time. John performed an analysis of her baseline needs and learned that she was on her own version of a Mediterranean diet. But instead of consuming lots of healthy fruits and veggies, she was drinking half a bottle of red wine every night to fall sleep and having three cups of coffee every morning to wake up.

The constant yo-yo of caffeine and alcohol was wreaking havoc on her metabolism and keeping her from getting restful sleep. She never drank to get drunk, so she didn't identify as an alcoholic, but still she was unable to kick the habit. She said she and her mother caught up on the phone nearly every night, and they simply enjoyed drinking a little wine together.

How could we help Brian and Amanda change their eating and drinking habits?

SLEEP: THE UNDERESTIMATED NECESSITY
Of the many fables of Silicon Valley, the story of the young entrepreneurs who are so committed that they eschew regular sleep

and only take short naps under their desk for weeks on end is one of the most dangerous. So, before we go much further, let us state once and for all: great leaders get enough sleep.

We've noticed anecdotally in our client work, and research concurs, that not getting enough sleep leads to irritability, poor decision-making, anxiety, and depression. In fact, not getting enough sleep can lead to even more severe health issues. According to a National Institutes of Health report, sleep deprivation leads to increased risk for hypertension, diabetes, obesity, depression, heart attack, and stroke.

One client who was the head of engineering at a prominent tech company came to us because he was unable to get along with other leaders on this team. As his boss told us, "Doug is brilliant and produces results as an independent contributor, but no one wants to work with him, and I can't have that."

John dove into our regular Leadership 360 analysis, in which we aggregate feedback from a client's colleagues, to assess what was going on, and sure enough, the data matched up with the boss's sentiments: low EQ, low emotional regulation, not a team player, only out for himself, and not for the company.

John read back the 360 to him in one of their first meetings, and Doug scoffed, "Give me a break! My job is to build product, not get along with people." The problem is that this young man was up for a promotion and needed to learn to collaborate and lead, not just write code.

"Actually, Doug, I beg to differ," John replied. "Your new job description explicitly states that you must learn to get along with people and not just write code, so maybe we should figure out what's going on here."

Nothing like a good ol' bucket of ice-cold reality to wake a client up.

Digging in with Doug, John asked him to describe what he

needed to do his best thinking. "I like working from midnight to 4:00 a.m. No emails, no Slack. I can finally get in the zone."

"Great, but when do you sleep?" John inquired.

"Sleep? I'm twenty-eight. I don't need sleep. I'm good on four hours a night."

Four hours a night? Almost anyone regularly getting four hours a night is going to be a foul, irritable pain in the rear end.

John was faced with a conundrum, however. The client needed more sleep, but he also got his best work done when he was uninterrupted. Asking him to work regular hours and go to bed at ten or eleven like a normal person wasn't going to work if other team members were pinging him over email and Slack late into the evening.

EXERCISE: THE CURE-ALL

Justin McLeod, the CEO of dating app Hinge, has a rigorous daily yoga practice that he views as fundamental in helping him show up for the daily struggles of being a start-up founder. When Justin seems a little off on a coaching call, Edward's first question is, "How is your yoga practice going?" And nine times out of ten, Justin hasn't done it in a few days. It's like clockwork.

While we're not physical trainers, keeping tabs on our clients' exercise routines is a crucial part of our practice because it is so important to emotional and mental well-being. How important is it? In one Duke study, individuals who treated their depression symptoms with medication were five times more likely to lapse back into depression after treatment than those who treated their depression with thirty minutes of exercise three days a week.

Since everyone in the medical and mental health community agrees that regular exercise is a key component to a healthy body and mind, why is it so hard developing a regular exercise habit?

We dug in on this question with Teresa, the founder of a well-funded direct-to-consumer wellness brand. Teresa had just raised a Series B, so you would think she would be jubilant, but to Edward something seemed off. Her positivity and ebullience had been replaced with pessimism and heaviness. Edward ran through our regular needs inventory with her, and she seemed to be eating and sleeping well. No recent breakups or family issues either (we dig deep into clients' personal lives if that is what they need to show up as better leaders). And although work stress was high, it wasn't any worse than it had been during the first two years of building the company.

What had changed?

Edward knew Teresa was a former college athlete with a regular running routine. She had a running club she went out for a jog with most mornings. She would even show up for coaching sessions in sneakers and athletic gear. But more recently Edward noticed she seemed to be dressing the part of the traditional tech CEO—black slacks, silk blouse, leather shoes.

When Edward asked how her running club was going, she guffawed. "Ha! You think I have time for that anymore? I have a team of over fifty now. I'm doing two media interviews a week and have stand-ups at eight a.m. every day. I barely have time to eat, let alone run. I can't be a college athlete anymore, Edward. I have to be the CEO now."

Was it not possible for Teresa to be the CEO she wanted to be and also maintain the running habit that made her feel centered?

MEDITATION: THE WOO-WOO THING THAT WORKS

Nestled somewhere along the redwood-dotted ridgeline that separates Silicon Valley and the Pacific Ocean, Stillpath is a Zen-inspired retreat center that is home every winter to an invitation-only meditation weekend for some of the most prominent thinkers and leaders in Silicon Valley. These top executives from

Facebook, Twitter, Google, Apple, and a dozen other firms come together to sit in silence for a weekend for one simple reason: It makes them better leaders.

The efficacy of meditation has been well studied and documented over the last thirty years. In 1990 Jon Kabat-Zinn did one of the first studies to show that meditation had a significant clinical impact on anxiety and depression. He also happens to lead the retreat at Stillpath.

Since then, hundreds of studies have replicated and expanded on Kabat-Zinn's findings. Scientists have shown that meditation abates stress, increases focus, reduces the risk of a myriad of chronic diseases, and generally makes you a happier person.

One recent study funded by the US Army showed that mindfulness meditation exercises helped soldiers better prepare for high-stress combat situations and improved their overall cognitive resilience and performance.

Meditation is so effective, in fact, that many leaders now put a daily meditation practice on the list of needs that they have to be maximally effective. CEOs Marc Benioff of Salesforce, Jack Dorsey of Twitter, Dave Heath of Bombas, and Justin McLeod of Hinge, as well as COO Mark Williamson of MasterClass, all have daily meditation habits.

Why? Because leading is hard. We weren't evolved for this volume of stress, information, or decision-making. To our nervous systems, the stresses of running a fast-paced company are akin to being in a constant state of war.

A 2015 study conducted by researchers at Stanford, UC Berkeley, and UC San Francisco found that entrepreneurs who participated in the study were significantly more likely than non-entrepreneurs to report a lifetime history of depression (30 percent of entrepreneurs in the study, as opposed to 15 percent of non-entrepreneurs), ADHD (29 versus 5 percent), substance use

(12 versus 4 percent), and bipolar diagnosis (11 versus 1 percent). Putting these stats another way, when compared to the general population entrepreneurs are twice as likely to suffer from depression, six times more likely to have ADHD, three times more likely to struggle with addiction, and eleven times more likely to receive a bipolar diagnosis than non-entrepreneurs.

One client named Daniel was having a lot of trouble with irritability and moodiness. Although he was almost always correct in his suggestions to employees on how to improve their workflows, he didn't exactly share his thoughts in the most supportive manner. During his 360 review, he was confronted with the reality that people across the business almost universally did not like working with him. In fact, many junior people actively feared him.

Digging into the topic, Edward posited various ways to address his caustic moods, but one that surprised him was the suggestion that he meditate. Daniel was not exactly the most touchy-feely guy, however, and the first time Edward mentioned meditation, he scoffed. Guys' guys didn't meditate, as far as he was concerned.

WHY WE DON'T GET OUR BASELINE NEEDS MET

Changing our habits around our baseline needs is hard. Carbs and alcohol are both physically addictive. Crying children and stress keep us from getting enough sleep. Exercise literally hurts and takes up a lot of time. And meditation can seem boring or hippie-dippie. We know.

Yet we also know that changing our habits around these baseline needs is in our best interest. Leaders who are well-fed, rested, in shape, and mindful are better equipped to perform the emotional labor of leadership—that is, to lead with heart—than those who are not getting their needs met. Full stop.

So why is developing new habits around our baseline needs so difficult?

Our own experience and a bevy of scientific research shows that our inability to change our habits even when our health or work is on the line has more to do with our belief systems than our willpower. Developmental psychologist Robert Kegan, whose groundbreaking work on habits formation is captured in the book *Immunity to Change*, described the underlying belief systems that keep us from doing the things we know are good for us as "competing commitments."

Looking back at the clients you just learned about, let's dig into what competing commitments they might have:

- Brian was committed to being "one of the guys" and thought it was effeminate to be the one at the table who orders a salad or asks for gluten-free pizza.
- Amanda was committed to having a nightly call with her mother back home, and she was convinced that sharing a glass of wine (or three) was "central to making a connection."
- Doug was committed to not being the one employee who asks for "Slack-off time," the term we use for turning off Slack for periods of focus during the workday.
- Teresa was committed to being the "serious CEO" who didn't have time for something that brought her joy and a sense of community.
- Daniel was committed to being a "guy's guy," not a hippie meditator.

Each of these clients was committed to the story that upholding an image about themselves was more important than getting their basic needs met. But those stories were hurting all of them, standing in the way of each of them feeling optimal, and their performance as leaders was suffering.

Having conversations around competing commitments can be delicate work. Behind each commitment is often an assumption about the person dedicated to it:

- *Brian*: I assume I won't be seen as manly if I have specific dietary needs.
- *Amanda*: I assume my mom and I will lose connection if we don't unwind over wine together.
- *Doug*: I assume people will think I'm weak if I have to ask people not to distract me.
- *Teresa*: I assume I can only get people to respect me if I am constantly available and poised.
- *Daniel*: I assume my football-watching friends will call me a California hippie if I meditate.

These big assumptions, also called self-limiting beliefs, are often at the center of our decision-making, especially when we find ourselves doing things that are not in our best interest, instead of actively getting our needs met.

CHALLENGING THE BIG ASSUMPTION

Looking at the assumptions our clients had about themselves, what do you notice? Each of these assumptions has to do with maintaining their standing in the eyes of other people. As we will see in the next section, we all have a powerful psychological need for acceptance and belonging, so it may not be surprising that those needs can come into conflict with getting our baseline needs met.

The problem is, our assumptions that we need to do X to be accepted or loved by Y are often relics of old stories we've been telling ourselves for decades. Maybe gluten-allergic Brian heard his manly father criticize his aunt after Thanksgiving for being a "picky vegetarian." Maybe Amanda grew up on a vineyard, and wine has been a part of her family story for generations, or maybe she saw her mother connect with her own mother over a glass of wine at family get-togethers.

Whatever the backstory is, our self-limiting beliefs are most often rooted in an old story we learned as far back as childhood about what is required for us to be accepted. Our task as coaches, and your task as a leader, is to help people challenge those assumptions head-on, often by spurring them to have direct conversations with those whose love, support, or camaraderie they are afraid of losing.

- Brian could say, "Hey fellas, turns out I'm allergic to gluten, and I don't want any flack when I don't eat bread when we go out."
- Amanda might try, "Mom, I'm finding drinking wine with you on the phone every night is keeping me from getting great sleep, but I still love talking to you, so I'll just have some tea."
- Doug could tell his team, "Folks, I get my best work done without distractions, so I'm going to turn off Slack from two to six p.m. every day."
- Teresa could share, "Wellness is one of our core values here, and everyone on the team is encouraged to exercise on a schedule that works for them."
- Daniel could remind himself, "Arnold Schwarzenegger and Clint Eastwood meditate, and they are no hippies!"

Here's when we turn this back to you. What baseline need are you having a hard time getting met? What's the competing commitment that keeps you from doing so? And going a layer deeper, what is the Big Assumption behind that competing commitment? Who are you afraid of disappointing or losing the respect of or connection with?

These questions might be difficult to answer at first, but they are crucial to uncovering the truth behind your behavior. There's almost always a good intention of wanting to be loved behind most of our negative actions or inability to change. Our task is to unearth those good intentions, name them, and challenge the assumptions behind them.

Turning to your team, these are the same questions you can ask of them to invite them into a conversation. The trick is seeing beyond what might seem like irresponsible behavior and getting to the unmet baseline need. Amanda being drowsy and unfocused in a meeting is less about her needing more coffee, focus, or discipline, and more about her not getting enough sleep due to some well-intentioned competing commitment and self-limiting belief.

When we begin looking beyond people's behavior and try to see deeper into the competing commitments and assumptions about themselves that they are making, we are taking the first steps toward leading with heart.

Let's dig a little deeper into the needs system and explore more of the emotional side of needs.

Emotional Needs

If meeting our physical needs helps us feel nourished, rested, fit, and centered, meeting our emotional needs helps us feel safe, engaged, and resilient. And just as we each have a unique recipe for meeting our physical needs, we each satisfy our emotional needs in different ways too.

Some people love seclusion and solitude, while others need constant human interaction. Some need lots of recognition and praise, while others are more intrinsically motivated. Some can't stand being told what to do, while others crave guidance and coaching. Some need lots of downtime and a vacation to feel whole, while others love staying busy and don't understand what people like about the beach.

There are also some psychological needs we all have in common, especially the need to feel safe and included. Having psychological safety is knowing that you won't be punished or humiliated for speaking up with ideas, expressing concerns, or making mistakes. Without psychological safety, there is no curiosity, no vulnerability, no creativity . . . no heart.

Our task in this section is to help you gain insight into your own emotional needs, as well as those of your team, so that you can begin to have open and productive conversations about your needs. The only hitch is that emotional inputs are not measurable like physical ones. We can portion out food, drink precisely the right amount of water, and use digitized jewelry to make sure we're getting the right amount of sleep. But emotional inputs are different. How do we measure how much sense of belonging we offer someone? How do we know how much praise is enough? Where can we find a meter to measure how psychologically safe a colleague feels?

These things are inherently unmeasurable. Instead, we have to rely on our sense of what is right. We must get radically curious and honest about what feels good and what doesn't, what makes us feel safe and what doesn't. We then have to be able to communicate to others what we need and help our teams feel safe enough to communicate with us what they need, as well.

We hope the stories that follow speak to you in some way. Whether you precisely see yourself or a team member in these anecdotes is less important than whether you can identify with the dynamics at play and the subtle revelations our subjects had about what they required to be their most creative and productive.

THE NEED TO FEEL VALUED AND RESPECTED

It was a sunny and unseasonably warm fall day in New York when Victoria realized she was done. After three years trying to make things work as an enterprise sales lead at one of the top tech firms, Victoria was ready to quit.

The deals she was working on were all on hold. Her colleagues seemed to be icing her out of meetings and information loops. And her boss had just submitted a performance review for her with the career-damaging "doesn't meet expectations" assessment.

She felt she was failing, and the shame was overwhelming. Growing up the daughter of Chinese immigrants outside Chicago, there were certain expectations her family had of her, which of course included being a doctor and married with children by the age of thirty. And as Victoria approached her thirty-second birthday, single, childless, and on the brink of being fired, she felt like she was drowning in a tidal wave of shame.

"It feels like I have missed every milestone I have ever set for myself, and it's killing me," she exclaimed on one of her coaching calls with Edward.

Now, if you met Victoria at a dinner party, you would think quite differently. From the outside, Victoria is the walking definition of success and good fortune: Ivy League educated. Working at a top-five tech firm. Owns a fabulous apartment in Manhattan. She's even learning to sail on getaways to Croatia. But at this moment, in this role, all she saw was a series of failures and missed expectations—hers, her boss's, her parents'.

As Edward and Victoria began to work together, he noticed a pattern. Everywhere in Victoria's organization, leaders were tapping out. Her closest colleague had transferred to another division of the company. A new female senior director who was recruited from Google and who had been hired to layer in between

Victoria and her boss left after just six weeks. Even the analysts hired away from the Boston Consulting Group were bailing.

The only thing all these people and Victoria had in common was the same boss.

Tim was a former consultant in his mid-forties who was brought in to run her business unit a few years before Victoria began. Tim had a great relationship with his boss and his boss's boss. This was due to the fact that he always delivered on his numbers and stayed in frequent communication with his superiors. Tim managed up very well. He anticipated what his higher-ups needed and got it to them before they had to ask for it.

With his direct reports, however, instead of anticipating their needs, he actively ignored them. Tim did what we call "managing the task" rather than managing the person. His exclusive focus on hitting the numbers at any cost unfortunately came at the cost of his team's emotional well-being.

What Tim and managers like Tim don't know is that management styles like that might work in consulting firms, where most associates only plan to stay for two years to get the experience on their résumé, but it can create retention problems at technology firms with long product development and sales cycles, where institutional knowledge is at a premium and hiring is costly.

To Edward, it was obvious that Victoria was not getting her emotional need to feel valued met, but to her she was the problem. When someone is working in an unsupportive or emotionally abusive environment, it's easy to mistake it for something else. All the blame and gaslighting can make employees believe *they* are the problem, not the other way around. From the outside, it was clear that Victoria was working in an environment that was unsupportive at best, and downright toxic at worst. But from the inside, she had a hard time seeing it.

Sometimes in a coaching relationship the questions "What part of this is your responsibility?" or "What part of this can you control?" lead to a stark conclusion: in this case, that the only part of this that was within Victoria's control was her decision to continue to show up at this job expecting things to be different.

At first Victoria had a hard time seeing that she was the victim of chronic neglect and emotional abuse. It was even harder for her to see that this behavior from men was something she had first experienced in her childhood home. Her father had been cold and exceedingly demanding for most of her upbringing. She had been conditioned at a young age to accept this as normal. In a subconscious way, it was familiar. But it was time for her to see this is *not* normal.

Sometimes we don't realize just how poorly our need to feel valued and respected is being met until we have an experience which satisfies that need in a deeply compelling way. Through her coaching conversations with Edward, Victoria began to see that men *can* be affirming and nurturing. Over time, as their conversations continued, she began to rewrite the story she told herself about what she deserved. She began to see herself as worthy of being treated in an affirming way. And at long last, she began to seek that out.

Soon after realizing that she wanted to work on a team that made her feel valued, affirmed, and safe, three things she had never felt at any point in her career, she decided to leave her job and search for a new position. After she alerted her network that she was looking for something new, introductions began to come her way. Female leaders in tech reached out to her on LinkedIn to discuss potential collaborations. Various VCs and other influential types began recruiting her. And soon she found an opportunity for a job at a new company.

As she got to know her new team, she could tell something

was different. Everyone was using language that communicated a sense of respect and collaboration. People didn't steal credit from each other. They laughed and celebrated small successes. And as talented and accomplished as they all were, they were also curious about and impressed with Victoria's experience and expertise. She had stumbled into a company in which leaders strove to make each individual successful, and didn't simply try to make sure the tasks got done.

Safi Bahcall, the best-selling author of *Loonshots*, talks about the importance of leaders thinking more about making their teams successful and less about getting tasks done. He shared on a call with us, "Leaders often think about what they need to do to get their teams to do things. But that's not scalable. You can't keep track of every task. What if instead they thought about their team members as delicate flowers? Suppose your job isn't to get this task done by this date, but simply to get this person to grow into the most beautiful flower they can grow into? That's scalable."

Today, having been transplanted into more nourishing soil, Victoria is a beautiful flower in full bloom. Of course she still has moments of self-doubt, like all of us, but gone are the days of chronic negative self-talk and shame.

The moral of this story may seem rather straightforward: Get out of toxic relationships, whether they be friendships, jobs, or romances. But many of us stay in situations that don't feed us for far too long.

When all we want to do is bloom, and when those around us are blaming us for not blooming, it is easy to think we are the problem. It often takes an outside party like a friend, coach, or therapist to hold up a big flashing sign that reads, THIS SITUATION IS NOT NORMAL! YOU ARE NOT GETTING YOUR NEEDS MET!

Since you might be wondering, let's close the loop on Tim's story, as well. It would be satisfying to say he was held accountable for his actions, but in spite of the massive exodus of talent from his organization and the complaints to HR about his behavior, leadership did nothing to reprimand him. This lack of action in the face of flagrant abusive behavior is what creates toxic cultures, and more and more it is catching up with executive teams and their boards throughout Silicon Valley and beyond.

All it takes is one Victoria documenting the abuse and having the courage to talk to the press for a brand to experience a deeply damaging hit to its reputation. Even if it doesn't get that far, the company will gain a reputation for having a toxic culture and lose its ability to attract top talent in today's ultracompetitive market.

As leaders we need to ask ourselves, what kind of culture are we trying to build? Do we want to have a team of creative problem solvers who show up to work every day energetically nourished and excited to help us build something special, or do we want an organization filled with people who are committed to doing the absolute minimum to get their task list done?

Bahcall sums it up this way, "The bottom line is leaders need to wear a different hat based on what will motivate and excite different people. You have a different way of communicating based on how different people will respond. If you listen to the 'music behind the words' of your people, they are telling you what they need to be successful."

Some questions that can inspire conversations on these topics are:

- What relationships or environments are not meeting your needs for affirmation and safety?
- Have you been accepting abusive or neglectful behavior, all the while thinking that you are the one with the problem?
- How can you experiment with finding different teams or people with which to spend time?
- Who or what makes you feel like you are really blooming?

PSYCHOLOGICAL SAFETY AND THE MYTH OF EXECUTIVE PRESENCE

A recent report by McKinsey found that "when employees feel comfortable asking for help, sharing suggestions informally, or challenging the status quo without fear of negative consequences, organizations are more likely to innovate quickly, unlock the benefits of diversity, and adapt well to change."

Yet, as fundamental as that sounds, only 26 percent of leaders create psychological safety for their teams. Or conversely, 74 percent of leaders do NOT create psychological safety.

Harvard professor Amy Edmondson broadly defines psychological safety as a climate in which people are comfortable expressing and being themselves. According to Edmondson, creating psychological safety first requires leaders to explicitly acknowledge the lack of answers to the tough problems groups face. When leaders highlight that there are no easy answers and that they don't have the answers, they send a clear message to the entire organization: It's okay to be flawed.

For far too long, we have been told that one of the keys to excellence in leadership is to have "executive presence," which is loosely defined as the charisma and gravitas that engender respect and inspire confidence. While that's nice and all, we have observed in our research and throughout our coaching careers that leaders who try the most to have executive presence often get the worst results and poorest engagement from their teams. In contrast, those leaders who are most comfortable being themselves have better outcomes and engender deep loyalty and engagement from their people.

Let's take Sue, for example. Sue is the newly hired CEO of a public company in the cybersecurity space. She was hired by the board because she has a reputation as a hard charger who gets results. As you might imagine, Sue has executive presence for days. She is charismatic, put together, and extremely well spoken.

While none of that is a problem, one thing is: Sue's new team thinks she is unapproachable. Sue is so perfect that her team of hoodie-wearing engineers and marketers has a hard time connecting with her. She never admits to making mistakes, and now her team doesn't feel like they can either.

Sue's management philosophy is "bring me solutions, not problems." While it is noble to encourage your teams to be solutions-oriented, the downside of this philosophy is that no one feels able to ask for help when faced with intractable problems. It bears repeating: leaders who make their people feel unsafe saying that they smell smoke will always be putting out fires.

And put out fires Sue does. She has built an executive team culture in which people do not feel psychologically safe, so they don't push back, admit mistakes, or question the norm. As a result, she doesn't catch wind of problems early so that she can deal with them quickly; instead, they come to her attention only when they are full-on emergencies. Which is why her team is constantly beset with outages, missed deadlines, and unhappy customers.

In her coaching sessions, Sue complained to John that she was "not working with A players" and could not seem to get a "spirit of excellence out of them." When John pushed back and posited that her leadership style and perfectionism might be making people feel unsafe and unwilling to come forth with bad news, she was at first quite defensive. "John," she said, "I should not have to babysit full-grown adults and make them feel like failure is okay."

With this one statement, John knew that Sue had a common misconception about what psychological safety is all about.

As Edmondson puts it, "Psychological safety is not about being nice—or about lowering performance standards. Quite the opposite: It's about recognizing that high performance *requires* the openness, flexibility, and interdependence that can develop only in a psychologically safe environment, especially when the situation is changing or complex."

Far from open, flexible, and interdependent, Sue was being closed, rigid, and antagonistic. And while that management style may have worked for her on Wall Street, it was leading her down a perilous path in Silicon Valley.

Sue was like many of our clients. They come to us with a question about getting their team to step up. They complain that their employees are delivering a second-rate work product—that they're always disappointed. Yet this is almost always a sign that this is a leader who isn't taking responsibility for their role in creating an unsafe working environment.

It was clear to John that Sue wasn't taking responsibility. She had blindsets of skepticism and denial. She was unable to see her role in all this. She was committed to the story that she was an effective executive surrounded by low performers.

The first step in changing this narrative is often getting raw, honest feedback from the team. When John performed a 360 feedback survey for Sue, he gave many people on her team their first opportunity to get a few things off their chest. Not all of it was constructive, frankly. Some people had long-simmering resentments that were just waiting to come out. But regardless, John now had a solid data set to review with Sue.

When they sat down to review the data, John made sure Sue got exactly the truth bomb she needed. Seeing words like *bully* in reference to herself was not easy for her, but it was important. Through the coaching and the 360 feedback, Sue was able to see for the first time how her leadership style was emotionally impacting her team. Her own need to look perfect was creating a perverse fear of imperfection on her team. And as we will see in the next chapter, fear can make people shut down and make poor decisions.

Sue's journey to taking responsibility and learning how to lead with heart and have conversations that create psychological safety on her team was a hard one. It began with taking off the blinders and seeing for the first time her role in creating an unsafe working environment. Everything she'd been taught about management over fifteen years working in finance was challenged by the idea that it was her job to create emotional connections with her team, and not just their job to deliver perfect work products on time every time.

In reflecting upon Sue's situation and journey, answer these questions for yourself:

- In what ways might you be creating a psychologically unsafe working environment for your teams?
- How often do you hear about problems too late? Could that be a signal that people don't feel safe coming to you sooner?
- How could you go about getting honest, anonymous feedback from your team that offers an unvarnished perspective on how your leadership style impacts them?
- What old stories about executive presence are keeping you from letting down your guard and being more connected and authentic as a leader?

IT ALL STARTS WITH TRUST

Nick found his way into the start-up world through hedge funds. After ten years in the feast-to-famine, testosterone-fueled world of high finance, he decided he wanted something "a bit less stressful." Why he thought running a start-up would be less stressful is beyond us, but nevertheless, here he is, a forty-eight-year-old father of two, sitting at his desk on the sixth story of a San Francisco office building, trying to revolutionize the travel industry.

"I feel trapped, Edward," he laments, staring out the window at someone in the building directly across from him, who himself is staring at someone else a few floors above Nick. The odd sensation that they are in a human aquarium is not lost on either of them. "I ask people to do simple things, and they always seem to come back half done, poorly done, or not done at all. Why am I the only one who seems to take what we are doing seriously?"

Nick's predicament is much more common than one would believe. Perhaps you've been in his shoes yourself. In fast-paced start-up environments, the leader seems to see what needs to be done and to what level of quality it needs to be done with absolute clarity. He is the holder of the vision. His team is doing something that's never been done before, so there's no standard definition of what good looks like. And Nick, like many other CEOs, has a hard time explaining what he wants. He knows it only when he sees it, and he rarely sees it.

In our work with leaders, we see this problem time and again. The CEO instinctually knows "what good looks like," but she doesn't know how to define it, so she spends most of her time pointing out what *isn't* good. This cycle of ambiguity and disappointment rarely leads to great results because all it does is erode one of the most important ingredients in a company's success: trust.

Without knowing it and with only the best intentions, Nick has created a culture that is destined to continue to disappoint him, make his team miserable, and deliver poor results for the company at large. He can't for the life of him see that he is failing to give his team what they need most from him right now: trust.

Researcher and author Paul J. Zak has done numerous studies around the importance of trust and how to go about building it at companies. He found that when compared with employees at companies that score low on trust, people at high-trust companies indicate they experience 74 percent less stress, 106 percent more energy at work, 50 percent higher productivity, 13 percent fewer sick days, 76 percent more engagement, 29 percent more overall satisfaction in life, and 40 percent less burnout.

Back in Nick's office, he and Edward are discussing his leadership style in greater detail. "How often do you praise your employees for a job well done?" Edward inquires.

"Praise? They never do things right, or on time."

"Okay, and how much do you challenge them with specific and attainable goals?"

"We are trying to change the entire travel industry here. Everything we are doing seems unattainable. So I set very ambitious goals and tell them to meet those in half the time I actually need, assuming they will be delayed."

"Got it. And how much do you let go and allow your team to figure out the best way to execute on those goals?"

"Edward, if I am not riding them and holding their hand the entire way, things never get done right. I'm trying to explain to you . . ."

When we write it that way, it may seem glaringly obvious that Nick is failing as a leader, but from Nick's perspective he is doing everything he can to get the team pointed in the right direction. What Nick doesn't know is that providing feedback only when you are disappointed, being vague in goal setting, and controlling how people go about doing their work creates a negative spiral of declining trust and performance. It also flies in the face of one of the fundamental rules of persuasion. According to author and social scientist Robert Cialdini, people are more likely to say yes to people they like, and being a controlling boss is no way to get people to like you.

This scenario is surprisingly common. Nick sees a team not performing. The team sees a leader who doesn't trust them and is bordering on being emotionally abusive. Thinking back on the story about Victoria, we see a similar story here with Nick, but from the perspective of the demeaning boss.

Nick doesn't know it, but he is violating the first three rules of building trust, as revealed by Zak in his research:

1. **Reward excellence.** Everything we know about motivation theory teaches us that we need to reward the behaviors we want more than punish those we don't. This holds true whether we're raising kids, training dogs, or motivating employees. Research indicates that for every bit of negative feedback, we need to provide five to seven positive comments.

2. **Issue attainable challenges.** Employees experience an incredible release of positive neurochemicals when they are given a difficult but achievable job. They get into flow (which we will explore more later) and circle up with their colleagues more. "Vague or impossible goals often cause people to give up before they even start," Zak points out.

3. **Let people decide how to work on the goal.** Freedom to decide how you get a job done is one of the key markers of trust. It's something nearly all employees crave, and something nearly all micromanagers get wrong. According to author Dan Pink, autonomy is one of the top three motivators we have as human beings. When we tell people how to do their work, we are removing the feeling of ownership that is crucial for higher-order thinking and innovating.

First-time CEOs often struggle with these points. They are nervous about getting it right, and feel a particular need to keep "their baby"—the company—from failing. Sadly, in committing these three core mistakes, they are ironically setting themselves up for failure.

Let's get back to Nick. After a long silence, Edward asks Nick the crucial question: "What would be different if your team felt that you trusted them?"

As soon as Edward asks the question, Nick turns away from the window and looks him in the eye. Reflecting on how important it is for him to feel trusted by his husband and his investors, he has a moment of clarity. He can see very clearly how not trusting the team is perpetuating the situation. He is caught in a negative spiral.

"Well, they would probably take more ownership and think more creatively."

"Exactly, and what do you need to trust them?"

"They need to take ownership and think more creatively," he says with a knowing chuckle.

Aha! Nick has been waiting for his team to behave in a way that makes him trust them more. But those behaviors on the part of the team will only be available to them if they have their need to be trusted met. It's a classic chicken-or-egg conundrum.

Nick now realizes that he is going to have to take the leap and give them the trust he isn't quite sure they deserve. It's a leap of faith that he knows he has to make. And as hard as it is, he can now see quite clearly how important it is.

But how can he show them he trusts them? Good question.

The good news is, all he has to do is start proactively performing the behaviors we discussed a few minutes ago: reward excellence, issue attainable challenges, and let people figure out the *how* by themselves.

By the end of the session, Nick has agreed to take fifteen minutes once a day and look for someone on the team to praise. We call it "catching someone doing something right." And when giving praise, he agrees to use the tried-and-true "situation-behavior-impact" method.

Hey Sally, I just wanted to drop you a quick note to let you know that today on the call with our top customer, you answered all their objections very well and made them feel at ease. It seems you've solidified that relationship for the long term. Great work!

He also agrees to sit down with the team and break their big-picture vision statements into smaller, more attainable goals. This seems fairly obvious, but many leaders with grand visions feel like they lose energy when they think about the details. Sorry to break it to you: As the leader, you don't get to only do the things that give you energy. You also need to work with your team to define roles and give them clear and attainable goals.

And finally, Nick agrees that he will ask the team to tell him to back off when he gets too up in their business about how they are going to execute on their goals. He will tell them very transparently that he is working on trusting them more and that he wants them to support him by telling him when he is being too controlling.

These aren't easy conversations to have, but they are cathartic. Many times, simply saying that you want to trust your team more causes a shift in the dynamic. They see you making an effort, and they do their best to step up and get more engaged in the work.

Today, Nick's company is doing much better. After getting radically curious about the team's need to feel trusted, he has made great strides in learning to trust them. As a result, the team has begun to work more collaboratively and creatively. And Nick is beginning to enjoy his job more. He feels less alone, less fearful, less trapped. By giving his team the trust that they need, he is finally getting the peace of mind he needs to do higher-level strategic work, even if he does still work in a human aquarium.

Reflecting upon Nick's efforts to build trust on his team:

- In what ways are you building or eroding trust on your team?
- What more could you do to "catch someone doing something right"?
- In what ways are you creating vague goals, yet holding people to specific expectations?
- What does letting go of the *how* look like for you?

Environmental Needs

On a September afternoon in 1972, Abraham Maslow was sitting in the natural hot springs at Esalen Institute, the legendary retreat center on the Big Sur coastline, watching the sun set into the Pacific Ocean. He was chatting with his new friend philosopher Alan Watts about the impact that spending time at Esalen had had on him. He had a newfound energy for continuing his research into human motivation and needs. He felt increased energy working in the vegetable garden perched high above the roaring ocean below. He was overcome with a natural high every time he meditated beside the stream beneath the soaring redwoods.

It was then Maslow realized he had left the entire natural world out of his original hierarchy of needs. Aside from food, water, and shelter, every other need he described was provided by other humans. He had overlooked the fact that our physical environment can have just as profound an impact on us. Natural light, soothing sounds, proximity to nature, a refreshing change of scenery—each of these are key ingredients that help us feel creative and resilient.

In the coming pages, we will explore various ways the places we work or seek inspiration affect us. We often take our physical environment for granted when we are doing "knowledge work." Few of us have work that is intrinsically linked to the weather, winds, or tides anymore, so we rarely pay attention.

And yet the air we breathe, the sounds that fall on our ears, the light that touches our face—these are what interact with our senses day in and day out as we try to build our companies, write our books, show up for our families, or inspire new social movements. Our environment is the context in which we create; maybe we should pay closer attention and make sure we're getting our environmental needs met.

Leading with heart requires having conversations about creating a safe and nourishing working environment for yourself and your employees—not just the emotional environment, but the *physical* environment too. We hope as you read these stories that you will begin looking at the relationships that both you and your team have to your environment through new, more honest lenses.

DESIGNING SPACES THAT MEET OUR NEEDS

About an hour north of Santa Fe, New Mexico, on a sinuous highway lined with piñon-juniper woodlands and imposing red rock cliffs, you'll find an innocuous turnoff with a sign that simply reads "Ghost Ranch." It was at this place, with its psychedelic sunsets and otherworldly eroded hoodoos and badlands, where famed American artist Georgia O'Keeffe did much of her best work over fifty years in the mid-twentieth century.

It comes as no surprise that visual artists have a unique bond with the places that inspire them. Claude Monet had the serene gardens and ponds of Giverny. Jackson Pollock found inspiration lying under the angular branches and falling leaves of East Hampton. Jean-Michel Basquiat was steeped in the graffiti and chaos of Greenwich Village.

We can literally *see* the places these artists created in their work. But what of modern knowledge workers? Can we see the offices they occupy in their work?

We would argue that we can. Although more of us are working from home now, thanks to the new hybrid office model many firms have adopted since the coronavirus pandemic, we all still have to work somewhere. And while budget-conscious start-up founders think that investing in more comfortable furniture, better lighting, and innovative office design is a luxury, research says otherwise.

Indeed, the productivity of employees is much more impacted

by the light, temperature, and design of their workspaces than one might assume. A 2017 study of software workers in Pakistan showed that, all other things being equal, workplace furniture and lighting accounted for an astounding 64 percent and 45 percent respectively of variance in employee performance.

Research has also shown that proximity to or even brief glances at nature have positive cognitive benefits for both adults and children. Green spaces near schools and children's homes promote cognitive development and improve self-control.

Another study showed that students who glanced out of their classroom window at a rooftop garden for a mere forty seconds halfway through a challenging task made significantly fewer mistakes than those who paused for forty seconds to gaze out a different window at a concrete rooftop. Still another study showed that college students who watched a short nature video were more likely to cooperate with each other on complex tasks than those who had not.

Employees seem to know this intuitively. A 2018 survey of 1,614 North American employees found that access to natural light and views of the outdoors were the most coveted attributes of an ideal workplace environment, beating out other perks like onsite cafeterias, fitness centers, and child care. A similar study from 2019 found that natural light and fresh air were the number-one and number-two most desired working conditions among survey participants.

Designers of today's office spaces have taken these studies to heart. One of our clients, London-based Second Home, has built a reputation for its coworking spaces that are full of plants and bathed in natural sunlight. Their Lisbon office has no less than a thousand plants in the main coworking area, with floor-to-ceiling windows and skylights to match. Another client has a gleaming new headquarters in New York's Meatpacking District that feels like a jungle, and it should—they spent close to $1 million on plants and even more on a design that allows natural light to permeate the entire space.

Light, air, and decor are not the only important characteristics of the spaces in which you and your teams work. Another work environment factor that has been deeply studied is how office layout impacts our ability to collaborate.

Many of today's offices were redesigned as a result of a landmark study in the 1970s, performed by Thomas Allen at NASA, to analyze why some engineering teams were more productive and collaborative than others. Surprisingly, the only data point Allen could find that correlated with higher productivity was proximity of the engineers' desks. Engineers who were able to see and hear their colleagues throughout the day without getting up and going to a meeting room or another floor were able to get questions answered and bounce ideas around quickly. Rather than working as a collection of individuals, they functioned more like a hive and took on problems together, resulting in better and faster problem-solving.

It's no wonder then that new office buildings like Google's massive headquarters in Mountain View, California, are being designed to create more "collisions" between employees with the goal of no two employees ever being more than a two-and-a-half-minute walk from each other.

During John's early coaching work at Apple, he saw firsthand just how obsessed Steve Jobs was with creating the right kind of space for people to harness their creativity. When Jobs returned to Apple in 1997 after a twelve-month hiatus, he brought with him a passion for creating spaces where people could collaborate more easily.

In those days, when John was working at Apple University, it was rumored that Jobs had a secret room at the Apple headquarters in Cupertino where he would sometimes gather his most important designers and engineers and "lock them up" for days at a time to resolve some important issue. It is said that the room was a comfortable space that allowed people to relax while they were brainstorming. Likely, many important design decisions for the iPhone were made in that room.

Steve was also committed to getting his team outdoors to create more opportunity for divergent thinking, so they frequented various retreat centers in the Bay Area where they could get closer to nature. Jobs and his friend/coach Bill Campbell did most of their sessions walking around the Apple campus or the open spaces surrounding Palo Alto.

Conversation starters about your physical work environment for you and your teams:

- What spaces and places make you and your teams feel most productive?
- How high of a priority has it been to create an inspiring workspace for yourself and your team?
- What impact does your furniture and lighting have on your ability to work comfortably for prolonged periods?
- Be honest with yourself: Does the light and flow of air in your place of work leave you feeling energized and inspired, or drained and unmotivated?
- What would be different if you mixed up your environment throughout the day?

THE SOUNDS THAT TUNE US

In the 2019 box office flop *The Sound of Silence*, Peter Saarsgard stars as eccentric New Yorker Peter Lucian, a man so attuned to the sounds of the city that he carries tuning forks around and has developed a map of all of New York based on its background tonal frequency. The West Village? A melancholic D-minor chord.

Central Park? A glistening G chord. The Lower East Side? A jarring E7#9.

In the film, Saarsgard's character makes a living helping people "tune" their apartments. Suffering from acute anxiety? It might be due to the combination of the buzz of your toaster, the hiss of your radiator, and the ceaseless whine of those compact fluorescents you have on a dimmer.

As silly as that sounds, both science and experience tell us that subtle differences in the soundscape around us can have massive impacts on our well-being and ability to concentrate. One study found that participants who listened to natural sounds like that of crickets at night or waves crashing on a beach performed better on cognitive tests than those who listened to urban soundscapes like traffic or a busy café.

A sudden crashing sound can release cortisol, a hormone that is meant to help us recover more quickly from stressful events, into our bloodstream. But when put on a slow drip by the incessant buzz of overhead lights or the hiss of an old radiator, cortisol gives us that sickly feeling of anxiety and stress.

Wherever you are right now, stop reading for a minute. Close your eyes, and just listen to your environment. What sounds are falling on your ears? Maybe you're lucky enough to be within an earshot of some birds, or the sea. Maybe you hear the sounds of jovial voices coming from a nearby café, or drilling from a construction site. Whatever it is, just take note of it.

Now, close your eyes again, and pay attention to the sensations in your body as those background noises ebb and flow. Are they noises that increase your sense of peacefulness and serenity, or do they send little unpleasant spikes or tingles through your body?

This may seem like an odd topic to explore in a book on leadership conversations, but it's actually quite important. Just as we gain a sense of safety from the people around us, affecting our ability to be resourceful and creative, we benefit from gaining insight regarding the sonic environment that suits us. Many people find that white noise or background music is conducive for creative thinking. Others say that droning background noises can eat away at their ability to concentrate and feel safe.

If you think about it, human beings had never heard anything but natural sounds until a few hundred years ago. Imagine what a violin sounded like to a farmer who visited Vienna for the first time in 1730. Or how frightened people must have been the first time they heard a combustion engine. Or a jackhammer.

Our nervous system is not evolved to deal with the cacophony of sounds and frequencies it confronts every day. That's why it's up to us to pay close attention to, and have conversations about, how sounds impact us. Armed with better information, we can then adapt our environment to suit our needs.

As you tune in to the soundscape that surrounds you:

- What kind of background noises are present in your work environment?
- Are they positive or negative for you? Do they affect others you work with differently?
- What can you do to manage sounds in your environment to maximize the creative and productive energy for you and your team?
- How do conversations about what people need in terms of their background sounds and music create harmony or dissonance on your team?

WHEN WE NEED A CHANGE OF SCENE

Commit to a strict morning routine. Choose one outfit and buy ten of them to reduce decision fatigue. Drink Soylent for three meals a day to save precious time "wasted" preparing food.

The life hackers, founder frameworkers, and stoics would have us believe that the key to success resides in having strict habits and time-saving techniques. While we agree that healthy habits and focusing on what's important are vital, we also fight back against what we consider the tyranny of monotony and routine. Taken to an extreme, habits can be the death of creativity, wellness, and joy.

To feel like we are flourishing, we also need to slow things down and have a change of scene from time to time. New places inspire divergent thinking by helping us create new neural pathways. Sometimes just working from a new desk or taking a new route to the office can help us look at a problem in a new way. Imagine what spending a month working from Central America or vacationing on a sailboat can do.

Sadly, most American knowledge workers are not mixing things up enough, and this lack of spending time away from the office (or the home office) is having a negative impact on their mental health, employee morale, and ultimately the bottom line of their companies.

According to a 2018 survey of 1,025 adult Americans, 55 percent of American workers left unused vacation days on the table. This accounted for a whopping 768 million unused vacation days in 2018—a 9 percent increase from 2017. And of the Americans who do manage to sneak away, a separate 2021 survey found that 56 percent of them checked in with their boss or colleagues at least once a day while on vacation.

But that's okay, because not taking vacation shows you're dedicated, right? You're more likely to get promoted the less vacation you take, right?

Wrong.

According to a 2015 study, people who take all of their vacation time have a 6.5 percent greater chance of getting a raise or promotion than people who leave eleven or more vacation days on the table.

Taking more vacation makes you more likely to get a raise? How could that be? Don't the people who are committed, work weekends, and never take time off get the promotions?

No. The people who deliver results do. And according to various studies, people who take everything from small breaks throughout the day to long vacations are more productive.

A Cornell study from 1999 showed that workers who were reminded at various times throughout the day to take a short break were 13 percent more productive than their non-break-taking colleagues.

And that's just ten-minute breaks. Employees who *really* unplug for a few weeks at a time report feeling more positivity, an improved ability to think critically and creatively, and decreased feelings of burnout, all of which have been shown to improve productivity by 31 percent, boost sales by 37 percent, and actually triple revenue.

Given all the data, why aren't more employees taking time off, working from elsewhere, or just choosing not to eat at their desks? It could be that their leaders are not taking time off themselves. Founders are infamous for working too many hours, not taking breaks, and generally not setting an example that shows that time off for vacation or parental leave is not just acceptable but expected.

Tony Xu, CEO of DoorDash, set a stellar example for the rest of his company in 2020 when, during the lead-up to the company's IPO, he took a month off for parental leave after the birth of his second child. Too few CEOs set that example. They do not understand that time off to get perspective is a very real need for themselves and their teams.

It's not just about vacation. We often advise our clients to mix up their working spaces throughout the day, as well. This is especially helpful when there is increased stress and pressure to complete a project or gain new insights into a problem. Writers and artists have known for ages that there is power in changing up the environment to accelerate creativity.

John had one client who was not seeing things in the best light and needed a change of scene. The client was a first-time start-up CEO who was distraught about a key employee leaving and didn't know how to handle the situation. John immediately said, "Let's go for a walk!"

As they left the building, John could tell that his client's nervous anxiety was beginning to dissipate. He began to talk more clearly and slowly and started reflecting on all that had happened leading up to the resignation.

They spent an hour walking and talking, and by the time they returned to the office, the client had a plan for how he was going to talk with this employee. We use this technique often to settle people down, make them less emotional, and help them gain more clarity on the problem in front of them. It's so simple, but it always helps us look at issues in a more logical and rational way.

Lin-Manuel Miranda was often seen walking the streets of New York to break the writer's block that sometimes stymied his progress on his masterpiece, *Hamilton*. It is said that he wore straight through multiple pairs of shoes over the years he spent writing the musical.

While all of this anecdotal evidence about the value of walking for promoting creative energy makes sense, what does the science say? A new study by Stanford researchers suggests that creative thinking actually improves both during and after walking.

We've experienced this ourselves. Many of the ideas and concepts contained in this book were conceived during our walks together in Santa Barbara, Santa Cruz, and New York. And we've both found that our most transformative conversations with clients are when we are walking together. In the age of hybrid work, we encourage our clients to take more meetings while out for a walk—either in person or with earbuds.

There's something special about moving through space and not having a particular destination in mind that puts us at ease and creates space for new ideas. The subtle release of endorphins during a brisk walk lowers stress, improves our mood, and creates moments of clarity that we cannot achieve sitting behind a desk.

Thinking about unplugging and getting a change of scene:

- When was the last time you *really* unplugged?
- What example are you setting for time off, regular breaks, and overall pace at the office?
- What signals are you unconsciously sending regarding what "committed" looks like at the workplace?
- What would be different if you and your team made changing things up more of a priority?
- What would be different if you took more meetings while walking?

Control: The Double-Edged Sword

Between 1957 and 1978, Angus Campbell and his team of researchers at the Institute for Social Research set out to understand what gave people the greatest sense of well-being. This was quite revolutionary at the time, given that most social and medical research in those days sought to understand what made people sick, not what made them well. Campbell and his team published the results of their painstaking work in 1981 under the title the *Sense of Wellbeing in America*.

While most of us might think that one of the traditional measures of "doing well," such as wealth, health, or strong social/

familial ties, would have been the most important predictors of personal well-being, we'd all be wrong. Instead, people wanted one thing: control over their own lives. "Having a strong sense of controlling one's life is a more dependable predictor of positive feelings of wellbeing than any of the objective conditions of life we have considered," wrote Campbell in the final report.

And in case you think people have changed a lot since the 1970s when Campbell did his research, a 2014 Citigroup and LinkedIn survey found that nearly half of employees would give up a 20 percent raise for greater control over how they work.

Clearly, our employees are clamoring for autonomy and independence, yet all too often our urge to get things "just right" prevents us from giving that to them.

Let's look more deeply at Joe, the CEO of the small public health-care company we discussed in the introduction. It didn't take a PhD to realize Joe was a bit of a control freak. His personal need for control stood in stark opposition to his team's clear need for autonomy.

In a culture survey we did of the entire company, we asked them to describe the one thing they wanted to change. Here were their replies:

"Trust people to do their job."

"Stop interfering and complicating things.
Simple is sometimes fine!"

"Empower your people to make more decisions."

You get the idea . . .

When confronted with the data from the survey, Joe was surprised and felt a little victimized. "How could they say I'm controlling? I'm just exacting. I'm just living up to our values of 'challenging assumptions' and 'seeking the truth through transparency.'"

Joe had written a set of core values when the company was young around transparency and candor, but in recent years, those values had become weapons he used to control the team.

Joe professed that he was just being honest with his team, but in reality he was just being controlling. Excessive control is one of the most damaging traits a leader can have. It impacts morale, leads to poorer decision-making, increases turnover, and ultimately keeps the company from scaling. As we will learn in the next chapter, the "need" to control is not a legitimate need at all—it is actually just fear, which is often the result of unresolved childhood trauma.

At this point, some discerning readers might push back and say, "But Steve Jobs was the ultimate control freak, and just look at *his* legacy." True, Jobs was known for being quite demanding. But there was a big difference in Steve Jobs's use of control before and after he was fired from Apple in the late 1980s. The predeparture Jobs was unbearable by many accounts. He was brash and arrogant. But when Jobs returned to Apple in 1997, he had learned when to be demanding and when to let go. He had also learned about the importance of personal development and coaching.

The moral of the story here is that we all have a natural need to control our own lives. As leaders, we need to temper that personal need to make room for our team's natural need for autonomy. Building a team that is independent and empowered is one of the key ingredients to the long-term success of any company.

Your job as the leader is not to control the process but instead to focus on the outcomes. Coaching your team to have a similar or better focus on quality, design, and brand than you would builds their capacity to do great work. Instead of telling your teams how to write a press release or how to design the packaging on your product, how can you let go and coach them to solve their own problems? How can you empower them to take your vision and build upon it with their own ideas?

CHAPTER 1 TAKEAWAYS

- Leading with heart is hard work, and we need to have our needs met to do the emotional labor that is required to thrive and show up as heart-led leaders.

- Aside from our very basic needs to survive, we all have needs that must be met for us to thrive. These fall into three categories: physical, emotional, and environmental.

- If we pay close attention to how we feel in certain environments, around certain people, and when eating or drinking certain things, we can develop a very clear idea of what we actually need to feel resourced and creatively alive.

- Getting our needs met on a regular basis requires discipline and rigor. Just as we don't wait until the houseplants are withering to water them, we can't wait until we feel the lack of something to remember that it is one of our needs.

- Some clear tells that we ourselves or our teams are not getting their needs met: irritability, disagreements, anxiety, lack of motivation, and lack of creativity, all of which make us susceptible to being triggered into fear responses.

CONVERSATION STARTERS

1. What impact are your needs (physical, emotional, or environmental) having on your productivity and creative well-being?

2. What works for you to monitor your own needs and make sure you are taking care of yourself to the best of your ability? If you don't have a good strategy now, ask around—who has a good one you could try?

3. What unmet physical needs do you see in your team or organization? What's your plan for getting those needs met on your team?

4. What is working or not working regarding getting the emotional needs of your team met? What happens when people don't feel included or psychologically safe?

5. What are you blind to regarding the degree of psychological safety within your team?

6. Thinking about your office or workspace, what key elements contribute the most to and detract the most from you and your team feeling fully engaged and creative? What can you do differently to meet the environmental needs of your team, and your own?

2

WHAT FEARS ARE
HOLDING YOU BACK?

It is not fear that gets in the way of showing up—it's armor.
It's the behaviors we use to self-protect.

—BRENÉ BROWN

In a sunbathed office on Palo Alto's University Avenue, Ken was pacing nervously in front of the floor-to-ceiling windows on the second story. Veins were bulging on the side of his head, and he waved his hands violently as he spoke. Onlookers from the street may have thought he was rehearsing a dramatic speech. But no, Ken was lost in a paranoid rant about a member of his team trying to undermine his authority. Let's just say it wasn't Ken's best moment.

Edward had just reviewed Ken's 360 feedback with him, and the results were quite hard to take. In a nutshell, Ken's team universally disliked working with him. They said he was controlling, irritable, reactive, and vindictive.

While things had started out well when Ken first got the job, they quickly devolved into distrust, paranoia, and micromanagement. Although on the outside Ken seemed like he had strength and conviction, Edward surmised that on the inside Ken was caught in a downward spiral of fear that expressed itself in spiteful, aggressive behavior.

We all have fears. It is part of being human. Fear is natural in the business world, where leaders continually worry about losing out to the competition or making a crucial mistake. The key is to have the right balance of fear in motivating yourself and others, and not to let your fears bring out the worst in you.

In our coaching work, we have found fears can be *motivating* in moderation but *debilitating* when taken to their extreme. Conversely, in companies where there is no fear at all, there is often no impetus to create change or drive results.

Our clients are often blind to their fears because they have built various coping mechanisms to keep them hidden from view. This can be harmful since, at the extreme, fears can often manifest in physical ways causing increased levels of anxiety, panic, excessive worry, and stress. And even when not so extreme, they can negatively impact productivity, decision-making, and the morale of the entire organization.

When leaders can identify and engage in conversations about their fears, it can be a turning point in their leadership journey. They can learn to use their fears as sources of energy and motivation rather than being held captive by them. They can use them as springboards into compassion when they see colleagues trapped by similar fears they have since overcome, unlocking even deeper levels of connection, empathy, and trust—which in turn lead to better business outcomes.

What Is Fear?

Everyone experiences fear. It is an essential part of the human condition. If you had no fear, you'd be dead by now. If your ancestors had no fear, you never would have been born. A healthy level of fear keeps us from walking out in front of oncoming e-bikes, getting eaten by dangerous animals, and swimming near rocks in a roiling ocean. Taken to an extreme, an unhealthy level of fear can keep us from going outdoors, from meeting new people, or from speaking up in meetings.

While most people look at fear as a negative thing and something to avoid, others love the rush that comes from triggering their fears on purpose—jumping out of a plane, driving fast cars, or watching scary movies. Fear responses release endorphins that are actually a bit addictive. There's a reason we call those people "adrenaline junkies."

Most reactions to fear involve one of three standard responses: fight, flight, or freeze. During a fight-flight-freeze response, the amygdala, the most primitive part of the brain responsible for core survival functions, takes over. When we experience something we perceive as fearful, like a scary dog or a bus coming at us in an intersection, signals are sent within milliseconds from the amygdala that stimulate the autonomic nervous system with physical responses.

Our fears are not activated exclusively by clear and present dangers to our physical well-being. We can have similar fear responses that are triggered by psychological events. A fear of failure may cause a person to *freeze*, to avoid any chance of being wrong. A fear of not being liked may result in *flight* behavior, causing a leader to avoid conflict or difficult conversations. A threat to a person's competence may result in *fight* behavior, which manifests as anger or defensiveness.

That's right: the tens-of-thousands-of-years-old fear response that helped your ancestors avoid being eaten by saber-toothed tigers is alive and well in you when you get triggered at work because Fred from accounting asked you in front of the entire company a tough question you didn't have the answer to.

Our challenge to you as a leader is to name your fears, to have conversations about them, and ultimately to make them your ally. And in doing so, you will also be more able to see and name fear responses in others so you can move the conversation away from polarizing triggers and back into the zone of constructive conflict.

A Little Fear Is Good

In an article on the positive benefits of fear, Andrew Colin Beck coined the term *EuFear*, for "positive fear" (*eu* being the Latin prefix for "good" or "positive"), building on the work of Hans Selye, who originated the concept of *eustress* in 1974.

Selye argued that there is a positive cognitive response to stress that is healthy and gives one a sense of fulfillment and focus. Similarly, Beck suggests that we need a new paradigm for fear, as well, one that looks at the benefits of fear, not only the negative effects. His model reframes fear as a motivator and proposes a fear continuum ranging from no fear to full fear, with EuFear being the desired functional state.

When there is no fear in a company, people aren't motivated to do much at all. With no consequences for inaction and nothing to lose, people often don't take risks or initiative.

In contrast, teams that are working at full fear often experience crippling declines in performance. What's more, living in a nonstop state of full fear can cause unwanted physical effects, such as increased heart rate and lower oxygen levels.

Beck's model suggests that neither no fear nor full fear are ideal. Instead, his research indicates that the ideal for **functional fear** is at a 4 out of 10, slightly to the left of middle. It is at this point on the continuum that people experience fear that is positive and actually helpful in maximizing performance.

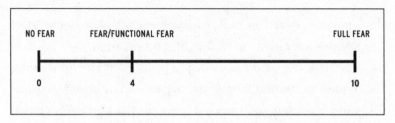

Beck EuFear Model

Turning Fear into Gold

To illustrate the potential benefits of fear and how to harness its power, let's go to a seemingly unlikely venue—a swimming pool.

Including relays, Michael Phelps has won a total of twenty-eight Olympic medals—twenty-three gold, three silver, and two bronze. That's ten more than the Olympian with the next highest lifetime medal tally, Larisa Latynina, a gymnast from the Soviet Union in the late 1950s and early 1960s. Which is to say, no one comes even close to the dominance Michael Phelps displayed over his sixteen-year Olympic career.

In trying to explain Phelps's seemingly superhuman feats in the swimming pool, scientists and journalists have explored many theories.

Some say it's his physical advantages. Phelps's "wingspan" (the distance between his fingertips) is eighty inches—six inches more than his height—while most humans have roughly equal wingspan and height. Additionally, Phelps is double-jointed in his elbows, knees, and ankles, giving him a wider range of motion than other swimmers. For example, his size 15 feet rotate a full fifteen degrees more than average, making them akin to flippers.

Yet when researchers analyzed the data, they determined that Phelps's physical attributes, while impressive, do not explain his dominance. Some swimmers who are similarly physically endowed don't perform nearly as well, while others with less noteworthy proportions have gone on to beat him on occasion.

So perhaps can we explain Phelps's performance by his training techniques? At the height of his training regimen, Phelps was swimming over eighty miles a week. He was in the water a fingertip-puckering five to six hours a day. Surely that is more than other swimmers? But again, we hear a resounding "nope." According to female gold medalist Jessica Hardy, *all* Olympic level swimmers swim six to twelve miles per workout, twice a day, six days a week.

Okay, so if it's not his physical attributes and it's not his training regimen, what else could it be?

US Olympic Committee sports psychologist Sean McCann has a theory. "The easiest thing for me is to predict the ones who will fail," McCann said in *Washington Post* interview in 2012. "The ones who are weak mentally never succeed at the Olympic Games because their vulnerabilities are exposed."

In contrast, according to McCann, Michael Phelps seems to have been born with an abnormal amount of mental strength. Basically, while many of Phelps's competitors apparently experience a freeze fear response under competitive pressure, a surge in nervousness or panic that tightens muscles, leading to the dreaded "choke," Phelps has a natural adrenal fight response to the same stress factors, generating a massive surge of energy and endurance. "Athletes who demonstrate mental weakness do not win medals . . . regardless of their talent or physical skills," McCann noted. When everyone else freezes, Phelps fights.

Growing up, Phelps was not the best at anything. Diagnosed with ADHD at nine years old, he had trouble in school. When his mother introduced him to swimming, at first he didn't even like getting his face wet, so he swam backstroke. He obviously overcame that fear quickly and learned that in the pool he could find focus and success that evaded him in the classroom. Leaving the frustration of not being able to focus in school behind, he became more and more determined to "prove them all wrong" while in the pool. His fight fear response was nurtured and developed over years of intense competition.

Phelps's incredible focus on competition came at a cost, however. When not winning in the pool, he felt as if his life had no meaning or purpose. When his Olympic career was over and the limelight waned, he became reclusive, withdrawing from friends and family. He fell into deeper and deeper levels of depression, even contemplating suicide at various points. It was as if his fear response when not in the pool was more flight than fight, fleeing from people and attention once he was no longer triumphantly winning races and setting records.

Miraculously, however, Phelps learned to flip the script on his fear once again. After hitting rock bottom, he sought help. He named his fear and depression, had courageous conversations with therapists and coaches about what ailed him, and has since become a global spokesperson for mental health. As a fighter against the stigma of depression, he is now a role model for people trying to overcome similar fears. He has found that the gift of mental toughness that served him so well in the pool can also manifest in a radical form of vulnerability. His bold openness about his depression and anxiety is helping to normalize mental illness and recovery for millions.

Although he will be remembered as the greatest Olympian of the modern era, Phelps's most enduring personal victory may be his willingness to confront his deepest fears and to choose a more productive response to them.

Leading with the Right Amount of Fear

So how does this idea of using fear to improve performance apply to leaders in the corporate world? When does fear cross the line from being positive to having a negative impact? When does it become destructive, causing personal and emotional harm to leaders and their organizations?

The challenge is to find that elusive point between inadequate fear, which can lull us into malaise and inaction, and too much fear, which can overwhelm us or our organization, leading to paralysis or toxicity.

Our experience in coaching is that many leaders are not aware of the fears that are impacting their behavior and the performance of their organizations. Let's look at some vignettes from a few clients we've worked with over the years.

Too little . . . A few years ago, we did some coaching at a company whose executive team was known as the Happiness for Lunch Bunch. When you spoke with anyone in the company, it was clear that there was no sense of urgency or accountability. People were happy, but productivity was low. The organization was not scaling, and the board lacked confidence that the leadership could produce the necessary profits.

We traced the problem to the CEO's love of positive news. His meetings lacked real, honest debate and conflict. Decisions were made by consensus to the point that people described the decision-making as "consensus paralysis." Crucial decisions took forever, and the tough calls were being avoided.

John worked with the CEO and the leadership team to integrate a healthy amount of EuFear into the culture, promoting more accountability and higher expectations. Through a series of feedback sessions with the CEO and the team, he held up the mirror to help them see what was really going on.

These sessions were difficult, but John established a set of rules of engagement that clearly specified what they needed to stop doing, start doing, and continue to do. As their team coach, John helped them apply these rules to their weekly leadership team meetings. Over time, the CEO and the team became more open, transparent, and accountable.

Too much . . . Another leader we worked with at a well-funded health-care start-up took ruling by fear to the extreme. In meetings he would literally shout down and brutally criticize his team. Small mistakes were met with scorn, and contrary opinions were derided with animosity and judgment.

As you might imagine, everyone in the company was basically in shutdown mode. Those who fought back at first eventually recoiled into silence. New ideas were not surfacing. No one was taking ownership. And since every little decision had to be run past the CEO, the company was unable to scale.

As company performance continued to fall, the CEO became more and more aggressive and accusatory. Executives fled in droves, and the company became caught in the dreaded death spiral. All because the CEO had no idea how to manage his anger, and thus manage the fear of his team.

According to Harvard's John Kotter, who literally wrote the book on *Leading Change*, triggering teams into paralyzing fear is one of the worst, and unfortunately most common, mistakes CEOs make. "I often see leaders who are trying to create change make the mistake of adopting a 'house on fire' mindset, and in the process they trigger a debilitating fear in their teams," said Kotter in an interview for this book. "An intense fear response from a leader who is trying to create action often creates inaction in the company."

Leading with *too much* fear it seems can cause people to have a freeze response, according to Kotter.

Just right . . . Steve Jobs has a reputation for having created fear and paranoia among his teams. Some thought it was too much, but looking at Apple's results during his tenure, it's hard to argue that it wasn't actually just right. When John started coaching at Apple during the early iPhone days, he saw Jobs's incredible gift for creating just enough fear on his team to engender indelible loyalty and sustain high performance.

It is not clear whether Jobs intentionally set out to create fear among his team, but he definitely had an intuition for it. As a result, leaders at Apple would spend hours or even days with their teams preparing for meetings with Steve, making sure that all the bases were covered. People were fearful of disappointing Steve and worked to bring their very best to meetings with him. This was EuFear in action, as Steve's behavior created a fear that motivated some people to perform at their highest levels.

The right amount of fear on teams creates what we call **constructive conflict**. If there is not enough fear and tension in the system, teams like the Happiness for Lunch Bunch fall into what Patrick Lencioni, author of *The Five Dysfunctions of a Team* and *The Advantage*, calls "false harmony": avoiding the tough issues, not having the hard conversations, and making decisions before controversial topics have been discussed.

At the other end of the continuum, teams can find themselves becoming polarized, like the health-care start-up we discussed

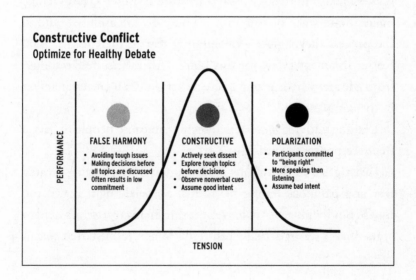

Constructive Conflict
Optimize for Healthy Debate

PERFORMANCE

FALSE HARMONY
- Avoiding tough issues
- Making decisions before all topics are discussed
- Often results in low commitment

CONSTRUCTIVE
- Actively seek dissent
- Explore tough topics before decisions
- Observe nonverbal cues
- Assume good intent

POLARIZATION
- Participants committed to "being right"
- More speaking than listening
- Assume bad intent

TENSION

above. This is dark territory where team members assume bad intent and are committed to being right because their fears are being triggered.

The ideal is to stay somewhere in the middle, in the zone of constructive conflict, as Steve Jobs so skillfully did with his teams. When teams have constructive conflict, there is enough fear that people are vigilant and take their responsibilities seriously, but not so much that they are hypervigilant and paranoid. There is psychological safety because the fear they experience is a healthy urgency to seize opportunities before the competition does, but not too much fear that creates uncertainty about their standing with the leader or their colleagues or sends them looking for other jobs.

The Leadership Fear Archetypes

It may be hard to imagine that leaders have fears just like anyone else. After all, many of them have built successful companies, negotiated huge deals, or raised gobs of money. Besides, they always appear so confident and in control. How could they have any fears?

In a *Harvard Business Review* article titled "What CEOs Are Afraid Of," Roger Jones reports on a study he conducted with 116 CEOs, finding that most executives have deep-seated fears: "While few executives talk about them, deep and private fears can spur defensive behaviors that undermine how they and their colleagues set and execute company strategy."

THE BIG THREE

There are three typical fear archetypes that leaders fall into, one for each of the fear responses: **fight**, **flight**, and **freeze**. Each archetype has an unexpressed underlying fear, as well as a "tell," a way of behaving that we can see quite plainly from the outside.

FEAR RESPONSE	ARCHETYPE	CORE FEAR	"TELL" BEHAVIOR
FREEZE	Perfectionist	Fear of getting it wrong	Chronic indecision & nitpicking
FLIGHT	People pleaser	Fear of not belonging or being accepted	Conflict avoidance & craving consensus
FIGHT	Impostor	Fear of being seen as incompetent	Arrogance, anger & irritability

To further understand each of these fear archetypes, let's meet three CEOs and learn how each of them manifested and managed their fears. As you meet each of these leaders, ask yourself: Which one do you most identify with? Do you identify with all three in different situations or environments?

And as we have throughout the book, since these are less than flattering stories, we have changed certain identifying details of our clients to protect their privacy.

CHRIS: THE PERFECTIONIST

Chris is the CEO of TeleSafe, a successful software security company. She graduated summa cum laude from an Ivy League school, where she played midfielder on the soccer team. Moving through her office, she gives off an air of grace embodied.

Google recruited Chris right out of school, and after twelve years she was considered an up-and-coming leader who could move easily into an executive leadership role someday. She was known for her thorough approach to products, making sure that things were not shipped until everything was exactly right. She describes herself as "process-oriented," putting into place the correct procedures and talking to all the right people to be sure every detail is considered and that all relevant parties are brought along.

A few years ago, her former classmate Phil approached Chris, asking her to consider joining forces with him to start a software security company. He'd already secured $1 million in seed capital and had notable early customer traction, but as a CEO he felt in over his head. Chris had always known Phil as an engineer, not a leader, but still she was surprised and humbled when he asked her to join him as a cofounder and become the CEO. He said he thought her extensive leadership experience and process rigor would complement his product and technical strengths.

Fast-forward a year later. One of TeleSafe's investors called us to see if we would consider coaching Chris. He indicated that she was struggling and that board members were raising questions about her effectiveness as a CEO. The investor indicated that Chris was open to coaching and aware that there were issues, but she was not sure how to deal with these challenges.

John started the coaching process by gathering feedback from Chris's team and members of the board. The feedback that emerged created a picture of a CEO stuck in freeze mode, unable to make key decisions. CEOs in freeze mode are often paralyzed by fear that they might make the wrong decisions.

The comments from Chris's team were telling:

"There is too much process in the organization."

"We avoid making key decisions."

"No one takes responsibility for getting things done."

*"We put off decisions and then fight fires at
the end when deadlines are missed."*

*"Chris wants to get every detail on our product
right, and we never ship on time."*

"We overcomplicate things; why can't we keep things simple?"

As Chris and John sat in her office overlooking the Embarcadero on a sunny day in San Francisco, she appeared somewhat
tense as they began their conversation.

John began by delivering the team's feedback, which was hard
for her to take. Initially she was defensive, claiming that the
problem was with her team. She felt that some members weren't
competent, and that she had been slow in moving poor performers out of the organization.

The Question. As they discussed some of the feedback that
was specific to her, John asked the crucial question: "Chris, what
are you afraid of?"

Her answer made it clear that her biggest fear was getting it
wrong and putting out a product that would not meet her or the
board's standards. She was fearful that if she didn't take time to
get things right, she would pay for it down the line.

But more than the words that she spoke, John remembers how
emotional she became as she explained herself. She choked up as
she spoke about how she had built her career on getting things
right and not putting out "crap" products. She paused for a moment and in a soft voice described herself as a perfectionist. She
argued that she would rather be late getting a product out than
not get it right the first time.

Her voice got louder and more defiant as she stressed the need
for meetings and thorough reviews to be sure that nothing was
missed. As she finished her thoughts, she said, "I'm afraid that if I
don't hold the line on making sure our products are high quality,
no one else will."

After some back-and-forth as to why this was important to her and where these beliefs and feelings came from, Chris and John proceeded to discuss the impact of her behavior on the team and the organization. She admitted that things were not good, and that she needed to make some changes. She was not happy about late launches, last-minute changes, slow decision-making, and team members' counterproductive behaviors.

Initially, she said she wanted "the team to take more responsibility and step up." But, as they ended their coaching session, she observed, "I think *I* need to change, but I am not sure how or if I can. My need to be thorough and scrutinize everything has always been a strength . . . it's one of the reasons I've been successful."

Chris's behavior clearly fit into the *perfectionist archetype*. She was so afraid of getting things wrong, she would freeze in indecision and never get anything across the finish line on time. Leaders characterized by this archetype perpetuate a culture of analysis and scrutiny that often paralyzes the team and the organization. Perfectionists rely too much on process, lack timely decision-making, engage in a pattern of firefighting, and continually miss critical deadlines.

These leaders fail to take responsibility for decisions and avoid making the tough calls. Perfectionists hide their fear and insecurity behind a veil of nitpicking, scrutiny, and criticism.

ANDRE: THE PEOPLE PLEASER

Andre is the CEO of EduSoft, a successful educational online learning company. EduSoft was founded two years before the Covid outbreak and is now well positioned to support teachers and students in online learning. In short, EduSoft's tools, resources, and software products are hot!

Andre started the company with a few friends after graduate school. Edward first met him after he raised a $40 million investment from a few of the top venture firms in Silicon Valley. In spite of the investment, the lead investor was concerned that

Andre, a first-time CEO, was having challenges with the team. He had just hired some new senior executives, and the board was hearing rumblings that things were not going well.

When Edward met with Andre, he experienced him as an outgoing, charismatic, and friendly individual. Andre smiled as he spoke, when he wasn't foused on listening intently. In general, he presented as a very affable persona. This guy is going to be great to work with, Edward thought.

As they began discussing their possible work together, Andre spoke extensively about the new team members and how they were not getting along. According to Andre, "Our biggest problem as a team is that people are not working collaboratively together. Team members demonstrate little respect for their peers."

After more discussion, Andre and Edward decided that Edward needed to focus on the team and that he should be a "team coach," with the goal of helping members become more effective. They agreed that Edward should talk to every team member and then observe the team in action.

As Edward proceeded to do interviews with each team member and to attend one of their weekly executive staff team meetings, he observed that the team dysfunctions Andre described were very real indeed, but that the issues were mostly the result of Andre's behavior.

It was clear that everyone liked Andre and that they respected his technical leadership. But it was also clear that Andre's leadership style, particularly in team meetings, was a major cause of the problem. It was more like an unstructured gathering of friends than a business meeting.

Without a clear agenda or focus, people just brought up topics they wanted to report on or wanted feedback on, and the team debated in circles forever. As a result, there were no clear outcomes, and no one knew what decisions, if any, had been made. As you might imagine, people began to dread Andre's endless, meandering meetings.

The trouble was that Andre wanted total consensus on key decisions. If there was no agreement, he would table the issue, and on many important topics no decisions were ever made. While Andre listened well and tried to hear all voices, when things got heated, he would back away and avoid the conflict.

As Edward observed the team, he saw visible frustration among the team members that key decisions were not being made. After the meeting adjourned, people shuffled out with their heads down and tight looks on their faces. Edward overheard one of the team members whisper to a colleague sarcastically, "Well, another great use of an hour."

As Edward and Andre walked back to the CEO's office, Andre expressed frustration at the team's inability to collaborate. "I try to give them space to step up and make decisions together, and instead they just debate endlessly."

Edward suspected that Andre was externalizing the problem and blaming the team for his own lack of decisiveness, but he wanted more data from the team to support his gut feeling. Interviews with the team members supported many of Edward's suspicions and pointed to additional CEO behaviors that were at the root of the problem.

Nearly every team member mentioned the excessive loyalty that Andre had for some of the early employees he hired, in one way or another:

> *"These people are no longer effective in their roles, and Andre doesn't have the backbone to get rid of them."*

> *"He's loyal to a fault."*

*"He can't deliver bad news and always
avoids difficult conversations."*

*"I love him, but he lacks the courage to make
the call when he needs to step up."*

*"His lack of decisiveness causes us to
constantly fight with each other."*

It was clear to Edward that Andre fell into the classic *people-pleaser archetype*, and that this feedback was going to be difficult for him to take. People pleasers have a baseline fear of rejection that leads them to avoid conflict, giving feedback, or sharing bad news. They want to keep everyone happy and drive toward consensus at the cost of progress.

Edward's feedback was going to hit at the very core of how Andre saw himself. Would he take responsibility and own these problems on behalf of the team? Would the feedback blindside him in a way that would paralyze his leadership? What was Andre afraid of? It was time to find out.

The Question. The feedback session started with Andre saying, "I am really looking forward to the feedback. I have a good team, and I know, even though there are issues, everyone has the best of intentions."

OMG, Edward thought. This is going to be even harder than I thought!

As Edward proceeded to share the feedback, it was apparent that Andre was stunned by all that he was hearing. He literally stopped talking and avoided looking Edward in the eyes. After a few minutes, he managed to utter a few responses and asked a question or two, but basically, he was devastated.

About forty-five minutes into the feedback session, Edward could see that Andre was beginning to tear up. In a very low and emotional tone, he started telling Edward how hard this was to hear—that he hadn't expected the feedback to be so negative. He knew that things were bad and that he could do better, but he had no idea that *he was the problem.* "Maybe I should just step down," he muttered. "Seriously. If they don't think I'm the right person for this, I can go do something else."

There's that flight again, Edward thought. The flight fear response often shows up as avoidant behavior: changing the subject away from the hard topic, not addressing issues head-on, or just up and quitting when things get difficult.

It was at this point that Edward said, "Andre, why don't you tell me what you're really afraid of? What's the fear that's coming up for you in relation to this team?"

The CEO then proceeded to talk about his need to be respected by the team. Not to have this respect would be hard for him. He elaborated about his great desire for everyone to get along and to like each other. He talked about the pride he felt in having built a culture where people were happy and worked together in a collaborative way. And after a long silence, he disclosed that he finds conflict uncomfortable and tries to do all he can to get everyone to reach a common ground.

Sensing a breakthrough was at hand, Edward pushed Andre to explore more deeply how and why conflict makes him so uncomfortable. He knew they were tapping into the real stuff. "Andre," he said, "I can tell that this is hard for you . . . Tell me a little about what comes up for you when you think about being accepted by a group. Why is it so important to you to keep the peace and make sure people get along? Sounds like that might be a pretty old habit."

With a big exhale and a glance up to the ceiling, Andre began to open up. He talked about wanting to be popular in school and doing everything he could to be accepted and liked by peers. He talked about his alcoholic father always fighting with his mother, and how he would get caught in the middle between his parents and his siblings. He described his role in the family as the peace-keeper, making sure that everyone got along.

With tears and a lot of emotion, he described how much he hated it when his parents fought. He recalled how his body would tense up, and how he would have this desperate feeling in his stomach. He hated it all so much, he would just run away. He said he ran away from home no less than five times before high school. And when he graduated, he went to a university on the west coast, getting as far from the stress and conflict of his childhood home in New Jersey as he could.

Edward could now see clearly where Andre's flight fear response came from. And his story hit Edward like a ton of bricks, since Edward grew up in a similar situation himself. It's uncanny how life sometimes brings us together with people who have the same core experiences so that we may facilitate one another's healing. And while we are not therapists and do not provide the long-term therapeutic relationship someone like Andre needs for deeper work, we can help clients see how their fears are affecting their work and point them in the right direction to do that healing work for themselves.

Listening and observing Andre as he talked, Edward could tell that he was experiencing some anxiety in the moment. "I can tell you're anxious just talking about these memories," he said. "Your breath is shallow, and your speech has sped up. Do you ever experience this same anxiety when you are leading the team?"

Andre's response was telling: he felt this anxiety all the time, especially when people were not getting along and fighting with each other. He was vehement as he expressed how much he hated it when people disrespected each other and couldn't find common ground. His anxiety was so high in these tense situations, he added, that he wanted to move as quickly as possible to resolve the conflict. In Andre's words, "I quickly employ my peacekeeping skills to bring the group back to finding a workable compromise. This works in the moment, but my team seems worse than it has ever been."

The people-pleaser archetype is characterized by a habitual flight response to fear. This doesn't necessarily mean Andre literally flees the room whenever he feels fear or anxiety, but he does his best to flee the moment, doing everything possible to keep everyone happy by changing the subject and avoiding tension or conflict.

Ironically, efforts to avoid open conflict only cause more of it behind the scenes. Because decisions are not made, team members engage in political maneuvering to advance their positions, often with mounting resentment. This is not an easy archetype to help. With people pleasers, we find the journey to change takes longer and involves deep reflection and healing.

LUIS: THE IMPOSTOR

Luis, a Harvard-educated doctor and entrepreneur, is the founder of HealthX, a health-care company whose mission is to use patient-centered analytics to make the health-care industry more effective and efficient for both patients and physicians.

John was introduced to Luis through a physician and investor who sits on Luis's board who was very bullish on the company, which had just completed a Series A funding round of $60 million. And although HealthX was growing fast, expecting to add fifty new employees in the next few months, the investor was concerned that Luis was continually stressed and having a hard time managing his role as a CEO in this fast growth period. It seemed like the perfect time to introduce Luis to a coach.

Upon first meeting him, John thought Luis seemed open to

learning how to better handle the challenges of his new role as CEO. Luis had never been a CEO before, and he was aware that he had a lot to learn. He wanted the coaching to provide him with some new tools so that he could better lead his company, and he emphasized how important it was that he be successful. "I don't want to disappoint anyone!" he said.

Our coaching agreements with leaders allow them to contact us at any time to discuss an important issue or decision that is causing them stress. We call this the 24/7 option, and Luis began taking advantage of it. A lot.

One afternoon, John and Luis met on short notice at Luis's request. Luis was noticeably stressed and upset as he talked about trying to balance everything in his life. As the father of newborn twins, he was finding it hard to balance the demands of family life with the pressures of work. His wife wanted him to be at home more. Luis was not sleeping and finding it hard to be calm and in control at work. He even described times where he experienced panic attacks.

In Luis's 360, the feedback John received from the team painted a picture of a leader who was quick to snap at people and often defensive, causing his employees to shut down in meetings. Team members found conversations with him difficult, as he "always had to be right" and "dismissed the ideas of others." His colleagues were becoming increasingly frustrated with his "command and control" style of leadership.

During the coaching session where John gave Luis this feedback, it was obvious that Luis was not in a good place. He looked tired and run-down. His eyes were red, and he was noticeably agitated. He started talking nonstop and, frankly, not making a lot of sense.

Seeing a need to change it up, John suggested that they take a walk. Luis agreed, and they stepped outside to take a stroll around San Francisco's South Park neighborhood, where Luis's company was headquartered. Luis really needed to talk, and walking set the stage for a meaningful coaching conversation.

When John asked Luis what was going on, he said that he wasn't sure what was happening, but that he was not sleeping. He said he had woken up the night before in a cold sweat, thinking about all the pressure he was feeling. "I had a dream that we had an all-hands meeting, and I had to tell everyone we were winding down the company. It was *way* too real, John!"

John just listened as Luis talked more about the stress he was under, repeating that he didn't want to disappoint anyone. As they sauntered along the San Francisco Bay behind the ballpark, there was a long pause. Finally John asked, "Who are you afraid of disappointing, Luis?"

Luis talked about how he was afraid that he would disappoint everyone, especially his parents. He described his upbringing in an immigrant Latino family in Albuquerque, New Mexico. His family was poor, and his parents both worked full-time. His mom held down two jobs—one that started early in the morning and the other a late-night shift.

Luis described his family as one full of love and support. His parents wanted something different for their children. He had two brothers and two sisters, and from an early age, they were all told that they had to get an education. The bar was set very high for all of them.

"My parents wanted all of us to have a better life, and for them education was the number-one priority. There's a reason why we all studied our butts off and went to Ivy League schools." Luis's energy shifted a layer deeper. Almost in a whisper, he muttered, "There's a reason why I went to Harvard and became a doctor. I've only ever wanted to make them proud."

They strolled along in silence for a minute, and Luis continued his story. He began to describe the challenges he'd had since leaving Albuquerque as one of very few "Brown kids" (as he put it) at Harvard, the only Latino in his medical school class. He talked about the undermining commentary from his classmates, who would hint that he was only there because of admission diversity goals. "What if they were right, John?!"

And now, as one of a small number of Latino entrepreneurs in Silicon Valley, he had similar worries. Even with a Harvard degree, he felt that he was often not taken seriously. He talked about how hard he had to work to convey the right image, and that he didn't fit the image of the classic CEO.

In his words: "If you haven't noticed, I'm not tall and white. I'm small and Brown, and I have an accent. So I compensate by using bigger words, by being loud, by talking fast all the time. I feel like I'm always selling . . . always faking it."

They continued their walk in silence for a few minutes as John let everything he'd just heard sink in. Luis was baring his soul here, and John wanted to give the topic the respect and space it deserved.

After another minute, John stopped walking and stomped his feet together to punctuate the moment. "So, Luis, tell me how these experiences and this belief that you are not taken seriously show up in your leadership. Tell me . . . what are you afraid of?"

Luis let his shoulders fall a little and looked down sheepishly. Then he shrugged and said quite plainly, "My biggest fear is that people will find out that I am not the smart person that they think I am. That I'm an impostor."

Bingo!

It was clear that Luis was falling prey to the *impostor archetype*. Being "found out" is one of the most common fears among all prominent figures, but especially new leaders who have never been CEOs before. A 2019 review of 62 different studies of over 14,000 participants showed that although impostor syndrome is uniformly common among men and women and across age groups, it is particularly prevalent among "ethnic minority groups."

The imposter syndrome has been more commonly spoken about in recent years thanks to the bold and personal revelations of prominent figures like First Lady Michelle Obama, actors Tom Hanks and Emma Watson, tennis champion Serena Williams, and former Starbucks CEO Howard Schulz, among scores of others.

People respond in different ways to feeling like an impostor. Some freeze. Some flee. But in our experience, the impostor archetype among leaders often shows up as a fight fear response, like they are trying to hide their fear of incompetency with antagonistic and controlling behavior.

Impostors often put on a thick coat of armor or even an aggressive bullying stance with their teams. "If I can point out the failures in others," they subconsciously tell themselves, "they won't have time to look at my potential failures." It's a classic overcompensation move.

The impostor archetype is extremely common among entrepreneurs, especially first-time CEOs, no matter their race, gender, or socioeconomic background, but especially so among the BIPOC founders we have worked with. In the words of one founder we coached, "We are all impostors; there is no way I could have had the success I have had without faking it. I just hope I don't get found out."

Luis masked his fear of incompetence by taking on the scrappy persona that has worked for him for most of his life. However, this time things were different. Both the physical and psychological effects were taking their toll on him and his company. Luis needed to embrace his fear, and our journey with him was only just beginning.

Making Fear Your Ally

This chapter has introduced you to three different leaders, all of whom struggled with fear. The question "What am I afraid of?" is a hard one to grapple with, and leaders can't always identify the fears that are impacting them, their teams, and their organizations. Of the five Leading with Heart conversations, this is often the hardest one to have and create change around.

Chris, Andre, and Luis all needed help identifying the role that their underlying fears played in their style of leadership. Each experienced and expressed their fears in different ways.

In Chris's case, her underlying fear and its impact on her leadership were not clear to her. She was aware that the team was not meeting deadlines, but unaware that her perfectionist behaviors, driven by fear of failure, were at the center of the problem.

With Andre and Luis, the fear was beginning to affect them both physically and psychologically, leading them to behave in ways that made them ineffective leaders who were hurting their organizations.

What are the strategies leaders can use to deal with their fears? How can Chris, Andre, and Luis apply these strategies to dealing with their own fears? How can you learn to manage your own fears?

We've developed a simple framework that we have found is helpful in coaching leaders to manage their fears. It involves:

1. Naming your fear and embracing it
2. Sharing your fear with a coach or colleague
3. Making a plan to choose different behaviors
4. Narrating your fear through storytelling

NAME YOUR FEAR AND EMBRACE IT
In our work, we find that we have more success when leaders are open to embracing their fears. This is not always easy to do, but

having a mindset of being open to naming and understanding fear is a good place to start.

Academic research supports the value of facing our fears. In her research on leaders and their strategies for dealing with fears, Tonya Jackman Hampton discovered that when they were able to name their fears, leaders were better able to explore and be open to strategies to deal with them. She discovered that while these fears never really go away, they begin to dissipate as leaders identify new ways to cope.

Leaders who view stressful events and fears as challenges to learn from rather than obstacles that could stymie their growth are more likely to improve their performance. Not all clients can embrace their fears right away. With some, it takes time to break down these barriers and move toward change. In other cases, leaders are unable to face their fears, which can result in the company failing.

For Chris, our work started making a difference when she was able to name her fear and recognize how her behavior was the primary cause for the poor performance of her team and the organization. By naming her fear, she could then have an open conversation with the team and engage them in helping her develop strategies for change.

This was hard for Chris to embrace at first. She and John worked together to write down and clearly articulate her fear and its impact on the organizational performance. This act of writing is critical in getting leaders to own and embrace their fears.

SHARE YOUR FEAR

Once the fear is named and written down, the next step is to share your fear with members of your team. We often ask leaders to choose a small group of people and ask them to provide feedback on whether fear is impacting the client's performance. These can be team members or others who work closely with the leader.

We usually coach leaders to use an open-ended process that begins with them naming their fears. We then encourage their teams to share how those fears might be affecting them. Here is the statement that Andre, the CEO identified as a people pleaser, used with his staff:

> *I have received feedback that our team needs to make decisions more quickly by engaging in more conflict and open debate. Our lack of decisiveness is causing problems among the team, with concerns that key decisions are not getting made. I realize that I am a big part of this problem and that my desire to promote collaboration and consensus can be counterproductive. I find conflict difficult and fear that too much conflict will destroy team morale.*

This opening statement set the stage for a number of questions that Andre used to gather additional feedback. Questions like:

- Can you help me understand the way you see it?
- What impact has my behavior had on you and the team?
- What behaviors should I *stop* doing?
- What behaviors should I *start* doing?
- What behaviors should I *continue* doing?

Gathering this kind of feedback helps leaders admit and embrace their fears. After collecting concrete feedback on specific behaviors that he should stop, start, and continue doing, Andre was ready to take things a layer deeper.

Working with Edward, Andre and his team were able to have a conversation about their dynamics. Edward established an environment to help everyone feel safe, and that enabled some people to open up and share their stories.

When we take the time to learn about each other's stories and fears, we are able to understand what's behind unproductive behaviors. Andre's vulnerability encouraged others to share. By creating this climate of openness and transparency, Andre helped his team to feel comfortable in expressing their opinions. They established a clear set of rules of engagement, which helped redefine the way that the group made decisions.

MAKE A PLAN

Fears run deep and are hard to change. Without a plan of action, nothing will change. The Naming My Fear model is an effective tool to help leaders move from understanding to real action. They start with a plan, but their teams help them expand upon that plan and make sure it is enforced. We find that when leaders are vulnerable about their fears and express a desire to do something about it, their teams respond in helpful ways.

The agreements identified in Chris's plan, next page, served as a "contract" to hold her and her team accountable.

NAMING MY FEAR

My fear: I am a perfectionist, and I have let my perfectionist behaviors negatively impact the performance of the team and the organization. These behaviors have caused us to continually miss launch deadlines, resulting in poor bottom-line performance of the company.	
My goal: To avoid analysis paralysis and commit to making decisions more quickly.	

STOP-START-CONTINUE BEHAVIORS	
STOP	• Overanalyzing and trying to make everything perfect • Having unnecessary meetings
START	• Assigning other team members to drive for closure on decisions sooner • Limiting the debate time on issues
CONTINUE	• To make quality decisions while getting product out more quickly • Support each other after tough debate

VULNERABILITY BEGETS VULNERABILITY

One of the observable outcomes from this process is that team members become more vulnerable themselves, often disclosing some of their own fears. One team member disclosed that he was reluctant to open up for fear that his comments would not add any value. He discussed his fear of not feeling smart enough, compared to the other smart people in the room. Once he identified and named this fear, he could begin to become an active participant in meetings. When leaders take off their armor and embrace their fears, it inspires others to reciprocate. With Chris, once she acknowledged her fear and committed to a plan to work on these issues with the team, change began to happen.

TELL YOUR STORY

One of the most powerful strategies for making fear your ally is to craft and tell your story to a broader audience. Stories inspire and motivate people, and help leaders connect with their teams. The fears that leaders have are often the same fears being experienced by others. Each of the leaders discussed in this chapter had compelling stories to tell about their fears.

Luis, for example, had a powerful story to tell—Latino heritage, humble beginnings, always having to work extra hard to prove himself, not wanting to disappoint anyone, especially his parents. His fear of being found out—of being an impostor—or failing was a key driver of his behavior. Luis had to overcome countless barriers on his journey.

Luis had to craft a story that was compelling and authentic, but that also let him display vulnerability while inspiring others. His story needed to show that he was evolving and growing as a leader.

John vividly recalls the coaching session with Luis when they first put the elements of his story together. They began with a brainstorming session in which John asked, "What do you want to say in your story?"

After an hour of back-and-forth dialogue, the following themes emerged from Luis:

- "I want to begin by talking about my family and my humble beginnings."
- "I didn't want to disappoint my mother."
- "What I lacked in size, I made up for in smarts."
- "I learned to never give up."
- "I wanted to be taken seriously."
- "I learned to be resilient."
- "I was knocked down so many times, but I always got up,"
- "I am learning to embrace my fears and let go more."

Luis created a ten-minute story from these themes, and committed to share his story at his company's next all-hands meetings. He asked John to attend the meeting, and it was one of the most memorable moments of his coaching career.

Luis began with his family story, and as he talked about his mother, tears began to well up in his eyes. His authenticity came through as he identified his own fears and how they have impacted his ability to show up and lead with patience and resolve. He concluded by connecting his own story of resilience to the culture of the company. The reaction was overwhelmingly positive, and his story became part of the company lore. From that point on, Luis never missed the chance to tell his story to new employees during employee orientation and onboarding.

Seeing and Working with the Fears of Others

Having read the stories of Chris, Andre, and Luis, you might not be surprised to learn that we believe that fears are the root cause of many unhelpful behaviors at the office—and yes, at home too.

The boss who rewrites your PowerPoint deck. The colleague who always seems to "forget" to CC you or invite you to important meetings. The direct report who has either gone noncommunicative or just complains to HR about feeling overworked and disempowered in his role rather than talking to you about it. The board member who writes scathing emails, but is always your best friend on the phone.

Learning to have the right conversations, conversations that allow us to see beyond disruptive or harmful behaviors and get to the underlying fears that motivate them, is a crucial skill that we all need to develop. The problem is, it's really hard—

especially when someone is stonewalling or throwing barbs at you.

People who are acting out of fear rarely do so gracefully. Instead, they often exhibit fight, flight, or fear behaviors that we have a hard time recognizing as such because we are most likely feeling attacked, confused, or abandoned by them—which in turn triggers our own fear responses and behaviors, and the pattern continues. Sound familiar?

If someone starts undermining you, your first instinct might be to undermine them back, or just to avoid them, depending on how you deal with fear. If someone starts ignoring you or cutting you out, you might give them the same treatment, or send off a hotheaded message.

We all know where that dynamic ends up: in toxic behavior—inability to work together or, worse, active subterfuge. It's amazing how poorly adults can behave when their egos are bruised. Because that's all it is, really.

We recently did a coaching project with the founding team of a leading retail start-up. Two of the three founders were no longer on speaking terms. They said they differed over strategy and vision for the company, but when you spoke with them one-on-one and asked about their visions for the company, they were maybe two degrees apart from each other.

It wasn't until we asked them to trace the relationship back to when it was most productive, or at least civil, that we began to see a pattern emerge. These mistrustful work relationships are often not due to one singular event. There is normally a pattern of behavior that erodes trust over time until one or both parties say "Enough!"

That's when the finger-pointing starts:

- "He always seems to take the credit."
- "She has the CEO's ear."

- "He says the same thing right after me, and only then do people pile on."
- "She plays politics behind my back."

But when we ask them about their own behavior and whether that might be upsetting their colleagues, they say innocently:

- "I'm just reporting on what the team is doing."
- "Am I not allowed to speak to my CEO?"
- "I'm done trying to change things."
- "I'm better at one-on-one meetings."

The problem with getting our fears triggered is that we assume negative intent on the part of the person who triggered us while remaining convinced of our own sterling intent. Our primitive fear response does not run through the prefrontal cortex; thus, it literally contains no sense or reason. It simply sees a colleague speaking over us in a meeting or not giving us credit, and it reacts as if that proverbial saber-toothed tiger is sprinting across the savannah at us.

Most of this chapter has been about learning to understand and manage your own fear responses. This section is to help you develop a keener eye for detecting when *you* are triggering a fear response in someone else.

Before we go any further, let us be clear: It is *never* your job to accept abusive or inappropriate behavior from anyone. This section is not about you turning the other cheek when someone is emotionally abusive or worse. What this section *is* about is helping you to develop the ability to recognize fear-based behavior when you see it and to learn to choose how you respond to it.

For simplicity's sake, let's break it down into two easy columns:

WHAT IT LOOKS LIKE . . .	WHAT MIGHT BE GOING ON . . .
Colleague cuts you out of meetings.	FIGHT or FLIGHT: Colleague might be feeling competitive and is experiencing a fear of being outshone by you.
Colleague redoes your work.	FIGHT: Colleague is fearful of making mistakes and feels a compulsive need to make everything 5 percent better.
Direct report continuously does subpar or late work.	FREEZE: Direct report is so battered by stress and nitpicking that she no longer tries.
Direct report surprises you with negative feedback in your performance review.	FLIGHT: Direct report does not feel safe enough to address his concerns with you and feigns agreement and trust.
Boss makes lots of last-minute and unreasonable demands.	FIGHT: Boss is triggered by the pace and stress of the job and can no longer think long-term, tries to control everything.
Boss gives terse feedback and always seems irritated with you.	FIGHT: Boss is triggered by feeling unqualified for the job and externalizes that impostor syndrome onto you.

Obviously, these are all random examples. Basically, the rule is that anytime someone comes at us with potentially hurtful or unhelpful behavior, we have a choice: **react** or **get curious**.

If we react, we will likely get triggered into fear ourselves, and we will escalate the situation by letting our own fears take over and run whichever fear script we are best at. Which means we will fight back, disappear, or just go quiet.

But when we get radically curious in the face of bad behavior, we sometimes have a chance to stop fear in its tracks. If we choose to get curious and confront our own fears and the fears of others, we have the opportunity to have compassion for the fear, which in turn gives us the chance to have a conversation about it.

People around us are acting out of fear all the time. Compassion and curiosity for that fear are your first line of defense. Once you see it and shine a light on it, it often disappears.

One client who was the CTO of a Fortune 500 company that was in the middle of a digital transformation process was dealing with a CEO who was deeply committed to his *shaming and blaming* behavior. Nothing was going fast enough. Everybody was "an idiot" (his words). Executive team meetings often ended in yelling. And anyone who brought his behavior up to him was met with ire. He was *not* leading with heart to put it mildly. The problem was that his *ideas* were golden, it's just that his *delivery* was fear-laden and toxic.

Normally, we encourage clients to have courageous conversations to resolve conflict, but sometimes the environment is too toxic for such direct communication. To resolve this, Edward suggested his client draft a deeply compassionate but anonymous letter that basically said, "You're the smartest person in the room. Your ideas are exactly what we need. But you are driven by fear right now, and you will drive most of us away if you don't fix it."

When the CEO first read the message, he was probably livid, but as the message sunk in, it began to have its intended impact. Sometimes in a hostile environment, it takes an "involuntary 360" to throw a bucket of cold water on a leader who is stuck in a fear response loop.

At the next executive team meeting, when he held the letter up, our client held her breath. But after a few defensive remarks, the CEO thanked whoever sent it, and promised the team that he would find a coach. Mission accomplished.

Sometimes, however, people are committed to their fear story no matter what you do. They are committed to feeling fearful, wronged, stressed out, or what have you. In that case, you may not be able to extinguish their fear, but you can still choose how you respond to it.

Your own knowledge that the person is coming at you or being hurtful in some way because *they* are committed to being fearful helps your brain avoid getting triggered into your favorite fear response, which keeps the situation between you from escalating. And that's a good thing for everybody.

You do not have to be perfect overnight at recognizing fear-based behavior, but commit to getting incrementally better at it over time. The first step is seeing that almost every negative behavior someone throws at you is in reality a fear response. They are either in fight, flight, or freeze.

Once you begin looking at people through that lens, you will see fear everywhere. Sometimes their fear is in response to something you are doing, but most often it is not. And armed with that insight, you will start choosing how to respond more appropriately.

Overcoming the Fear of Asking for Help

Of the many fears that hinder teams, the fear of asking for help is one of the most dangerous and deserves special mention here. When people feel like they have to have all the answers, they often sit on problems too long and create even bigger problems. The best way for leaders to address this issue organizationally is to role-model asking for help themselves.

One particular coaching session John had with one of his top CEO clients, let's call him Neal, was not like the others. Almost as soon as they got on the call, John could tell that Neal was not in a good place. Neal is usually upbeat, always generating positive energy, and this was a new Neal that John was seeing.

Neal was describing the pressure he was under to scale the organization. He felt a big burden to deliver to investors who had just given his company over $200 million to expand internationally. As they explored Neal's frustrations and sticking points, it became clear that Neal was not spending enough time on the important big strategic decisions that would define the company's trajectory over the next few years. Neal wanted to take the company public in the next eighteen months, but instead of thinking about the big picture, he was stuck in the weeds.

As founder of the company and a naturally gifted strategist, Neal thought putting together the strategic plan was something that he should be able to do on his own, but he was uncertain. "As a first-time CEO, I had the answers during the early start-up stages, but I have never done this at scale. I have ideas but no real answers."

John asked Neal if he knew of someone who could help him resolve some of these strategic dilemmas, but Neal was a little resistant at first. *Aren't CEOs supposed to have all the answers? Wouldn't I look weak to my team or the board if I asked for help?*

The fear of asking for help is all too common in the business world. People worry that they will look bad or weak in the eyes of their colleagues. But research suggests the opposite is true. A 2015 study showed that when people in leadership positions ask for help, their perceived competence actually goes *up*, not the other way around, as one might fear.

Sitting there with John, Neal realized that he wished other members of his team would ask for help more often. They were all such brilliant people, and they weren't using each other as resources enough. Perhaps if he modeled that behavior himself, he could signal to the rest of them that asking for help is not just okay—it's preferred.

He thought for a moment and then mentioned an investor who we'll call Jim as a possible person he could go to for help. Jim was a seasoned and successful former CEO himself who had weathered many of the challenges Neal was facing. The more Neal and John discussed this idea, the better Neal liked it. They spent the rest of their session generating the strategic questions that Neal wanted to ask Jim. By the end, he said he was committed and ready to have the conversation.

A couple of weeks later, Neal reported back to John on the meeting. Jim didn't have the answers to all of Neal's questions, but he had given him guidance on the critical things to focus on now and in the future. Jim was able to help Neal see things more clearly and discern where he should be focusing his energy.

As coaches, we often encourage our clients to reach out to mentors to ask for help during inflection points in the business. Recently, we connected Tony Xu, CEO of DoorDash, with Tim Cook at Apple, who was helpful in giving him guidance on the business challenges he was having.

When leaders are stuck, their first instinct is often to go inward. What they don't realize is that they are modeling that behavior to their teams. Fear of asking for help can be contagious, and it can infect the entire organization. When you get stuck, who might be the right person to talk to? If you have a board, maybe a board member might be of help, or be able to recommend others.

If you look around, you are sure to find someone who has successfully navigated similar challenges. Asking for help shows strength and humility and is the perfect behavior to model for your team.

Postscript:
What Happened to Chris, Andre, and Luis?

We often get asked about the real impact of our coaching with leaders. Did the coaching make a difference? Did anything change? Was the change sustained?

Chris: Chris made great strides in her leadership and began to let go of her perfectionistic behavior. Products got out on time. She credits the hiring of a COO and the stop-start-continue activity with her team around her fear as major factors in removing barriers and changing her behavior. Her company went public two years later.

Andre: Andre made good progress in the earlier stages of the coaching: more healthy debate and constructive conflict arose in his group meetings, and new ground rules helped the group make key decisions sooner. But this only lasted for four or five months, and then Andre began to fall back into his old behaviors. Frustrations began to mount among the team members, and people talked more about leaving the organization. The crowning blow happened when Andre was unable to get rid of a longtime underperforming leader who was a close friend.

A year after the coaching ended, the board brought in a new CEO, and Andre became a member of the board. Andre's high need for approval and conflict aversion had made it increasingly difficult for him to make decisions and scale the company. While he was not successful in sustaining changes in his behavior, the coaching process did help Andre embrace the transition and support the need for a more decisive and operational leader.

Luis: Once Luis embraced his fears, he was able to continue to grow and learn. His behavior didn't change overnight, but as the company grew, he was able to trust his team and empower people more. He learned that he didn't need to be the smartest person in the room all the time. He considers his storytelling event as the single most important element in helping him take off the armor that was hiding his fears. Luis's company became wildly successful, and he ended up selling it for a high-nine-figure sum. He has since started a second company, where many of his original employees have joined him.

We hope this chapter has provided you with insights on the fears that may be holding you back as a leader. Once you identify your fear, name it, share it, and develop a plan, you will be able to tell your story and grow as a leader. When you stop to ask what fear may be motivating someone's behavior, you can sometimes diffuse it. Fear can be scary, but leaders who face it head-on are more likely to make lasting changes.

- Fear is a natural thing, something that all leaders experience.

- Underneath all fears are deeper underlying emotions and unmet needs; uncovering these emotions is critical to understanding what is keeping you from becoming the leader you can be.

- Not all fear is bad, and finding the right balance of fear on your team can help you maximize your performance and the performance of the organization.

- Understanding fight, flight, and freeze patterns and their corresponding archetypes can be helpful in understanding and managing your fear.

- The perfectionist, people pleaser, and impostor archetypes are common patterns for leaders; identifying your type can be helpful in developing strategies for managing your own fear and that of your teams.

- Naming, embracing, and sharing your fears are important elements in helping leaders manage their fears.

- Storytelling is an effective way to normalize fear in an organization. Sharing your story can be a powerful step in embracing your fear and sparking conversations about fear with others.

- Most unproductive or hurtful behaviors we experience in others are motivated by fear. When we get curious and try to see the fear behind the actions that hurt us, we have a better chance of resolving the conflict without being triggered into fear ourselves.

CONVERSATION STARTERS

1. When you are feeling stressed or in some conflict, what is your go-to fear response? Are you more likely to get annoyed and argue, get quiet and pretend nothing is happening, or leave the situation altogether?

2. Which CEO story did you most identify with, and why? Are there parts of more than one story that you connect with?

3. How have your fear responses worked against you or the company in the past six months?

4. What deeper questions or old stories that you tell about yourself might you want to explore with a therapist or coach to uncover where your fear responses come from?

5. What questions or interventions from others bring you back from the brink of having a fear response?

6. What are your team members most afraid of? What has been your role in triggering your team's fears? How can you change this?

7. Think of someone you sometimes have conflict with at work (or at home). What fear response might they be having, and what could you do or say to address their fear with compassion instead of with your own fear response?

3

WHAT DESIRES DRIVE YOU, AND WHICH MIGHT DERAIL YOU?

Love can make you do right.
Love'll make you do wrong.

—THE REVEREND AL GREEN

At his peak, his name was synonymous with resilience, dedication, and victory. He was one of the most decorated athletes of all time, and most certainly number one in his sport. His entire personal brand was about pushing the limits, working hard, and never giving up.

His training regimen was the stuff of legend. Up to eight hours a day. Weights, running, cycling. Anything to extend his aerobic threshold, that point of exhaustion when the human body stops using oxygen and food to create energy and switches over to the anaerobic process that burns stored glycogen. The longer you avoid going anaerobic, the more endurance you have.

Scientists would invite him into their university labs to study him, as if he were an alien. They would poke and prod while he ran on treadmills, wires dangling off his chest and back. But mostly the men and women in lab coats would scratch their heads in wonder. How could his body use oxygen so efficiently? How could he convert food to energy so quickly? How could he cruise to victory with ease and grace on his face, while his opponents wore furrowed brows of anguish? How could he bounce back from cancer so quickly and regain his title?

Indeed, he seemed superhuman. And when asked what the secret to his success was, he would say plainly, "It's simple. Success comes from training harder, living better, and digging deeper than the others."

Train harder. Live better. Dig deeper. What an inspiration.

But then, after over a decade in the limelight, after nearly everyone in the United States, from Oprah to John Kerry, wore one of his yellow bracelets, after his fans donated over $500 million to his foundation to support cancer survivors, after being talked about alongside one-name sports legends like Babe, Ali, Tiger, and Jordan, it was revealed that Lance, the pride and joy of Austin, had been cheating.

Not just as he got older.

Not just to aid him in recovery from testicular cancer.

But the entire time.

And just like that, Lance Armstrong went from being the most revered athlete in the world to the most reviled. In the aftermath, he lost his titles, his sponsorships, his wife, and his good name. He also brought down the reputation of the entire sport of competitive cycling and ruined the lives of many of his team members, not just from the fallout of the controversy but also from his abusive behavior before the curtain came down.

But why? Why did Lance Armstrong, the greatest cyclist who's ever lived, a perfect human specimen with aerobic superiority, need to cheat? What drives someone to betray the trust of the entire world?

Reading through articles about him, it becomes clear: "I wanted to win the Tour de France. And when I won it once, I wanted to do it again, and again, and again. It just kept going."

He simply wanted to win again, and again, and again. And eventually his desire to win became so strong, it overpowered his ethics, his sense of duty to his fans, and his moral obligations of fairness and sportsmanship to his team and his competitors.

The negative impact Lance Armstrong had on cycling as a sport and on his former teammates cannot be understated, especially given how well he has fared despite his downfall. Even after paying penalties and having his titles stripped, he still has an estimated net worth of $50 million, while many of his former teammates, the victims of his abuse, have been left destitute.

The natural and healthy human desires to win, to grow, to help, to create, to be loved and admired can propel us to do great and admirable things. But when taken to an extreme, those same desires can become unhealthy, turning us into shadows of ourselves—into people who destroy relationships, say hurtful things, and drive companies and careers into the ground.

Heart-led leaders learn how to keep their desires in check, harnessing their productive drives and moderating their less healthy and unproductive ones to ensure they don't get derailed—or derail their teams—with negative behaviors.

This chapter will help you gain deeper insight into the nature of your own desires, and give you tools to have conversations with your teams about their deepest desires, through powerful stories, exercises, and questions. Of all the chapters in this book, this one has the most cautionary tales of leaders who have fallen from grace. Why? Because it is precisely satisfying our basic human desires, doing the things that feel good in the near term, that can lead us astray and derail us in the long term.

What Is Desire?

If we assembled a hundred people in a room and asked them about their deepest desires, we'd likely get some wild and diverse answers. No two people are motivated by the same core desires. But to write a chapter that discusses our desires, we do need to narrow down the field and talk about what we find, and what the research suggests, are the most important.

Since antiquity, philosophers and scholars have tried to distill the core drivers of human behavior into a few discrete themes. Aristotle and other Greek philosophers believed our core desires could be split into two categories: desires of the body (food, water, sleep), and desires of the intellect (curiosity, morality, and belonging). In the 1800s, Freud argued that all motivation came down to one thing: sex. And the so-called hedonists of the twentieth century believed that all human behavior could be explained as either pleasure-seeking or pain-avoiding.

While it would be nice to explain all human behavior in one or two memorable snippets, recent research indicates it's a bit more complex than that. Being overly reductive when we are trying to achieve fine-grained insights about what makes specific individuals tick puts us at risk of grossly missing the mark. Our core desires and drivers are much more nuanced than body versus intellect, pleasure versus pain, or sex versus celibacy.

In the early 2000s, psychologist Steven Reiss performed an extensive study of over six thousand individuals on four continents to enrich our understanding of what really drives people. Rather than landing on two or three core drivers, he and his team uncovered sixteen different desires that motivate us.

Many of them, like food, aesthetic beauty, and exercise, we put into the needs category. In our framework, needs are those things we must have to feel fully *resourced, resilient,* and *ready* to do our best work. Desires, on the other hand, are those things within us that *motivate us* to do our best work. If getting our needs met is like tuning up and putting gas in the car, our desires can either press the accelerator pedal or slam on the brakes. It's a subtle but important distinction.

For our purposes, we will explore five groupings of desires Reiss and his team outlined that we see alive and active in our clients and the companies they work in:

- **Acceptance, love, and intimacy.** We all want to be loved and accepted. It drives us to be kind, accepting of others, and collegial. It can also derail us by making us people-pleasing, insecure, and lascivious.
- **Competition, resentment, and revenge.** The drive to "win" is one of the most basic human desires. It's what creates the thrill of the game. It motivates us to seek mastery. However, wanting to win at all costs or seeking to punish those who best us can bring out the worst in us.
- **Curiosity, learning, and variety.** When we have a growth mindset, we see ourselves as infinite . . . there's nothing we cannot learn, no skill we cannot develop, no problem we cannot solve. But taken to an extreme, this can lead to navel-gazing and perfectionism. The paralysis of analysis sets in, and we either take no action, or too many unfocused actions.
- **Power, status, and recognition.** Someone always needs to lead . . . that's why we are writing this book. It's also fine to be motivated by recognition. But when leading becomes more about the leader than about those being led, we can fall into power grabbing, status seeking, and other unhealthy behaviors.
- **Service and justice**. Although we still have a long way to go, where would we be today if no one sought to abolish slavery, supported women's right to vote, or put an end to unchecked air and water pollution? The desire to serve and do what's right becomes derailing, however, when we become self-righteous

BEHAVIORS THAT TELL US WHEN OUR DESIRES
ARE MOTIVATING OR DERAILING

DESIRE	MOTIVATING	DERAILING
ACCEPTANCE AND LOVE	• Responding well to feedback • Expressing gratitude • Showing generosity of spirit • Demonstrating healthy sexual boundaries • Focusing on the team	• Constantly seeking feedback and credit • Hoarding information or budget • Demonstrating unhealthy sexual boundaries • Focusing on self
COMPETITION	• Commitment to excellence • Being intrinsically motivated to be the best • Focus on efficiency • Creativity and innovation	• Irritability and a tendency to criticize • Morally ambiguous decision-making • Obsessive focus on rivals
CURIOSITY AND LEARNING	• Delegation of decisions • Openness to new ideas • Creativity and innovation	• Inability to delegate • Creative chaos • Systemic indecision
POWER AND STATUS	• Focusing on getting things done • Mentoring and coaching • Being willing to get hands dirty • Making respectful requests of team	• Focusing on titles and perks • Giving orders and overdelegating • Behaving as if "above" some tasks • Making unreasonable requests of team
SERVICE AND JUSTICE	• Using language of inclusion • Being open to dialogue • Embracing science and data	• Using language of exclusion • Focused more on being right, than doing what's right • Embracing fringe theories

or self-destructive. We need not sacrifice ourselves or our
relationships in the name of service.

Is this list of human desires exhaustive? Not at all. Nor it is
meant to be. Maybe you have an unshakable desire to live alone
and collect comic books or classic cars or bits of driftwood. That's
cool—we're not seeking to address every potential human desire.
Instead, we've tried to distill the list down to those desires that,
in our experience, drive leaders to lead well or derail them altogether.

As you read through the following stories, ask yourself: In what
ways can I see some aspect of this applying to me or to my teams?

Acceptance, Belonging, and Love

"I just want to be loved. Is that so wrong?" If you are old enough
to remember late-1980s *Saturday Night Live*, you'll remember Al
Franken's Stuart Smalley whining self-affirmations into his mirror and begging to be loved.

We all want to be loved and accepted. The question is, to what
lengths are we willing to go in pursuit of that love and acceptance? What are we doing unknowingly that actually makes love
and acceptance elusive for us? Or what do we need to do as leaders to make the people we work with feel accepted and included?

Our desire to feel acceptance, belonging, and love is biologi-
cally hardwired in us. Human beings are social beings. Before we
built big cities, our ancestors banded together in tribes. Being
accepted by the tribe was an existential matter to a young person
living in a forest filled with wolves, bears, or jaguars. Only by
working together are we able to take on many of the essential
aspects of survival. Only together do we create culture, feel love,
and play games.

In today's world, our coworkers are as close as most of us we will ever come to having a tribe. Studies have found that the most successful companies are those that engender feelings of loyalty, camaraderie, or even a cultlike devotion among their employees. When people feel like they belong to and are accepted by a "tribe" they believe in, they work harder than they would otherwise. When they feel a lack of connection and inclusion, they check out.

Think about your company or team. Whether you are the CEO or the receptionist, you know if you are working in an inclusive working environment. If you're unsure, pay attention. Do critical decisions happen behind closed doors? Is there a focus on *what* needs to get done and a lack of context around the bigger picture and *why* things are happening? And while we'll talk more about purpose later, what's important to know here is that clarity around purpose, context, and the path to success makes people feel *in* on the plan.

BEING INCLUSIVE IS WORTH THE SQUEEZE

Inclusive cultures are not just more equitable—they are good business. Rick, the CEO of a soon-to-IPO company in the media space, reported to us that he had a very high-performing executive team but was dealing with what he called "a lack of quality execution" at the VP level. As is often the case, that was only the beginning of the story.

The executive team, composed of the C-suite and a few of their chiefs of staff, was very close and had deep trust. Many of them were "OGs," meaning they had been at the company since the early days. They had a regular cadence of high-quality meetings with healthy, rigorous debate and generally arrived at ambitious and strategic decisions. We were very proud of the coaching work we had done to get them to that point.

But in the broader culture and engagement surveys from the

company at large, we noticed a problem. Whereas the exec team was reporting a lack of execution at the VP level, the senior directors and VPs were universally expressing dissatisfaction with the lack of communication and context coming from the C-suite. Although good decisions were being made, the way in which they were being made did not feel inclusive. VPs with twenty years of industry experience were being handed marching orders, not interesting problems to solve. In the words of their VP of digital marketing, "This isn't what I signed up for. I feel like I'm a short-order cook, not a respected thought partner."

A lack of inclusion can take many forms. In some companies, the fracture between those who feel included and those who don't falls along racial or cultural lines. In this company it was falling along lines of tenure—the longer your tenure at the firm, the more included you were. In some ways, this makes sense. Trust builds over time. Getting through the early days of uncertainty, teetering on the verge of bankruptcy, and still sticking with it bonds people together.

But unknowingly, these OG teams hoard information and decision-making authority and starve the next level of leaders in the company of much needed context and empowerment. Not only does it create resentment, but it often results in suboptimal business outcomes. The VPs and directors are often closer to the work itself. They know the customer. They see the bottlenecks and operational challenges. When senior teams don't involve these junior leaders in decision-making, they can be flying blind to many of the on-the-ground realities of the business.

Many of these second-level leaders are also often high performers who were poached at great expense from other successful companies. They are recruited for their domain expertise, their contacts, or their knowledge of how to scale processes. And yet all too often they languish as disempowered middle managers.

Looking at the data with John, Rick realized that something

needed to change. Having spent most of his time developing relationships with his C-suite members, he had not realized that
there were a couple dozen highly qualified and very well paid
leaders in the company who felt left out in the cold.

John and another one of our coaches embarked upon a multi-
week process to document the VPs' unspoken resentments, frustrations, and feelings of being excluded. They interviewed both
the VPs and the C-suite members and captured verbatim quotes
that were emblematic of the problem.

At an off-site at a Napa Valley retreat center, they all spent a
few days walking through the data and having clearing conversations. Once the topic was broached, it felt like everyone could
relax for the first time. The toxic undercurrent that wasn't being talked about was finally on the table and, knowing that they
weren't alone, people finally felt comfortable sharing.

A lack of inclusive behavior in senior leadership teams like this
often comes down to one common but unhelpful assumption: *It's
easier if we just do it ourselves*. As we've mentioned, many senior
teams at fast-growth start-ups are composed of people who have
been working together for a long time. They have high trust.
They've developed their own language. They are the *in* crowd.

They are busy too, and delegating takes time. There's also uncertainty about the quality of the result. To do it well, you have
to provide adequate context, support through coaching, and en-
trust someone with the final decision. What if they make a bad
decision after all that? It can often feel like the juice isn't worth
the squeeze when the answer seems obvious.

But over time a lack of delegation and inclusion erodes operational leverage and creates an entire organization of doers with
very few decision makers. This is by definition *not* scale. If the
next level of leadership is included in decisions, they learn "what
good looks like" and soon are making better decisions than more
senior leaders could make without them.

As a result of this off-site, the company decided to commit to more inclusive processes and behaviors. The C-suite got clear about the kinds of decisions they should be making (i.e., ones that impact the next three or four quarters, not just three or four weeks) and began delegating the rest to their VPs.

Although the changes created a lot of anxiety and uncertainty at first, the long-term results were nothing short of miraculous. Within a few months, the mood around the office began to shift. More creative ideas started bubbling to the surface in staff meetings. People started taking bigger risks. And that jovial sense of camaraderie they all craved began to emerge.

Leading with heart requires stepping back, widening the lens, and getting curious about what's going on under the surface. All too often we make decisions based on what feels most efficient for those closest to us in the near term. But, as we know, shortcuts rarely yield the best results. Being more inclusive might feel less efficient at first, but it is ultimately where true scale comes from.

Suggestions for starting a conversation about inclusion on your team:

- In what ways does your team box people out or make them feel excluded?
- Is there an in crowd at your company who seems to make all the decisions?
- How would things be different if your team invested in more inclusive processes?

THEY WANTED AN ANSWER TO A DIFFERENT QUESTION

Edward likes taking clients on walks for their coaching meetings. Getting moving helps generate new ideas. As Nietzsche said, "All truly great thoughts are conceived while walking."

In one walking meeting, Amy, the chief product officer of a fast-growing health-care start-up, was telling Edward how the glacial hiring process for their new CTO was creating a lot of swirl on her team. She was being asked questions on a daily basis that she simply didn't have the answers to: When will they fill the position? How will the engineering team composition change? Who will be the new contact in engineering for X project? When will we be able to move forward with Y project?

So many appropriate questions, but when Amy ran those questions up to the CEO or COO, she would get the same response over and over: "Unclear. Sorry. We will let you know when we know more."

One of the fun things about working in start-ups is that you are constantly doing and building things that have never been done before; one of the hardest things about working in start-ups is that you are constantly doing and building things that have never been done before. All that newness brings with it uncertainty and ambiguity.

Comfort with ambiguity has long been touted as crucial for executive success, especially in today's fast-growth start-up environments, where nearly everything can change quickly. But in Amy's case, she was dealing with middle managers who had not yet developed that skill, and she wasn't going to be able to train them up in a matter of weeks. Yet the more she passed down the we'll-let-you-know-when-we-know response, the more anxious and distracted her team became.

That's when Edward asked her, "What if they want an answer to a different question?"

Staring blankly, Amy took the moment in. "What do you mean?"

"What if they want an answer to a different question? You're spending all this energy trying to get them the information they are looking for, but what if they don't really desire clarity on that question, but rather on a much deeper one?"

She blinked a few times, and they kept walking. Edward let the question steep a little.

After a few minutes Amy asked, "What other question could they be asking? Why wouldn't they just come out and say it?"

One of the many interesting things about humans is that we often aren't fully aware of the emotional processes or desires that drive our actions. We say we are just bored when we pick up our phones and scroll through social media or dating apps, but what we are more often seeking is approval. We say we are hungry when we open the fridge to find the chocolate ice cream, when what we are really feeling is lonely. Sorry if that stings a little.

Sometimes when we ask for definitive information at work, what we are actually seeking is reassurance that we still belong— that we are safe. What Amy's team really wanted was assurance that the shake-up on the tech team wouldn't negatively impact their jobs, or that she would have their back if it did. They wanted to know that she would fight for them because, as far as she was concerned, they were important members of the tribe.

That's when she stopped in her tracks, held her hands to her brow, and exclaimed, "Wait, what? Of course!"

She could see it all clearly now. All the overly specific "What is going to change?" questions about the hiring process on the other team really translated to "What is going to change for *me*?"

It seems so simple, but in the moment, we often take the bait. Someone asks a specific question, and we try to find a specific answer. But when the answer to their question doesn't exist, it behooves us to try to look deeper and determine whether they really want the answer to a different question.

Push yourself to develop the habit of always looking a layer deeper:

1. When was the last time you took the bait and didn't look a layer deeper for what people were *really* asking?
2. What would be different for you and your teams if you kept in mind that when people ask for specifics around changes in the business, they are really asking about their own desire to belong?

CONFLATING INCLUSION AND CONSENSUS CREATES BUREAUCRACY

It bears repeating that making people feel included is one of the core tenets of leading with heart. Effective leaders showcase and reward inclusive behaviors across the entire business. Why? First, because it's the right thing to do, but second, it's also good for business.

According to Deloitte, inclusive companies have 2.3 times higher cash flow per employee than their less inclusive peers. A Gartner study determined that inclusive teams' performance is improved by up to 30 percent. And a BCG study found that companies with diverse and inclusive management teams had a 19 percent increase in revenue compared to their less diverse counterparts.

Author and relationship expert Esther Perel says that diversity of relational styles needs to be added to our understanding of diversity in the workplace: "In every group you have people who will jump at the chance to talk, and people who have no less important things to say, but are either more deferential, more shy, more perfectionistic, more unsure, or come from a culture where you let others speak first. And that's totally normal. All of this makes for a healthy group. It's important for leaders to name and normalize that."

And yet, despite all of its proven benefits, attempts at inclusion can also have negative outcomes when not planned and executed thoughtfully. Let's look at a case study from one client as an example.

Stacy is the CEO and founder of a hot direct-to-consumer skin-care brand. Since founding the company she has been careful to prioritize diversity and inclusion in her hiring and management practices and has enjoyed many positive cultural and bottom-line business outcomes as a result. When we last spoke to her, she was courting various acquisition offers from larger heritage brands. Today, the company is humming, but it wasn't always that way.

When we first met Stacy, she was experiencing the typical difficulties of scaling with which many clients come to us: lack of role clarity, confusing dotted-line reporting structures, inefficient thirty-person meetings. Frankly, these issues are common at most companies, but they are especially acute in many of the fast-growth start-ups we work with.

Stacy defined the problem she was facing when she and Edward first sat down: "We have three times as many people as we did two years ago, but it feels like we move at half the speed. There are so many meetings, so many approvals. We're too young of a company to have this much bureaucracy."

If you've ever studied math or data science, you'd know that complexity in a system goes up exponentially with every additional "node." In any group of n people (like your company), the number of possible relationships is $n \times (n-1) / 2$. So a company with four employees has six possible relationships, but a company with eight has twenty-eight. A team of sixteen has a hundred and twenty, and so on. CEOs try their best to design organizations to offset that complexity, but all too often bureaucracy results.

In the fight against bureaucracy in the United States, bureaucracy appears to be winning. According to *Harvard Business Review*, since 1983 the number of managers, supervisors, and administrators in the US workforce has more than doubled while the total number of people in all other roles has increased by a mere 44 percent. And employees can feel it. In a recent study, two-thirds of workers said their companies had become more, not less, bureaucratic in recent years.

Certainly, part of Stacy's problem was structural, due to the sheer number of people and the organizational design. But a confounding factor is that she and her leaders had begun to conflate inclusion and consensus.

In practice, this conflation takes many forms. It starts with workflows having too many specialized steps and levels of approvals, so that everyone who has an opinion "feels heard." Each additional step or approval becomes a possible bottleneck where great projects languish. Conflating inclusion and consensus can also result in meetings with dozens of people who "want to be in the room where it happened," but have no functional reason for being there.

When Edward first introduced the idea that Stacy was possibly conflating these two concepts, she recoiled in shock. "One of our core values is Inclusion, Edward. I don't understand how to do that without *actually* including people."

It is crucial for leaders to be very clear about what their values mean in practice. Transparency can be conflated with having no privacy. Honesty can be conflated with oversharing. And inclusion can be conflated with consensus.

As they spoke about it more, Stacy began to see where Edward was coming from. The problem, they determined, stemmed from Stacy allowing every individual in the company to determine what inclusion meant to them, rather than leadership letting the team know what it meant to the company.

Healthy inclusivity means making sure that the people who have real value to add are proactively invited to do so. Inclusive leadership means making room in the conversation for quieter voices, for the traditionally disempowered, and for the underrepresented. For dealing with especially difficult topics, Esther Perel advocates passing around note cards and asking people to write on them—this ensures those quieter voices will be included.

Inclusive leadership doesn't have to mean making room for every person who wants public exposure or creative control, however. Sometimes meetings get to the point where "everything has been said, but not everyone has said it," as the old adage goes.

Stacy's challenge was to make it crystal clear, through role-clarity exercises and workflow redefinition, exactly how many people should be involved in each decision, and not to let individuals overcomplicate things just because they wanted to provide input. At the same time, she had to ensure that people who had value to add were not purposefully or accidentally excluded from conversations or decisions in which they should be included.

Making this transition was hard for Stacy and her team. The process required many difficult conversations in which Stacy had to tell individuals that their contributions were valued but not required on a particular workflow. She removed dozens of people from various meeting invitations, while being vigilant about maintaining a diversity of voices across the board and ensuring that the right people were in the room. She also instituted new asynchronous information-sharing processes so that no one could ever again say dryly, "This meeting could have been an email."

Stacy made these changes while still holding her values around inclusivity close. She was committed to helping the team understand that the changes she was implementing were in the name of speed and agility, and not to quiet dissent. She still wanted rigorous debate and a meritocracy of ideas, but not at the cost of progress and bottom-line outcomes.

Having a conversation about inclusion and consensus doesn't have to be hard:

- In what ways is your organization conflating inclusion and consensus?
- How could you reduce complexity and bureaucracy while still ensuring diverse voices are heard?

- What processes move through too many hands?
- Which meetings have become bloated?
- What would it take to start a conversation on this topic?

Competition, Revenge, and Resentment

Throughout history, rivalries have been core drivers of innovation and excellence. John F. Kennedy never would have committed to putting a man on the moon by the end of the 1960s if Nikita Khrushchev's USSR didn't seem like it already had a leg up. Basketball great Magic Johnson would not have been so magic were he not constantly pecked by Larry Bird. The iPhone might *still* not be waterproof if not for Samsung's 2015 ads of people dropping their Galaxy S5s into their sink, drink, and toilet . . . and using them again.

Rivalry can also bring out the worst in us. Studies have shown that rivalries greatly increase the chance that otherwise ethical people will engage in unscrupulous behavior. That makes competition a very powerful but potentially dangerous tool for leaders to wield in motivating their teams.

This section will explore a few stories that explore various ways to use conversations about the desire to win as a motivator. People get creative and find untapped stores of energy when it's all on the line—which is often the case in winner-takes-all business categories. We will also delve into a couple cautionary tales of rivalries that went too far, and discuss how leaders can see for themselves where to draw the line.

APPLE VERSUS . . . THE WORLD

Say what you want about him, but few leaders did a better job fanning the flames of corporate rivalry than Steve Jobs. From the now-iconic 1984 Super Bowl ad that sought to smash IBM's oppressive grip on computing to today's ongoing arm-wrestle with Google and Samsung for smartphone market share, no company has picked more fights with competitors than Apple. When you google "Apple rivalries," your search brings back stories about Apple versus IBM, Apple versus Microsoft, Apple versus Dell, Apple versus Facebook, Apple versus Adobe, Apple versus Samsung, Apple versus Google, and many more.

And with reason. "Steve Jobs is perhaps the most competitive human being I have ever met in my life," said management guru Tom Peters. Adopted as an infant, Jobs is said to have always felt he had something to prove. "Steve carried a chip on his shoulder throughout his life. He felt insecure and was constantly seeking ways to move ahead in life and prove his existence," recalled David Kottke, a college friend of Jobs and employee number twelve at Apple.

In our work with successful founders, we find many of them also feel like they have "something to prove." Indeed, the best teams are often composed of people who have a similar chip on their shoulder. One CEO client told us it was the most important thing he looked for when hiring: "I look for folks who don't come with the classical pedigree. They have a much more natural urge to prove all the naysayers wrong."

This competitive drive to "prove them all wrong" is perhaps one of the most important cultural elements that Jobs instilled into the culture at Apple that lives on to this day. At Apple, it's never been about competing directly by imitating or "keeping up." Jobs wanted to stay out front, way out front. "You can't look at the competition and say you're going to do it better. You have to look at the competition and say you're going to do it differently," said Jobs in the 1990s.

If you talk to employees inside Apple today, their relationship with competition has changed very little. "We don't actually look at what competitors are doing in a certain category and try to copy them. We focus on investing in new categories," said one product manager who asked to remain anonymous due to Apple's secretive culture.

Apple employees are so focused on staying out front from an innovation and customer-delight perspective that they spend little if any energy wondering what Facebook, Google, or Samsung are doing. And even though Apple is the most valuable company in the world, they maintain that mystique of the renegade, way out in front, being chased by the rest of the world.

Let's talk about using competitive pressure well:

- No matter what company you're with or what category you're in, how do you think about competition as a driver?
- Do you hire and reward people who have a healthy chip on their shoulder?
- Are you focused on innovation? Or are you paying too much attention to the competition and trying to keep up?

RAUL'S RACE AGAINST RUMORS

Simon Sinek, building on religious scholar James Carse's ideas in his book *Finite and Infinite Games*, argues that business should be treated as an infinite, not a finite, game. Unlike sports where there is most often a clear winner or loser at the end of the match or game, in business you are only ever winning *for now.* Someone else could crop up tomorrow to eat your lunch.

Some business leaders find great solace in the fact that the game never really ends—they can always try again. Others hate the lack of a definitive endpoint. One client who could not stand the ambiguity of the start-up world was Raul. Raul found his way into tech after a successful career in politics where he developed the work ethic of Paul Bunyan and his mythical blue ox all wrapped into one.

For Raul, never clearly knowing if he was ahead or behind in his nascent product category did not inspire a whole lot of confidence. Every time he caught a whiff of a rumor that a new competitor was launching, or an existing competitor was building a new feature, he would call his CTO in a panic. Or worse, he'd contact individual engineers and instruct them to scrap whatever they were working on and build a similar new capability into the product.

Needless to say, the feedback we received about him from his team members was less than stellar. Far from being motivated by the fierce competitive landscape, they were completely defeated by the constant thrash. The slow burn of meaningful rivalry can create focus and high performance. But erratic leadership fueled by rumors and paranoia burns teams out due to the lack of focus and constant reprioritization.

When John asked him if he could see how his panic and "guardrail-to-guardrail" leadership style was impacting the team, Raul was at first indignant. "John, we have one shot to do this right. The competition gets more intense every day. I don't understand why I'm the only one who feels any sense of urgency. I'm the only one who sees it!"

There it was. "I'm the only one who sees it." A little bit of paranoia is healthy—just ask any successful Silicon Valley CEO. Yes, it *is* a highly competitive environment. Yes, someone else *is* trying to eat your lunch. Yes, you always need to be watching your back and anticipating competing moves. But taken to an extreme, over-the-top paranoia about competitors is one of the key blindsets that keeps leaders from seeing things clearly.

Instead of being customer-focused and product-led, Raul was obsessed with the competition. Instead of delighting his customers, he was building a Franken-product that made less and less sense to them. Instead of giving him an edge, his constant paranoia over the competition was driving away talent and customers and building a mountain of technical debt. And he couldn't see it.

John worked with Raul to help him step back and gain more perspective. They went on a listening tour to have conversations with Raul's leadership team so he could hear for himself what the top talent he'd paid top dollar to recruit thought about his "race against the rumors." Hearing directly from his team showed him the impact he was having. He realized he'd been spending all his time looking *outward*, at the competition, and not *inward*, at his company's customers and team.

Working together, Raul and John laid out a plan for Raul to refocus on the right things. He would no longer pay attention exclusively to the moves of competitors, whether real or imagined; instead, he would spend more of his time engaging directly with top customers and product leads. He got curious about customers' needs and engaged them as partners in building the perfect product. He also made an agreement with his CTO to no longer go around him and tell the engineers what to do.

It hasn't been all roses since then, but Raul has stayed committed. And the changes he instituted seem to be working. At the time of publication, Raul's company has raised another $100 million and is getting ready to make a public stock offering.

A few more questions to get you and your team talking about what healthy competition looks like:

- In what ways are you focusing too much on the competition?
- When has a competitive rivalry become all-consuming?
- How can you use rivalry to make you more focused, rather than more paranoid and scattered?

WHEN COMPETITION DISTRACTS FROM THE CORE BUSINESS

Few companies in the last twenty years have earned the reputation of underdog as much as Under Armour. Coming seemingly out of nowhere in the late 1990s after founder and longtime CEO

Kevin Plank started the company in his grandmother's basement in the DC suburbs, Under Armour earned a reputation early on for attention-grabbing celebrity deals and smart Hollywood product placements.

While sports apparel giant Nike likely paid the company little notice in the early days, Plank surely got Nike CEO Phil Knight's attention when he started stealing entire college and professional sports franchises away from them. By the year 2000, just five years after founding the firm, Under Armour was making the uniforms for eight Major League Baseball (MLB) teams, close to two dozen National Football League (NFL) teams, four National Hockey League (NHL) teams, dozens of NCAA teams, and oddly enough the US Olympic Archery Team.

While Plank and others may credit these team deals with launching the company into the stratosphere, some longtime employees who asked to remain anonymous argue that at some point all the attention on high-profile deals and sponsorships became a distraction.

"Sometimes, to be cool at Under Armour and have the attention of the CEO, you needed to be working on designing the Olympic outfits and not just selling product at Dick's Sporting Goods," said one former UA employee. "But ninety-five percent of our business was selling at places like Dick's. Leaders show their teams what the company's priorities are by where their attention goes. And if most of the CEO's attention is going into doing Olympic uniforms because Nike does Olympic uniforms, lots of people *not* working on the Olympic uniforms will feel like their area of the business is not important. It's demotivating."

High-profile projects need to be put in perspective, he says. "It would have been different if Kevin had said, 'Hey, guys, we're doing this important PR thing with the Olympics, and we're going to put two percent of the budget towards it. But everybody else is making cool products for high school athletes . . . you're doing the real work here. You're keeping the lights on, and thank you for your focus!' But he sometimes didn't stress that enough."

After fifteen years of steady growth, Under Armour sales eventually plateaued around 2016. It seemed that Plank's narrow focus on Olympic uniforms had finally caught up with him. The founder announced that he was stepping down from the CEO role in 2019. By 2020, under new leadership with a new focus on the fundamentals, sales were on the up again.

Questions for you as a leader:

- How do you balance stealing thunder from the competition with creating excitement around your more mundane business priorities?
- At what point do competitive PR stunts become an energy suck and distraction?

THE DARK SIDE OF COMPETITION

Competition is a potent force that can bring out the best in us. It can also bring out the worst in us, as one longtime Uber employee found out.

Sitting with John at an outdoor café in Palo Alto, Zach, an early Uber employee who asked that we not use his real name, looked back with mixed emotions upon his six years helping the company expand its footprint around the world. "Most people don't remember this, but in the beginning we were just this little company that everyone from regulators to the mob was trying to crush," reflected Zach. "We worked so hard for so long. Everything seemed like an emergency . . . It was fun, but it didn't always bring out the best in everyone."

Zach explained that from the outset everyone at Uber felt like they were fighting for their lives. "We were better than the entrenched cab system in every way, and they knew it. So they tried to do everything to kill us any chance they got."

This dynamic, of being the proverbial David fighting against Goliath, has motivated teams to do the seemingly impossible since the beginning of time. Every decade seems to have its iconic story: Nike taking on Adidas in the 1970s. Apple taking on IBM in the 1980s. Netflix taking on Blockbuster in the aughts. And then in the 2010s, Uber taking on Big Taxi, as the Uber PR team came to call the loose collection of hundreds of cab companies around the country in an effort to demonize them.

Few things are more motivating than the threat of existential risk. Early employees at all the major tech companies tell stories of "fighting for something," "taking on the man," or "putting a dent in the universe." And Travis Kalanick, founder and CEO of Uber, was more talented than most at using this core desire to win to get unreasonable amounts of productivity out of this team.

Kalanick purposefully recruited people who had that proverbial chip on their shoulder. And as the company grew, he used their competitiveness to drive higher and higher performance from the team. First, the bogeyman was Big Taxi, but Uber's ubercompetitive team found its ultimate common enemy clad in a fuzzy pink mustache.

"When Lyft first launched, they tried to rip off our entire business model, including our tech," sneered Zach, still visibly upset, seven years later. "We always knew we were better. We had better tech, more money, more market share . . . but the fact that they were trying to eat our lunch drove everyone crazy."

And that's when some Uber employees began to cross the line and fight dirty. Things came to a head in 2014 when Uber executives in New York were accused of requesting thousands of rides from Lyft drivers, only to either cancel last minute or take the rides and try to convince Lyft's drivers to switch to Uber. Some might say that was simply being creative, but riders didn't look so kindly on it. Calls to boycott Uber sprung up around the country, and riders switched over to Lyft in droves.

Over the next few years, the rivalry continued to boil over, earning Uber more and more of a schoolyard bully reputation. CEO Travis Kalanick's increasingly aberrant behavior did not help the situation, and he was eventually forced to step down.

The Uber story is an interesting case study for leaders who would like to stoke the competitive fires on their teams. What's the best way to use competition as a driver? How far do you take it? Where do you draw the line?

The line between healthy and unhealthy amounts of rivalry is blurry. Not enough competitive spirit, and people can be lackadaisical. Too much competition on your teams, and you have people sabotaging each other by withholding resources and information.

While studies have shown that appropriate levels of competition can increase excitement and creativity, competition that elicits feelings of anxiety and fear makes employees significantly more likely to cut corners or sabotage their colleagues.

In one study, researchers found that how a company uses carrots and sticks to stoke competition effects employee behavior. The prospect of winning a bonus is likely to drive salespeople to send those extra emails or make those extra calls, whereas the threat of being publicly embarrassed for being the lowest-performing team can "trigger anxiety and prompt people to resort to mis-selling, fraud, and lying to customers."

Uber obviously accomplished something amazing. It fundamentally redefined how we all get around. Before Uber, Big Taxi operated in a world of zero accountability. If you requested a taxi to the airport in San Francisco in 2010, there was only a 50 percent chance one would come. Uber also made a lot of people, including Zach, rich beyond their wildest dreams.

But at what cost? Were the years of burnout worth it? Was engaging in unscrupulous business practices necessary?

Zach isn't so sure.

"Working at Uber was such an amazing challenge. I worked with so many incredible people," Zach says, looking off into the distance. "But there's also a scar. I'm afraid to go back to work now because I never want to feel that way again . . . all the anxiety and stress, the moral ambiguity. It's left me avoiding getting involved in another startup, and that's a damn shame."

Curiosity, Learning, and Variety

We are all born with a natural curiosity and desire to learn. Just watch kids exploring tidepools at the beach or hunkering down with a new book. As adults, few things get us more excited than learning a new computer language, figuring out a tough problem, or deciphering how to order "deux croissants au beurre, s'il vous plaît" from the corner bakery while visiting Paris.

Conversely, few things sap the energy of a group of talented people more than working on a dull problem. Researchers from Montclair State University who performed a survey of 211 randomly selected employees found a statistically significant relationship between self-identified feelings of boredom and "counterproductive work behavior."

Great leaders learn how to tap into our natural desire to learn and grow and keep us from being bored, while also not letting us cascade into navel-gazing or never making decisions. Let's explore the subtle differences between encouraging exploration and learning and creating a constant state of indecision.

CURIOSITY AS A COMPETITIVE EDGE

In a faded polo shirt, crumpled khakis, and tan Birkenstocks over black socks, Sundeep looks just a little out of place sitting in his well-lit corner office in an anonymous office building in Redwood City, California, conveniently about halfway between San

Francisco and Palo Alto. In fact, he looks like he just rolled out of bed. You'd never know he's the research director of a secretive innovation lab and is most likely worth well over $20 million, and he likes it that way.

"We tell people to dress comfortably," Sundeep says with dry wit, knowing that in this very moment, he is the living embodiment of comfort. "We want nothing getting in the way of them feeling creative."

Over the last ten years, "the Lab" (we promised not to use the real name and changed many other details) has created several innovations that have made it into our lives in big ways. Some are new consumer products, others financial innovations. Each one spun out into the market as new businesses, each with market size potential of generating no less than $1 billion in annual revenue. "We make no small plans around here," Sundeep quips.

As we work with Sundeep and his team, it's obvious that things run just a little differently at the Lab. Whereas you might imagine an innovation hub to be filled with lab-coat-wearing scientists or messy workspaces littered with pizza boxes, the feeling here is more like that of a therapist's office. Rather than people running from office to office, stressed and strung out, if you do happen to see someone in the hall here in the Lab, they unhurriedly stop to chat and then saunter on as if they have all the time in the world.

And that is exactly how Sundeep wants it. "We don't consider ourselves venture capitalists . . . we are scientists." By the looks of the long roster of PhD mathematicians and physicists that the Lab employs, Sundeep's statement rings true. "My job is to hire the smartest and most curious people in the world and create a sandbox for them to play in," he says. "None of these people would last a day in other tech jobs. They take too many risks. Their projects take too long. But here, we give them the time and space to have fun and explore. And every so often, they come across a billion-dollar insight."

In an industry known for tight deadlines, demanding bosses, and grueling working hours, the Lab has anomalously chosen to give its employees the freedom to work on scientific problems that interest them at a pace that suits them. One team member has spent the last eight months developing a model to predict how climate change will impact rainfall patterns and crop prices in South America. Another is trying to determine how frequent global pandemics will be over the next twenty years, and the impact they will have on policy and population patterns.

Whatever the topic, Sundeep wants them to explore it. Because you never know where the next big idea will come from.

Not every company has the luxury of basically unlimited budgets, no firm goals, and no solid deadlines. In fact, most companies would go out of business in a matter of months if they tried to imitate the Lab. But what kernels of wisdom about how Sundeep supports his team's desires to learn and satisfy their curiosities can we take away from this story?

First, there is gold in them thar hills of unstructured time. Google execs realized years ago that the best innovation and problem-solving was done in engineers' free time—after hours or on the weekends. In a story that is now the stuff of company legend, an intractable bug in their ad-serving algorithm was solved late one night by an engineer who wasn't even on the ads team. When asked why he worked all night on something that wasn't even part of his job description, he replied blithely, "It seemed like a fun problem to work on."

Today, in response to the seemingly endless curiosity of their team, every Google employee is encouraged to spend *one day a week* working on whatever strikes their fancy so they don't have to explore that curiosity exclusively after hours.

Second, allowing team members to get curious and run experiments requires not just unstructured time but also an explicit understanding that failure is okay. As Tom Watson, CEO of IBM for over forty years, spanning two world wars and the Great Depression, said, "If you want to succeed, double your failure rate."

Yet too many companies today have not made it clear to their employees that failure is not just okay but is something to be celebrated. Failed experiments yield new insights. Employees who are not failing are not taking enough risks. Like a skier who never falls, they are more focused on looking good than on pushing the limits and seeing exactly where the edge is.

Some of the researchers on Sundeep's team spend the better part of a year chasing down an idea, only to come up empty-handed. And Sundeep chooses to celebrate those failures every time. "As soon as we lose the integrity of our research . . . as soon as we stop trying to solve nearly impossible problems, we lose our competitive edge."

WHEN CURIOSITY CREATES CHAOS

One client we've done extensive work with over the last couple of years has an extremely talented and creative executive team. They love nothing more than "spit-balling" new ideas, rolling up their sleeves, and getting their hands dirty.

And yet when we first met them, they weren't functioning well at all. Burdened by too many creative ideas, they had a hard time making decisions, especially strategic ones. Their executive team meetings were the living definition of rabbit holes.

When Edward asked the CEO why he allowed his executive team meetings to be so chaotic, he responded plainly, "But this is where all of our best ideas have always come from." Edward pushed him to go one layer deeper, since obviously great ideas were no longer the result of these meetings. The CEO looked out the window wistfully and said, "This is what gives us energy . . . we love putting out fires."

This was a problem.

The job of the leadership team of a company with over 100 employees is to develop strategic priorities and make sure the organization works on those priorities, not to send the company in myriad directions, following their creative whims.

"But, but . . . being creative and solving problems *feels so good*!"

Yes, we know. Problem-solving and dreaming big are literally intoxicating. The creative process releases neurochemicals like oxytocin, endorphins, and dopamine that leave us feeling emotions akin to those we experience falling in love or playing sports. Why wouldn't you want to feel that way all the time?

A key insight many leaders fail to reach, however, is that when they reserve all of those creative problem-solving moments for themselves on the executive team, they are robbing junior leaders in the organization of those same yummy neurochemically drenched moments and effectively relegating those junior leaders to the role of execution.

Yes, that's right. Every time you solve someone else's problems for them, you rob them of neurochemicals associated with joy, satisfaction, self-worth, and belonging.

Is the solution for the executive team to no longer meet? Should they no longer solve problems? No. They simply need to know what kind of problems they should be solving.

Andy Katz-Mayfield, the CEO of Harry's, the David to Proctor & Gamble's Goliath, came up with a simple framework for answering this all-too-important question that we absolutely love. He posited that the Harry's executive team should be working at the intersection of *intractability* and *impact*. Meaning, how hard of a problem is this? Can anyone else solve the problem almost as well or better than us? And how big of an impact on the business will this decision have? Does it impact our performance for the next quarter or half year, or just for the next month? Is it regarding our core product or a tiny product line? Does it affect our employees globally, or just a handful on one team?

If the problem meets both criteria of impact and intractability, the Harry's executive team works to solve it. If not, they delegate it.

Leaders and their teams get into trouble when they think either that a problem will be "fun to solve" or that they "don't trust anyone else to solve this problem as well as us." As leaders your job is to solve the important, strategic problems, not just the fun ones. And for the smaller matters that still prove difficult to delegate, it's best to coach your teams with Socratic questions to increase their problem-solving capacity. That is where true scale comes from.

Questions for leaders and leadership teams on sharing the problem-solving:

- What problems are you keeping for yourself unnecessarily?
- In what ways are you robbing your teams of their desire to learn and be challenged?
- How does this habit impact your team's overall capacity for problem-solving?

Power, Status, and Recognition

Power, status, and recognition in the workplace are often thought of as having negative connotations. We speak critically of people who are "power-hungry" or "status-seekers."

While it's true that too much desire for power, status, and credit is correlated with negative outcomes, it is quite normal and healthy for leaders to seek and enjoy a certain level of influence. For many, the enhanced ability to get things done and to see their vision come to life that results from having more power is the core reason for being a leader in the first place.

The challenge is keeping things in balance. For every high-flying CEO who came crashing back down to earth as a result of their obsession with power (Elizabeth Holmes of Theranos, Travis Kalanick of Uber, Adam Neumann of WeWork, and so on), there are dozens of examples of humble, hardworking, don't-need-to-be-in-the-spotlight leaders who build incredibly successful companies with vibrant, healthy cultures.

The academic research into power is fascinating but contradictory. Early social science research into the dynamics and behavioral impact of power tended to support Lord Acton's famous assertion: "Power tends to corrupt, and absolute power corrupts absolutely." The famous Stanford prison experiment of 1971 in which some test subjects were "prisoners" and others were "guards" had to be called off early because the guards became so abusive toward their prisoners. Other studies have shown that small increases in perceived power heighten "hypocrisy, moral exceptionalism, egocentricity and lack of empathy for others."

Another more recent study attracted our attention, however, because it is reminiscent of our own experience working with sound and effective leaders. Katherine A. DeCelles, professor and researcher at the University of Toronto, set out to answer the question "Does power actually corrupt, or does it simply reveal one's true character?" or to put it differently "Is power less of a character modifier, and more of a character amplifier?"

Her findings were conclusive. DeCelles and her colleagues found that "people's sense of 'moral identity'—the degree to which they thought it was important to their sense of self to be 'caring,' 'compassionate,' 'fair,' 'generous,' and so on—shaped their responses to feelings of power." It seems people who were caring, fair, and generous before being given power were even more so after. People who were not that caring before being given power were even less so afterward.

The implications for us as coaches and for you as a leader, investor, or employee is to encourage all of us to screen for character first, and not simply for vision and charisma, when we are choosing to hire or promote would-be leaders. The power-hungry among us are often out for power for the wrong reasons.

Let's take a look at a couple of leaders who learned to cope with power in different ways.

POWER BUILDS WHEN SHARED

Claudia is confident and credible—you trust anything she says. If she wasn't running a trendy coworking space in Los Angeles, you might imagine her as an anchor on the local news.

When we met Claudia, she had a clear problem: she felt terribly alone. She bemoaned that no one had her eye for design, so she had to make every decision regarding the aesthetics of her spaces, from wall coverings and furniture to candle scents and fixtures in the bathrooms. She had also purposefully built a "flat organization" that created a sense of equity and democracy, but it also meant she had no other leaders on her team whom she felt she could trust.

We put the words "flat organization" in quotes like this because these companies are often flat in name only. While there is certainly a flatness at one layer in these organizations, the leader often sits high above the rest of the org looking down. And while the leader may believe that she has created a consensus-driven, democratic system, what she has actually done is created a dictatorship.

In 2002, Google attempted to have a completely flat organization by eliminating all engineering managers in an effort to break down bureaucracy and go back to the start-up culture they enjoyed in the early days. That experiment lasted only a few months; too many people were going directly to CEO Larry Page with questions about coworker conflicts, expense reports, and other annoyingly mundane issues.

Claudia unknowingly ruled her fiefdom with an iron fist, and as a result, in addition to her personal feelings of loneliness and the need to do everything, she had problems with low morale, lack of creative problem-solving, and high turnover.

Have you ever wondered why the military has so many ranks in its hierarchy? There are captains, majors, corporals, first lieutenants, second lieutenants, sergeants, and so on. Why isn't there just one general and a few thousand soldiers?

Without going into an entire volume on military theory, the simplest answer is that one-to-many works in the transfer of knowledge, but not in the organization of labor. An author can write one book and transfer her knowledge to 10 million people, but to organize a group of humans to get things done, we need to divide ourselves into smaller groups.

Today, the average corporate executive has between five and ten direct reports. The number of layers of leadership under each executive is theoretically infinite, but it depends on the size of the company and the complexity of workstreams.

While it might seem ludicrous that we would advocate for a management hierarchy in a company of fifty, the alternative was what Claudia was dealing with: a lonely burned-out CEO on one hand and a gaggle of disempowered employees on the other.

When John and Claudia sat down to discuss her conundrum, he asked her point-blank, "What would be different if you had a few people in the business whom you trusted and viewed as peers?" Peers? What a crazy concept! Sharing power and decision-making? The whole idea made her nervous.

What she hadn't considered, and what John opened her eyes

to, is that sharing power doesn't have to mean accepting subpar outcomes. In fact, if done well, it creates *better* outcomes.

John's first step in helping Claudia become a leader who shared power was to get her to document her own thoughts on the company's brand and aesthetics. No one can know "what good looks like" if it is all in the leader's head. Sitting down and putting one's tastes and preferences on paper can make us feel vulnerable. It's often difficult to put it into words. Mood boards and other visual examples can be helpful. Even better is hiring a branding agency.

The second step is to identify who in the company naturally has the trust of both the leader and the other staff. Even in a flat structure, certain individuals have soft power or influence. They instinctively hold space, provide support, and offer feedback. And with any luck, they understand the tastes and preferences of the leader better than most. Claudia decided that Stephanie, her head of community, was her most trusted team member.

The third step is to experiment with letting go. Leaders who have been holding on to all the power for years do so out of fear that the company will drift away from their vision if they let go. Throwing off the bow lines all at once can rock the boat too much, leading to anxiety, and they tend to grasp for control again. In Claudia's case, she first gave Stephanie control over the tablescapes in the lunch buffet. That job seemed rather insignificant at first, but from there she entrusted Stephanie with redesigning the community chill zone. Little by little, Claudia felt more and more comfortable.

The fourth and final step is making things official. In a company like Claudia's that has never had a formal transfer of power, making Stephanie the new head of customer experience was a major milestone. With this, Stephanie was given control over design of new coworking spaces in the pipeline, which freed up Claudia to work on larger strategic questions like fundraising and hiring. This show of respect and trust from Claudia buoyed

Stephanie's confidence and deepened her loyalty to the company. Others in the firm also now saw a clearer path forward for career development.

Within a few months, Claudia had run similar processes to name a head of marketing and head of business development. By learning to share power and provide formal status and recognition to her team, she took the first steps toward forming an executive team that gave her operational scale and lowered her feelings of loneliness for the first time in a long time.

Reflecting on the use of power and control at your company:

- How are you holding on to power and control in your company or on your team?
- What does holding on to that power cost you and the company in terms of scale and efficiency?
- What would running small experiments with trusting and empowering certain members of your team look like?

ODE TO THE RELUCTANT LEADER

While narcissists attract the ire and the headlines, the more typical CEO we encounter does not have enough desire for power and does not do a good job giving employees power, status, and recognition. These CEOs are often engineers or designers—people who built a product that the company sprang up around almost by accident. They now find themselves leaders by circumstance, rather than by design.

Let's take Charles, the CEO and cofounder of a multibillion-dollar FinTech company. When his colleagues talk with us, they say, "Charles is such a strategic visionary. He really knows how to guide great decisions. But he doesn't do that enough. In fact, he doesn't really engage as a leader at all. We never really get any input from him. We never know if we are doing a good job."

Far from being one of the megalomaniacs who captures the

headlines, Charles is a reluctant leader. Like many of our clients, Charles is an intense introvert who had a critical insight about a market opportunity a few years ago and launched a business around it. But he never envisioned he'd be running a five-hundred-person multibillion-dollar company. The CEO role forces Charles to be more extroverted than he's comfortable with. It also asks him to provide more formal structure and authority to his team than he feels is necessary.

"I don't need a job title to know what is important or what I should work on. I don't understand why other people do," explains Charles when he and Edward sit down in his to go over his 360 at the company's headquarters in San Francisco's financial district.

Reluctant leaders like Charles need to learn that empowering people is more than trusting them to do a good job. The word *empower* literally means "to give formal or legal authority to."

To do that, leaders must do three things:

1. Make it known to employees what formal authority they have.
2. Trust them to make their own decisions within the scope of that authority.
3. Reinforce that authority with public praise and recognition.

What Charles was doing, however, was giving people titles with vague job descriptions, second-guessing and reversing their decisions, and giving zero praise or recognition—which is the definition of disempowering behavior.

In a meeting between Charles and his C-suite, one team member took a risk and tried to help Charles comprehend the full impact of his disempowering behavior. "Since we know you are going to redo everything anyway, my team doesn't spend much time coming up with great ideas. We do the minimum and wait for you to tell us what to do."

Just think about that. Charles is not a maniacal microman-ager. He's not a cunning narcissist, making people feel used and abused. He's just disengaged and unaware how his quietly under-mining behaviors are generating exactly the opposite behavior he wants from his direct reports. Reluctant leaders like Charles need to step out of their comfort zones and give employees the kind of clarity, feedback, and praise they don't feel they need themselves. This can feel foreign or even inauthentic, which causes many of these leaders to push back. "I feel like a fake giving people all these pats on the back. They should just do their jobs!" Charles would say.

Leading with heart involves meeting people where they are. Some people like lots of praise and feedback. Some not so much. It is the job of the leader to learn the various preferences and motivators of her team members and approach them in their preferred style and language.

Reflecting upon the varying levels of desire for recognition in your company:

- In what ways are you failing to feed your team's desire for power and recognition?
- How are you innocently undermining your colleagues' sense of autonomy and self-worth?
- What "languages" regarding influence and recognition do you see spoken at the office that don't feel natural to you? What would you or the team gain if you learned them?

Service and Social Justice

On May 4, 1961, thirteen men and women ranging in age from eighteen to thirty boarded various Greyhound and Trailways buses in Washington, DC, heading toward New Orleans. Their objective was simple: to get into "good trouble," as then-twenty-one-year-old civil rights leader and eventual congressman John Lewis, who was among the thirteen, came to describe civil obedience.

Throughout that summer, over 450 "Freedom Riders," including teachers, members of the clergy, college students, and even a Wall Street banker, rode the bus systems of the South, violating local segregation laws, getting themselves arrested, and in many cases getting beaten, all with the goal of protesting unfair segregation practices.

What motivates people to leave their homes, abandon their careers, and put themselves in harm's way in the name of fighting for a cause they believe in? A cause that, for white Freedom Riders, wouldn't even improve their own standard of living.

Perhaps you've experienced this sensation of wanting to support a cause or be of service yourself. Major advances in social justice would never have come about if it were not for the tireless and selfless dedication of legions of volunteers and organizers who were mobilized simply to fight for what is right.

The best leaders we've worked with have that sense of purpose, and we will spend an entire chapter later in the book exploring the many ways one can tap into and have conversations about purpose. For now, we want to explore how you can get into the right mindset to encourage others to be of service, how to tap into people's natural desire to "be the hero." One insightful investor we spoke with has a simple strategy for getting in the right mindset to do just that.

WE COULD BE HEROES

When your first two investments are Twitter and Digg, people say you are either lucky or a genius. But spend more than five minutes with Mike Maples, founder of Floodgate Fund, and you realize this guy is more than just lucky. Since those early investments, Maples and the Floodgate team have gone on to invest in companies like AngelList, Clover Health, Lyft, TaskRabbit, and many more.

Over his fifteen-year career as an investor, having met thousands of would-be Jack Dorseys and Kevin Roses (the founders of Twitter and Digg, respectively), he's developed a simple method of sussing out who has the right stuff to be a successful start-up leader. And it comes down to one question: Do they see themselves as the hero?

The idea of the hero's journey has been around for millennia, but it was Joseph Campbell who popularized the concept in his 1949 book *The Hero with a Thousand Faces*. Think of a movie or book that depicts a fabulous, epic journey and battle between good and evil built around a central heroic figure, and that story most likely follows the hero's-journey structure to a T.

Maples believes that building a company is akin to going on a heroic journey, and that it's important for founders to know what character they play in the story. "What many inexperienced leaders get wrong is they look at the magazines with Steve Jobs or Mark Zuckerberg on the cover, and they think the CEO is the hero," mused Maples on a Zoom call in the middle of the global pandemic. "They think the CEO is Luke Skywalker. But great leaders, the ones that you really respect, they realize their role is to be Obi-Wan Kenobi"—Luke's mentor in the Star Wars movies—"not Luke."

Start-up leaders, according to Maples (and we wholeheartedly agree, but had never thought of it this way), are the mentor figures. They are Obi-Wan to Luke, Gandalf to Frodo, Morpheus to Neo, Athena to Odysseus. And if they are really good, founders make everyone they touch, from early employees and investors to clients and customers, feel like they too are heroes.

Maybe this is why when you ask Silicon Valley employees whether they think their company is making the world a better place, an overwhelming 67 percent say yes. This may be surprising to anyone who observes the legions of people mindlessly staring into their smartphones in restaurants and public spaces and questions the role of technology in society, but to the men and women building the apps and technology that we all engage with every day, most of them really think they are on a heroic quest to change the world.

"Insightful leaders see a different future than the rest of us," says Maples. "They inspire us to go on the heroic journey of building the company with them by helping us understand that there's something broken today that needs to be fixed. The gap between today and that future state . . . that is the journey."

A critical mistake leaders make is when they see their teams or their investors as tools to utilize on *their own* heroic journey. We see this all the time in our coaching: leaders who make the work of the business about themselves, rather than about the heroic journey of their employees, customers, or investors. It may seem like a subtle difference, but it is a 180-degree change in perspective.

Leading with heart requires accepting your role as the mentor or coach in the story of your company, not as the hero.

- How does that lens change how you think about your job
- Do you tell people about why this journey is important to *you*, or do you help them connect with how the journey is important to *them*?
- Armed with this insight, what can you begin doing differently to satisfy your teams' desire to be of service, to be part of making the world better?

Try this test: Are your employees overly focused on compensation and benefits? Yes, people deserve to be well compensated—if they have to worry about putting food on the table, they will likely have a hard time focusing on your noble vision to disrupt the "broken" dry-cleaning industry. But if you sense too much chatter in the org about comp and promotions, it is a classic tell that you are not delivering in your role as Obi-Wan Kenobi. Employees who feel connected to the purpose, who believe they are on a mission of meaning, will spend more time and energy focused on metaphorically slaying dragons than asking what's in it for them.

CHAPTER 3 TAKEAWAYS

- Our core desires are powerful motivators, but they can also derail us.

- Our desire for love and acceptance has the greatest potential to inspire long-term loyalty, but it can also distract us if we get caught up in fantasy and intrigue.

- Blindsets like fantasy, paranoia, and denial keep us from seeing what's actually going on and can contribute to us getting derailed by our desires.

- Healthy competition is a potent driver to keep people united, but it can also create incentives for unethical behavior.

- Our curiosity and desire to learn can only thrive in an environment where we are given unstructured time and freedom to fail. However, if we overindulge that desire, it can lead to a lack of focus.

- Power and status are as motivating as they are intoxicating. Overreliance on them as motivators can create unhealthy dynamics and abusive behavior.

- The desire to be of service and to fight for justice taps into our sense of purpose and connection to something bigger than ourselves. Using it as a motivator requires allowing people to see themselves as the hero in the story.

CONVERSATION STARTERS

1. When you look back at your life and think about the periods of greatest effort and focus, what was the core driver that motivated you the most? How does this show up to others?

2. Looking around at your work colleagues, what are the core desires that you see them as being most responsive to?

3. What are the conversations you'd like to have with your colleagues to leverage their core desires in an ethical and authentic way to help them be more successful?

4. When have you been derailed by your desires in the past? What support can you ask for today to ensure you don't get pulled over the line again?

5. What blindsets keep you from seeing clearly, and could contribute to you letting your desires derail you?

6. In what ways do you see your colleagues overcome by their own blindsets? What can you do to help them break through their blindsets and develop a healthy relationship with their desires?

4

WHAT ARE YOUR GREATEST GIFTS?

When I had to fill in my immigration papers . . .
I had nothing to declare except my talent.

—OSCAR WILDE

Aristotle was one of the first to posit that the key to happiness and fulfillment was to gain a conscious awareness of our talents and gifts and to put them to good use. Yet, here we are, over two thousand years later, and most people have no idea what their natural gifts are, nor what to do with them.

We consider this one of the essential leadership conversations we all should be having. If we can learn to see the gifts in ourselves and others, to discern what makes us truly special and how we can make a difference, we can unleash untold potential to do good things for the world.

But most of us never get there for the same reason we don't buy cheap wine. To explain, let us transport you to Pop the Cork, Edward's favorite wine shop in New York's West Village.

Jorge and Yolanda Rueda are the kind of New York wine-shop owners Hollywood directors attempt to depict in the movies.

They call you by name when you walk in and remember your preferences. They do a cute little routine where she flirts, and he rolls his eyes disapprovingly. They love to hear about your latest travels and adventures. And they never bat an eye if you walk in dressed in a tux or in a robe and slippers—they've seen it all.

And in their quaint wine shop on the corner of Charles and Seventh Avenue, they don't stock a single bottle of wine under $13. When on an unseasonably warm October evening Edward asks them why, Yolanda says with a laugh, "People in this neighborhood pick up a perfectly fine eight-dollar bottle and ask, 'Is it decent? Or am I supposed to *cook* with it?'"

Jorge shakes his head in disbelief. "If you put a glass of that cheap wine down next to the expensive stuff, most people could never tell the difference." But they *feel* there's a difference. They feel in their gut that the more expensive the wine, the better it must be.

Behavioral economists call this phenomenon "price signaling." Given the option between something dirt cheap and a similar product that is moderately expensive, many people choose the more expensive product. In general, we assume price is a signal for quality.

Bringing it back to our gifts, just like we instinctively conclude that inexpensive wines must be of low quality, we similarly undervalue the things we are naturally good at because they are, in a word, free, and therefore not of any value. In contrast, we sometimes overvalue the skills and knowledge that we paid for with hundreds of hours of concerted effort or hundreds of thousands of dollars in student loans, like learning to code, practicing the piano, or studying to become a doctor or lawyer.

This is important for leaders to remember because, as we will see in the pages ahead, outsized results for ourselves and our teams often come from building upon natural talents and abilities, not simply grinding away at developing newfound skills.

Yes, we should all have a growth mindset and know that our skills, talents, and intelligence are elastic and can be expanded with concerted effort. But that expansion is more likely to happen faster and be of greater value and impact if we build upon a foundation of innate interest and ability.

If you can learn how to see and utilize your own gifts, and those of the people around you, you will begin to unlock a near limitless fountain of possibilities.

The Myths about Gifts

Let's first dispel a few common myths to help you reframe the entire concept of what it means to "have a gift."

MYTH #1: GIFTED PEOPLE ARE THE BEST IN THE WORLD AT SOMETHING (AND STARTED YOUNG).

Bobby Fisher dominated the US Open of Chess at fourteen years old. Serena Williams won twenty-three Grand Slam singles titles by the age of thirty-six, more than any other player, man or woman. The Beatles created one of the greatest libraries of popular music the world has ever heard, all before they were thirty years old. (Mind-blowing side note: they ranged in age from twenty-seven to twenty-nine when they broke up, and had only been together for a little over six years.)

When most of us think about gifted people, we usually think of individuals who have a best-in-class ability, whether it's singing, acting, speaking, or doing impressive things with a ball of some kind. They are the best of the best, we tell ourselves. They are people at the top of what they do, and they probably started doing that thing early on in their lives.

In other words, we put gifted people on a pedestal and tell ourselves they're not like us. This often leads us to develop the story that whatever gifts *we* have are insignificant or unremarkable in comparison.

Let's set this straight right now: everyone has some special gift, whether or not you are the GOAT (Greatest of all Time). Being gifted at something doesn't mean you have to be the best in the world, the best in your country, or even the best in your hometown. You simply have to be good at something that other people might find difficult. The value is in that contrast.

MYTH #2: GIFTS INVOLVE A PERFORMATIVE ART OR ACTIVITY, LIKE SINGING, ACTING, OR ATHLETICS.

We often think about gifts as something that can earn us fifteen minutes of fame on TV. But most people's innate gifts are subtler in nature and come out only in certain situations or conditions. For example, John has an uncanny ability to create frameworks and tools for coaching—but that won't earn him a spot on *America's Got Talent*.

Despite our deification of athletes, musicians, and actors in popular culture, you don't have to be exceptional in athletics, music, or acting to be gifted. Instead, you may have a gift for negotiation, for organization, or for putting others at ease in stressful moments. You may have a gift for listening, or for empathy. A "gift," as we define it, *is any innate ability that you can build upon with effort and practice.*

MYTH #3: IF WE ARE GIFTED AT SOMETHING, WE DON'T NEED TO PRACTICE OR WORK ON IT.

When you see someone do something seemingly effortlessly and intuitively—your colleague who commands a room every time she speaks; the guy who always comes up with the wittiest taglines; the boss who always makes you feel valued and motivated—it's easy to tell yourself that he or she was probably "born" being able to perform at that level. But scratch the surface with any of these people, and you will find a foundation of innate talent built upon with hundreds, if not thousands, of hours of practice. Why do we know this is true? Because we all tend to do *more* of the things we feel we are good at. We naturally put in hours exercising our gifts, because it feels good to be good at something.

The next step is to put some *intention* behind that practice. Just because you have a head start due to being a touch more charismatic or intuitive with numbers doesn't mean you don't have to cultivate and nurture that talent to become truly exceptional.

If you don't commit to developing your gifts with practice, they risk amounting to nothing in the long run. John, for instance, has always been a natural public speaker, having been a communications major in college—but he honed his skills even further at a young age by joining an after-dinner speaking club in Long Beach, California. Through regular weekly practice, he developed an ability to speak with exceptional clarity and confidence.

What misconceptions about gifts are keeping you from identifying and developing yours, or those of your teammates?

It's in the Way That You Use It . . .

Now that we have outlined three common myths about gifts, let's review how people actually *use* their gifts. How you deploy yours will make all the difference in the kind of impact it will have for you and for the world.

LEVEL 1: IN SERVICE OF OURSELVES

Jordan Belfort, also known as the Wolf of Wall Street, used his exceptional gift of persuasion to pillage the retirement funds of the elderly. Televangelist Jim Bakker used his gift of public speaking to enrich himself and hide his extramarital affairs.

While not everyone who uses their gifts strictly to serve themselves is corrupt or a crook, they might still be robbing the world of a part of themselves that could be of great service to others.

We find that when people are using their gifts solely for themselves, they most likely have some unmet need. If you or a team member is using their gifts in service of themselves, why might that be? What need is not being met? What might change if that need were met through other means?

LEVEL 2: IN SERVICE OF A PRACTICAL PURPOSE

At the age of twenty-three, Mozart was an organist for hire. At the age of thirty-eight, J. R. R. Tolkien, author of *The Hobbit* and the Lord of the Rings series, was a university professor who graded secondary school tests on the side for extra cash. Both went on to do pretty well when they figured out how to use their gifts for more than practical purposes.

People who are stuck using their gifts for practical purposes may wake up one day and realize they have been "playing it small" for too long. Or they may remain blind to their own potential and never come to that realization at all.

You can tell if someone is using their gift solely for some practical purpose if you find yourself saying they are not "living up to their potential." While using our gifts in service of ourselves can easily cascade into unethical behavior if we are not careful, using our gifts for practical purposes can just as easily devolve into mediocrity.

This essential truth is easy to ignore, however, because "using one's gift for practical purposes" often translates to "doing what one needs to in order to pay the bills." Mozart was broke in his early twenties, so he worked as an organist for hire. Tolkien made ends meet by grading papers.

This is how millions of people get trapped into living in their zone of excellence but never arrive in their zone of genius, to borrow from Gay Hendricks. That is to say, they do things they are good at and get rewarded for, but they do so simply to get by. They never take the risk of finding the greatest expression of their gifts, and as a result never feel like their work is effortless and of maximal impact—two markers of living in your zone of genius.

When we are using our gifts for a practical purpose, we get just enough reward and recognition to keep going, but never enough to feel truly fulfilled. True fulfillment generally only comes from using our gifts in service of a higher purpose.

LEVEL 3: IN SERVICE OF A HIGHER PURPOSE

When we think of people using their gifts for a higher purpose, any number of notable figures come to mind. Martin Luther King Jr., Abraham Lincoln, Wolfgang von Beethoven, Maya Angelou, Marie Curie . . . the list is endless. But as we discussed earlier in this chapter, one need not impact millions of other people to be gifted.

When we "right-size" our conception of what a gift is and what a higher purpose might be, we see truly gifted people using their gifts in service of a higher purpose all around us: the supportive coach, the empowering manager, the brilliant product designer, the busker on the corner who brightens your day with a Bob Dylan cover.

The common thread among these examples is that they are taking their gifts of support, empathy, design, and musicality and sharing them with others. That's really all it takes to use your gift in service of a higher purpose: to claim it and share it intentionally with the world at whatever scale feels right for you.

At this point, you might be saying, "But what about the organ player at my church, or my kid's high school teacher? Are you saying those people aren't using their gifts for a higher purpose, in the same way that Mozart and Tolkien weren't?"

Yes and no. It really depends on what your organ player and teacher feel like they have inside them. Are they perfectly content expressing their gifts on a small but impactful stage? Then more power to them.

But when they are honest with themselves, do they see a potential within themselves to have even more impact? Do they see a path to be of even greater service? Then yes, in that case we would say they are "playing it small" relative to their potential—the potential they, or their friends and loved ones, see for them.

Using Our Gifts to Get into Flow

Of the many things we can thank Thomas Edison for—phonographs, light bulbs, telegraphs, movie cameras, X-ray machines, and even tattoo pens—perhaps the most important was the modern work ethic, memorialized in his quote, "I never did a day's work in my life. It was all fun."

In modern-day Silicon Valley, we find that the most impactful people we work with actually *love* their jobs. While there are dozens of theories as to what makes for happy employees, research shows that people feel happiest when they are challenged, when they feel like they are learning, and when they are using their gifts to their highest and best purpose.

As the author and psychologist Mihaly Csikszentmihalyi would say, today's most impactful workers spend more time in a "flow state" than workers did a hundred years ago, and this is in large part what drives employee satisfaction and productivity. Whether you call it "flow state" or "deep work," the concept is the same: when we are challenged to use our gifts to dive into hard problems for large, uninterrupted periods of time, we get into a state of mind that many people can only describe as deep satisfaction.

One of our clients who spends a lot of time in flow is Mark Williamson. As the COO of MasterClass since 2017, Mark has played a pivotal role in the spectacular rise of the company from a single writing class by author James Patterson to a global household name that today boasts classes taught by Serena Williams, Martin Scorsese, Anna Wintour, and dozens of others.

Although Mark keeps long hours, he derives energy from the grueling pace of his work because he feels like he's expressing his gift of curiosity. "I approach most things with a 'beginner's mindset,'" Mark explains. "This means life becomes a fun, never-ending game where you are constantly accumulating knowledge and looking for truth that you can put to work to help change the world for the better."

Mark's mindset is common among many of our clients in the tech sector. Most talented engineers see their core gift as solving intractable technical problems. When their work revolves around truth-seeking or problem-solving, it no longer feels like, or even resembles, work. They see their work as a fun yet challenging game that puts them into flow.

The challenge for all of us is to figure out how to use our gifts to get into flow on a more regular basis. Csikszentmihalyi says the key is making sure our work is challenging enough to push us to the limits of our skills. In practice, this means finding the most challenging tasks and problems your company can offer and matching them with the greatest expression of your team's gifts.

In our experience, this is the secret sauce to making sure people are doing the best work of their lives—keeping them challenged just enough to make sure they are not bored, but not so challenged that they are riddled with anxiety and self-doubt.

When Our Gifts Are Underutilized

One client, the CEO of a social networking app, knows a lot about the challenge of finding the sweet spot where he is challenged enough by his work, but not so challenged that it becomes overwhelming. By just about any measure, he has every reason to relax and be content: the company is growing, his team is happy and competent, he has a wonderful wife and family.

Of course, it is unrealistic to be engaged and challenged all the time, and he still periodically experiences anxiety and boredom. The problem is, he is so gifted at so many things that he can easily get bored when things are going a little too well, or exasperated when his team isn't keeping up with his 500-horsepower brain.

As a result, he instinctively looks for other problems to solve in the business. He admits that this can also spill over into his personal life too. We might say he sometimes *creates* problems to fix, just to have something to do. Like the time he reached out to the head of HR to rebuild the entire compensation system, even though no one had complained about it. Or when he sometimes rewrites ad copy after a committee of five people on his team has worked on it for over a month.

Maybe you know a little about this yourself. When work or life starts feeling a little boring, we create some drama in our relationship or look for a new project to work on. While it's human nature, it's also a really dangerous habit for a leader to fall into.

The best response to this need for stimulation is to use our gifts to look for big strategic questions about the future of the business. The idea is to shift your focus longer into the future, and not look for problems to fix in the here and now. When Edward discussed this simple idea with the CEO, it was revelatory. Now he digs in with his product team and develops new revenue streams within the app that are projected to hit the bottom line in a huge way in the coming year, or sketches out plans for an entirely new product he can incubate within the company.

And for times when this doesn't work and he sees himself slipping into old habits of micromanagement and creating undue stress for his team, Edward has helped him sketch out a series of projects he can work on at his new farm in upstate New York. He now has a place to park all that energy and intellect to get himself into flow.

A client at a marketplace start-up had a similar issue, but it was his team that was starting to feel underchallenged. He had focused so much on creating an egalitarian and supportive culture that he was starting to lose his star players because they weren't feeling challenged enough.

This is what happens to many companies that grow to a stage in which people start to feel invisible or like cogs in a machine. Processes become too arduous, tasks too repetitive. Managers seem a little checked out, so employees start checking out. It's a dangerous downward spiral, but what is actually happening?

While a million things could be to blame, the culprit is often the loss of fun and flow. Employees are not growing. They are not learning. They are not using their gifts or being pushed to their limits. In short, they are not doing the best work of their careers.

The good news is that this is fixable. We all want to feel like we are growing, not stagnating.

Ask yourself these questions to learn whether you are doing too much or too little:

- When do you feel like you are being pushed to the limits of your skills?
- What do you do when you feel yourself being sucked into boredom or propelled into anxiety?

- When you look around your teams, how do you see this tension between boredom and anxiety at play?
- How can you help people to use their gifts better to serve your company and your customers?

Finding the Gifts in Our Flaws

In the late 1100s, the central Italian port city of Pisa was living high on the hog. Having sacked the Sicilian capital of Palermo in 1063, and capitalizing on the recent increase in maritime trade, the Pisanos were eager to flaunt their worldly success.

To signal that their city was a force to be reckoned with, they decided to build a "Field of Miracles" outside the town center. It would be home to a collection of impressive new buildings ranging from a cathedral to the world's tallest bell tower, which Pisanos would stock with treasures that local soldiers had looted during their Mediterranean sojourns.

Accordingly, in 1173 Pisanos drew up plans for the Field of Miracles. Possibly unaware that the word *pisa* derives from the Ancient Greek word meaning "marshy land," they were surprised when five years after construction began, the Tower of Pisa started to lean. The mushy sediment beneath the structure had compressed, and the half-built, would-be-highest bell tower in the world began listing to one side.

Dismayed and embarrassed, the Pisanos stopped work. For the next two hundred years, the tower stood there, an unfinished stump, until it was completed in 1399 by builders who employed various advances in engineering, plus a few optical tricks, to make the tower's sideways sag a bit less obvious.

Today, the Leaning Tower of Pisa, as it came to be known, is considered a mixed blessing for Pisanos and Italy itself. While the oddity draws millions of visitors to a town that is otherwise seen as an uncomely stepsister to nearby Florence, to many Italians, the world's best-known tower is still a source of national embarrassment.

But that's not the interesting part.

More interesting, at least for our purposes, is that in the 850 years since Pisanos first broke ground, or marsh as it were, on the Field of Miracles, their leaning tower has withstood no fewer than four major earthquakes, including one over 6.0 on the Richter scale. During these convulsions, hundreds of shorter structures throughout Italy toppled, but the Leaning Tower of Pisa kept its figure and its bittersweet dignity.

Why?

While the propensity of Pisa's tower to tilt is widely perceived to be a magnificent flaw, seismologists agree that this same imperfection is what has allowed it to survive. Without going into all of it, the softness of the soil combined with the structure's angle reduces how much it shakes during quakes.

If the Leaning Tower of Pisa had been built according to plan, it surely would have been knocked to the ground centuries ago. Its most conspicuous fault is, it turns out, its greatest strength.

The same goes for people. Every one of us has qualities or characteristics we're not proud of, or that we believe get in the way of our success: A short fuse. Hypervigilance. Impatience. In some situations, these can be seen as flaws, but in others they can be catalytic gifts.

One of our former clients—we'll call him Pat—had the gift of being a tireless maximizer. He never accepted things at face value. He constantly pushed his team to go one layer deeper: What does that data really say? How do we know if that is really true? What if what we think is happening is not what's really happening?

This is a gift many successful entrepreneurs have, but they often express the gift in such a way that it is viewed by team members as a fundamental flaw. Pat's skepticism could be demoralizing. And it was getting worse as the company grew and the stakes became higher. His skepticism had become so daunting, it risked toppling the entire company. If your team feels like nothing is ever good enough and you never celebrate success, they will quickly become unmotivated.

The challenge John issued to Pat was to learn how to use his gift of skepticism more strategically and surgically. Rather than always being skeptical with everyone, Pat had to learn to discern which situations called for skepticism, and which actually called for celebration. Pat's response to John was telling: "What you call skepticism, I call vigilance. If I'm not vigilant about double-checking everything and questioning everyone's assumptions, who will? That's my job!"

We've seen this situation before, haven't we? The mistrustful CEO who is taking all the joy and creativity out of people's work by nitpicking and litigating every single decision. Pat's gifts of analysis and detail-orientation were having a troubling unintended consequence when he overplayed them. Like many leaders, he was overly focused on "getting everything right" and not focused enough on "helping his team be successful." Pat's myopic focus on task completion coupled with his perfectionism were driving the really good people, those who demand autonomy and want to be trusted, away, leaving him with the B players who don't mind being told what do to all the time.

John bottom-lined with him: "If you don't change this pattern soon, you're going to run every last one of your best people away, Pat. What would be different if instead of nitpicking them, you helped them learn to have the same discerning eye you do? That would give you true scale."

This moment was a real breakthrough for Pat. He saw the writing on the wall, and promised to make the needed changes ASAP. He realized his job was to make other people in the company as good at asking the hard questions as he was. Pat attributes this insight to keeping his team satisfied and intact while they positioned the company for IPO—always a stressful period.

Apply this lesson to your own life:

- Which of your "flaws" may actually be a gift?
- Is there some benefit you get from not being perfect?
- How can you keep your flaw in balance, so you and your team get the benefit of it, without being toppled over by it?
- What flaws are your teammates having trouble finding the gift in, and how can you help them find value in something they think of as a liability?

Sometimes our gifts are born not just from our flaws but also from hardship. Let's look now at how our most difficult moments can surprisingly help us develop gifts that are actually of great service to us and others later in life.

Claiming the Gifts Born from Our Pain

Snow was falling outside the windows of Classroom 104 of the Harvard Kennedy School on a brisk December afternoon in 2008, as seventy-five students crowded in for the final class of Professor Ron Heifetz's Exercising Leadership course. There is no classroom experience more polarizing or exhilarating at Harvard's public policy school than Heifetz's, and that day would be no different.

The syllabus for Exercising Leadership indicates that it is a normal graduate-level course: readings will be assigned, discussions facilitated, papers written, grades given, and so on. However, Exercising Leadership is anything but a normal graduate-level course. While some would call it a real-time experimental laboratory for learning, others liken it to *Lord of the Flies* meets

Survivor. For example: sometime during session 2 or 3, the professor quizzically sits down, apparently refusing to lead the class any longer. Students look around at each other, dismayed: *Are we supposed to discuss the readings? Is this a test? Maybe one of us should get up and facilitate a discussion?*

Invariably, chaos ensues. Various attempts to establish order by one student or another are shouted down. Factions arise. Voices rise even higher. Harsh words are exchanged. And at some point, the person you thought to be the calmest in the room storms out in a red-faced rage.

Given the state of politics these days, perhaps it's actually the perfect dress rehearsal for the real thing. In fact, many of the students in the classroom can tell you exactly how it compares—no graduate program in the world has more elected officials among its alumni than the Harvard Kennedy School.

But on that cold winter day, things were a bit calmer. Since it was the last class of the semester, Heifetz was doing his best to bring it all home. After a long pause, as he was prone to make, the professor casually observed, "And over the course of the semester, you may have learned that some of your classmates have surprising gifts or superpowers you weren't entirely aware of before. Let's take Edward, for example . . ."

Yes, as in Edward Sullivan, coauthor of this book. Who, upon hearing his name, sat up and smiled uneasily.

"At first, many of you may have assumed that Edward wasn't much more than another privileged white man getting through life more on style than substance," the professor continued, as Edward sank back down into his seat. "And so maybe you were surprised to learn that Edward actually has an incredible power of empathy and insight unlike many of us have ever seen. It's almost like he can read your emotions from across the room."

Edward's eyebrows rose slightly as he started to wonder where this was going.

"But that's what often happens with the children of abusive alcoholics. Never knowing if Daddy was in a good or bad mood, little Eddie had to develop a Spidey-sense for his father's emotions, discerning in a split second whether he was safe or if he had to run and hide. That's the way it is with our gifts—they often begin as defense mechanisms."

At that moment, Edward felt like a character in a Hitchcock film when the camera seems to zoom in and pan out at the same time. He had visited the professor during office hours to talk about his progress in the class, and Heifetz, a trained psychologist, had prodded him about his home life growing up.

It's true: Edward's father was an abusive alcoholic. Not all the time, but episodically for years, enough to instill in young Eddie the need to be hypervigilant.

While the immediate impact on Edward of being outed as the son of an alcoholic and the victim of child abuse was a wave of shame and disbelief that the professor had violated his confidence, the long-term impact was nothing short of transformational.

Edward had never viewed the difficult moments from his childhood as having any value at all, let alone as being assets. What's more, never had he thought of empathy as a superpower. In many ways, that moment was the catalyst for a multiyear process of personal transformation and improved self-awareness that led Edward to where he is today: the CEO of a top coaching firm.

When we look across the landscape of high-performing individuals, both within the ranks of our clients and beyond, we can see a very distinct pattern. Many of the most successful and impactful adults had childhoods that were compromised in some way by neglect or abuse.

At least three of our top CEO clients were raised in horrific conditions of poverty and neglect. Oprah and Maya Angelou (not clients) were both sexually abused as young girls. Elon Musk and Steve Jobs had emotionally and physically abusive fathers. Jim Carrey and singer Jewel were homeless as teenagers.

If you look around at many of the truly gifted people in your life, you will likely find that many of their gifts arose out of difficult circumstances. That coworker with a vivid imagination perhaps needed to invent an entirely new world for herself as a child to escape a traumatic home life. The colleague with an incredible knack for organization and follow-through may have had to learn to create order and consistency for himself while growing up in a chaotic and unpredictable environment.

The first step in claiming the gifts we derive from painful experiences is to reframe the stories we tell ourselves about those experiences. For Edward, it took a grad school professor to help him reframe his painful childhood as one that had given him certain gifts he had yet to comprehend.

What painful experiences might you want to reframe? Whose help can you solicit to help you accomplish that, if it doesn't seem immediately obvious that any good came from your painful experiences? And as a peer, leader, or mentor, how can you help walk another person through the process of reframing their old painful stories of loss or trauma? In our experience, doing so requires two important ingredients: vulnerability and trust.

Just as Edward gained *your* trust by being vulnerable and sharing a difficult story from his own childhood, to build trust with your peers and teams, you will be challenged to get vulnerable and share your own stories of how you overcame hardship and found the gift within yourself. We know this may be uncomfortable. It can feel like oversharing, but our experience and vast amounts of research have shown it to be crucial.

In the 1960s, researcher Elliot Aronson found through a series of studies what he called the "pratfall effect"—the counterintuitive concept that when people in authority commit a blunder or show their flaws, their "interpersonal attractiveness" increases. Another study showed that when subordinates are vulnerable and ask for advice at work, they seem more competent and credible to supervisors.

Edward's professor knew that after a full semester battling it out with his classmates, sharing and hearing various stories of struggle, loss, and resilience, Edward had developed a deep feeling of trust in that room. That was the only reason he chose to help Edward reframe his story and claim his gift in such a public setting. He was also certain that Edward had done the requisite healing work but needed a push to take the critical next steps.

In reflecting on your own life, ask yourself these questions:

- What healing work do you still need to do before you reframe your painful stories and claim your gifts?
- What nuggets still remain buried under years of shame? Whom do you need to forgive and develop compassion for?

We know these are profound questions. Who can you talk with to explore them? If you have had deeply traumatic experiences, we encourage you to see a trained trauma therapist who can help you unpack those experiences in a safe setting.

Too Much of a Good Thing

In our work with clients, we find that at least 50 percent of the "problems" leaders have stem from using their gift a little too much. We call them "overdone strengths," and they plague all of us because it is natural to want to do more of what we are good at. Breaking free of that cycle often takes the input of a helpful friend, coach, or board member. It's not easy to hear that the thing you are good at and proud of is actually driving people crazy.

Our client Aaron, the CFO of a major tech firm, suffered from that problem. Aaron is intellectually gifted, to put it mildly. When most people are still trying to figure out what the data on a graph means, Aaron has already derived ten insights from said data and has made a plan in his head for three new product features, two new hires, and one layoff.

In short, Aaron is a machine.

But if you've ever worked with a machine, you know that people like Aaron can be overwhelming to us mere humans. Knowing that Aaron most likely already has the answer makes you not want to bother coming up with your own. Fearing that Aaron will see right through your feeble plan makes you not want to share your plans with him. Worrying that Aaron sees deeper into the data than you could ever aspire to makes you not bother looking at the data at all.

In short, Aaron was a "diminisher," to borrow the term coined by Liz Wiseman in her groundbreaking book *Multipliers*. According to Wiseman's research, diminishers tap into just 50 percent of their capabilities by micromanaging, telling people what to do, hoarding all the decision-making power, and generally underusing the brilliant people they painstakingly hire. And in our research, we have found that they do so because they are often overplaying their own gifts.

Aaron may have been one of the smartest people at his company, but he was taking the joy out of working there for many of his colleagues. And while this harsh reality was hard for him to hear about in his 360, it was also an incredible opportunity. He had no idea he was shutting out other great minds at the company. He was unaware that his attempts to "add value" to the conversation were demoralizing to more junior members of the team.

Armed with this information, however, Aaron was able to make some adjustments. He began by focusing more on coaching and supporting his team rather than directing and delegating. He started asking the kinds of questions that get people thinking and learning, rather than pointing to the answer. In short, he learned to have conversations that helped his team *see* the data and business through his lens, rather than simply telling them all what they were missing.

By making that one simple change and no longer overplaying his strengths, he was able to add capacity and scale to the organization in a way he never had before. Some leaders subconsciously resist developing their teams in this way because they secretly like being the ones with all the answers, but we cannot express enough how damaging this is. It damages morale, it creates groupthink, and it ultimately erodes the bottom line.

Overdone Strengths in Teams

Not only do individuals have overdone gifts, but teams do, as well. Sometimes a group of people can learn to be so good at working together that they exhibit what can only be called a one-of-a-kind competency as a unit. And sometimes it is exactly that extreme competency as a team that becomes their Achilles' heel as they try to grow the company.

We recently worked with the C-suite of a health-care start-up having trouble scaling. As a team, they'd been through a lot together over five years of managing and growing the company. From opening offices around the country to dealing with Covid and taking on one of the biggest names in health care, they had done it all.

Just like a platoon of soldiers that had been to battle together, this executive team had developed *deep* trust in one another.

They knew each other's gifts and flaws. They could finish each other's sentences. They made exquisite decisions together. The only problem was that there were three hundred other people in the organization who didn't enjoy the same trust from the members of the executive team that they had for each other. So while the exec team was incredible at making great decisions together, no one else in the company got to make any decisions at all. Their gift was being overdone.

By failing to delegate decision-making, the exec team was beginning to experience decision fatigue. Simple HR or product questions that should have been made two levels down were gobbling up precious exec team time. They found themselves making decisions about the website design. They even wasted an hour debating what the office holiday vacation schedule should be.

Lucky for them, they realized that something was amiss and reached out for help. Through our analysis we were able to help them realize that many of their incredible gifts as a core team had begun to hamstring the rest of the organization. What were once strengths when they were a small company had become liabilities as they grew.

Working with Edward, they put awareness into action. First, they developed a new charter for how they would work together. They defined exactly what kinds of topics they would discuss, how they would make decisions, and how they would hold each other accountable when one of them tried to pull the rest off track. Next, they talked to the rest of the company about it, so everyone was able to support them changing their leadership habits. And to make sure it wasn't something they talked about once and forgot, they created a schedule of quarterly accountability check-ins to gauge how well they were doing on instituting the changes.

That three-step process really works for developing new habits as a team:

1. Defining new expectations
2. Communicating those expectations broadly
3. Establishing a process and schedule for accountability

For this team, it worked wonders. The new charter gave them a document to hold each other accountable. The public scrutiny that came from sharing it with the team emboldened others in the company to remind them when they were "doing that micro-managing thing again." And the schedule for accountability kept the agreements top of mind going forward.

Every Poison Has an Antidote

One client learned through a feedback exercise that his superpowers included his gifts of empathy and authenticity. He was able to get deep into the hearts and minds of his users and create some of the fastest-growing apps of the decade. He could have raw and real conversations with his team to dispel ambiguity and give the kind of insightful feedback that moves things forward and helps people break out of negative patterns.

At an extreme, however, both of these gifts can become weaknesses. He learned through feedback conversations that his empathy could spill over into people-pleasing, and his authenticity could be seen as oversharing or being overly critical. To help keep himself from overdoing it, he developed simple antidotes to keep his gifts in check.

His process looks like this:

1. What are your gifts?
2. What might their "shadow sides" be?
3. What is the antidote for those shadow sides?

For overdone empathy, his antidote is humility: he doesn't have to make everyone happy, nor does he have the power to. And for overdone authenticity, his antidote is kind restraint: just because he thinks or observes something doesn't mean it is kind or necessary to share it.

Using these tools, and others, he has fundamentally changed his relationship with his gifts, and he now enjoys some of the highest employee engagement and happiness scores in the country.

Questions for further exploration by you and your team:

- What gifts or strengths might you be overdoing?
- How do your best intentions to be helpful shut down the participation or collaboration of others?
- What core strengths does your team or organization have that might be overplayed?
- Who can you speak with to get some perspective on how your gifts can be better deployed?
- What "antidotes" can bring you back from overplaying your gifts?

Assembling Constellations of Gifts

Early in 1984, thirty-one-year-old Debi Coleman stepped into Apple's Macintosh computer factory in Fremont, California, and took a deep breath. In the three years since Steve Jobs had hired Debi as a financial controller, he'd promoted her various times, but always within the finance organization. Until that day.

Now he was entrusting the English literature major from Brown with the crown jewel of the Apple empire—the brand-new manufacturing plant of the machine that Apple had just announced to the world in a Super Bowl ad was going to shatter IBM's hegemony over the computer industry—the Macintosh.

The only problem was, Debi had literally no experience in manufacturing and no idea where to begin. Three other manufacturing professionals in close succession had attempted to rein in the unwieldy plant, and all had failed. Construction on the building was only half completed. And although demand for the new Mac was going through the roof, throughput of the assembly line was only at a fraction of what it was designed for, and the company was already missing shipping deadlines.

But bit by bit, Debi and her crack team of soon-to-be manufacturing experts cleaned up the factory, armed only with clipboards, pencils, and brooms. They analyzed the assembly line and worked out the bottlenecks. They installed better systems to reduce inventory and initiate just-in-time manufacturing. They even painted the walls a gleaming, shiny white that dust could not cling to.

And to everyone's surprise, by September Debi had whipped the plant into shape, so much so that Jobs threw a party for Debi and the plant workers with a banner that read "September—the month we ran the factory, the factory didn't run us."

But here's the real question . . . why did Steve Jobs trust a financial controller with zero experience in manufacturing, aside from what she knew "in theory" from a few classes in business school, with running his most important factory? Debi had the same question.

Asked at the time what she thought about Jobs hiring her for the role, she said, "There's no way anyone else in the world would give me this chance to run this kind of operation."

Steve Jobs was many things, but he was not an engineer. Nor a designer. Nor a project manager. Nor a finance whiz. In fact, he didn't really have any marketable skills that would have earned him a job at Apple if he had applied off the street. But none of that mattered because Jobs had one crucial skill that made him perfect for his role as CEO: uncovering hidden gifts in people and putting those people in the right roles.

If you look across the history of Apple, you see stories like Debi's over and over. Jobs hired people who were "insanely good at their jobs," whether or not they were trained professionals in those roles. In fact, Jobs thought most of his early hires of more seasoned professionals were mistakes. "It didn't work out at all. Most of them were bozos. They knew how to manage, but they didn't know how to do anything."

Perhaps he didn't use our language for it, Jobs did what we've seen other great leaders do over the years: *they all hired people with specific gifts and created a constellation of complementary gifts.* Debi Coleman's gift was how precise and meticulous she was. She looked for new ways to solve problems, even the smallest and seemingly insignificant ones. And she drove those solutions through to completion.

Other great Apple hires from that era had complementary gifts. Guy Kawasaki, a contemporary of Debi's, was hired as Apple's "chief evangelist" in the mid-1980s. His gift is punchy, impactful, and memorable language. Guy is a taglines and frameworks guy, not the meticulous process optimizer Debi is.

This is how the best leaders think about assembling teams. Like Danny Ocean in *Ocean's 11*, they look for the best person in the world for each specific role. They purposefully don't hire people just like themselves. This point is specifically important because, as we saw before, Jobs couldn't really *do* anything either. Maybe he wasn't a "bozo" professional manager, but he also wasn't a manufacturing or human resources expert. "I've built a lot of my success off finding these truly gifted people and not settling for B or C players," Jobs said in an interview in the early 1990s. "I found that when you get enough A players together . . .

they really like working together because they never had a chance to do that before."

This is what we call building a "constellation of gifts." This is what happens when you bring truly gifted people together.

In 1983 and 1984, being on the Mac team for Debi and dozens of others was an example of working on a team that had a constellation of gifts. "I think if you talk to a lot of people in the Mac team, they will tell you it was the hardest they've ever worked in their life. Some of them will tell you it was the happiest they've ever been in their life. But I think all of them will tell you that it was certainly one of the most intense and cherished experiences they will ever have in their life," reflected Jobs. That is what happens when you bring together a constellation of brilliant, gifted people and let them work on hard problems together.

Bringing it back to you:

- When have you worked on a team that felt like a constellation of gifted people? What was special about that experience?
- If you're not having that experience now, what could you be doing more of to cultivate a team with a constellation of complementary gifts?

Let's explore next what happens when teams fail to see each other's gifts. And conveniently, we don't even have to leave Cupertino to do it.

When We Fail to See Each Other's Gifts

For Jon Rubinstein, or Ruby to his friends, the call to get his team more focused on seeing each other's gifts came in the early stages of developing the iPhone and other Apple products. His team of engineers and designers was mired in disagreement and not working effectively together.

And Ruby's boss, Steve Jobs, was not happy.

At his wit's end, Ruby called John to help with his team. John was Ruby's coach during one of the most crucial periods in Apple's growth.

Ruby's team suffered from one of the most common pitfalls facing teams of high performers: they were not seeing and valuing each other's gifts. What's more, they weren't seeing how their own behaviors were impacting other team members, and they were blind to how their behavior was blocking progress and sabotaging their collective success. John and Ruby needed to come up with a way to help this team see each other as colleagues and not as adversaries. And they only had a short time to do it.

The core problem, as John saw it, was that the team was almost *too* good. It was one of the most talented and elite collections of individuals ever to work on a project together. For example, the team had Ruby, a seasoned engineer and product developer who launched the iPod (they called him the "Podfather"), who would go on to be the CEO of Palm; Tony Fadell, the whiz kid (at the time) who would later launch Nest; and Jony Ive, Jobs's hand-picked head designer. When you have a team of superstars working together, they either achieve a once-in-a-generation level of success like the Mac team we just discussed, or they blow up and never want to speak to each other again. And it was clear what direction this team was headed in.

Armed with that insight, John decided that the best strategy was to help the team members begin to value each other's gifts and learn to build upon them, instead of competing with each other. This is when he came up with what would become one of his signature team tune-up techniques, a technique he's deployed in dozens of boardrooms, off-sites, and virtual retreats over the years: feedback speed dating.

It's really as simple as it sounds. You take the team, pair them off, and give them ten minutes to sit alone together and discuss two prompts:

- What I appreciate most about working with you is . . .
- A few ways you could support me more in my work are . . .

After ten minutes, you rotate the pairings until everyone has had one-on-one time with everyone else.

While this may seem too rudimentary to work, its genius is in its simplicity. No trust falls, no retreats, no sob stories about being bullied as kids. Just two simple prompts designed to force team members to look for each other's gifts and to have a conversation about them.

Players can get competitive with each other. Egos can flare. People can become skeptical and blind to each other's gifts, which erodes trust even further. This is why many teams become mired in politics and animosity. Instead, they need to affirm one another's strengths. As John showed Ruby's team—and hundreds of teams since then—sometimes they just need to create structure and process around having conversations that show they value each other.

After running this exercise a few more times, Ruby's team members were able to see each other in a different light. Even more importantly, they each began to see that their colleagues viewed *them* as having value. This enabled the team to have more rigorous and productive debate, rather than becoming mired in continuous conflict. As a result, they could commit to plans and hold each other accountable. And if you've ever held an iPhone in your hand, you know they delivered exceptional results.

Also, if you've ever worked on a team, you also know that the kind of dysfunction afflicting Ruby's team is all too common. Sometimes, even when we have the perfect "product insight," and what we're building is truly visionary and industry-changing, our lack of insight about ourselves and our teams can put us on the path to failure.

Thinking about Ruby and his team:

- How have you failed to see the gifts in others?
- How are your teams failing to see the gifts in each other?
- What will you do to change this? Maybe some feedback speed dating?

The Apex Gift: Seeing Other People's Gifts

Jessica Encell Coleman has one of those smiles that lights up a room. Not in the self-conscious "take my picture" sense, although she's certainly photogenic, but more in the "I see you and want to get to know you" sense. Her smile makes you feel like everything is going to be okay.

We got to know Jessica in the ski town of Eden, Utah, halfway between Salt Lake City and the Idaho border, in the summer of 2018. It was her third or fourth time facilitating one of her now-ubiquitous Magic of Human Connection workshops at a Summit Series event, a weekend retreat for entrepreneurs, artists, musicians, and other tastemakers.

It's hard to describe exactly what Jessica's workshop is without experiencing it, but the best approximation we can think of is that it is a "vulnerability accelerator." In one hour, she can take a group of complete strangers and turn them into old friends who hug when they see each other. We've never witnessed anything like it, and we've been to and facilitated a lot of workshops.

Through a series of exercises, she slowly opens the group up—it's like watching a time lapse of a flower blooming. There's the milling around and making eye contact with people as you pass. The invitation to treat everyone like a best friend you haven't met. The stopping in front of a stranger and appreciating the "divine spark" within them. And, if you are open to it, the transformational hugs.

It's a sublime experience from start to finish.

Jessica's workshop culminates in what she calls "the Inner Voice." One participant lies down on the floor or sits in a chair, and two others flank them, whispering positive observations about them directly into their ear. Having done it a few times, we can say without hesitation . . . it's a trip!

Somehow, Jessica has created a safe place for three complete strangers to make each other giggle, weep, and generally glow within an hour of meeting. There is something so special about hearing positive and unexpected things about ourselves, and even more so from strangers.

More than special, it's actually motivating. Social scientists have been telling us for years that positive reinforcement is the best way to get others to adopt new behaviors. One study on handwashing compliance in a New York State hospital showed a 900 percent increase in the frequency of handwashing by employees when an electronic board displayed a message reading "Good job!" on their way out of the bathroom if sensors in the sink confirmed they had indeed washed their hands.

Yes, we are really all just waiting for someone to say "Good job!" Even an electronic placard.

What's magical about Jessica's Inner Voice exercise is not just that complete strangers are saying you have great style or swagger, or some other superficial observation. It's that they are very often noticing beautiful traits or gifts that you may not see yourself. Or if you *do* see them, they might be fleeting, and not something you give much credence to. *You put people at ease. Your presence lights up the room. Your welcoming smile makes me want to tell you things that are hard to say.*

Very often it takes someone else spelling out the gifts they see in us for us to begin to believe in those gifts at all. By letting us in on this little secret about ourselves, they give us a reason to aspire to more. As author and business school professor Phil Rosenzweig says, "Holding a self-belief that is somewhat exaggerated . . . can often help us achieve higher performance. Believing you can run a bit faster than you've ever run before can help you do better."

For most of us, that "self-belief that is somewhat exaggerated" has to be sourced externally. This is where leading with heart comes in.

Leading with heart includes helping people see their own gifts and expand their sense of what they are capable of. One of John's clients who has proven one of the best we've ever seen at this is DoorDash founder and CEO Tony Xu.

To tell Tony's story, let's go back to a sunny fall afternoon in 2012, when Tony, then a Stanford Business School student, was in a macaron shop on University Avenue in Palo Alto, interviewing the owner about the "pain points" of running a small business. Tony was looking to start a company to support local economies, and he didn't know where to begin.

Aside from wanting to make enough money someday so that he could afford to take a box of macarons home to his girlfriend, Tony was inspired by how hard small-business owners have to work to make ends meet. In fact, he knew firsthand. His mother had given up her career as a family doctor in China when his family emigrated to the States when Tony was four years old. She worked in local restaurants during most of his childhood, and young Tony would join her from time to time washing dishes.

When the phone in the macaron shop suddenly rang, the owner jumped up to grab it, and Tony overheard her utter four words that would change the course of his life forever: "Sorry, we don't deliver."

In that moment Tony had a simple but pivotal insight: restaurateurs should focus on their gifts, namely making amazing food, and he should build a company to support them by getting their food into more mouths.

Within a few months, Tony and three friends from Stanford started PaloAltoDelivery.com, which today we know as DoorDash. In the beginning, Tony and his cofounders typed the menus of local businesses onto their new company's website, giving many of their clients their first presence on the web. They also delivered orders personally.

By 2021, DoorDash had become a $50 billion public company with well over five thousand employees. And while DoorDash has had to do countless things right to get to this point, it's one thing that Tony Xu does over and over that we believe is the secret to the company's success: he's never stopped asking the right questions and looking for how to leverage the gifts of others.

From the outset, Tony's mission at DoorDash was to make small businesses more successful by helping them deliver their ramen, macarons, pizza, wraps, and smoothies to the homes of would-be customers. Today, as CEO, his mission is still to do that, by focusing his attention on making his team as successful as possible.

Like the Mac team that Steve Jobs led through the early 1980s, Tony's management team at DoorDash is an incredible constellation of gifted people who complement each other. Through our work with the DoorDash team, we discovered that no matter how difficult the decision or seemingly insurmountable the obstacle, Tony's unwillingness to accept failure forces his team to dig in and find creative solutions. Tony does not bark orders, but he does hold his team accountable and push them beyond what they think they are capable of.

That's what great leaders do. They recognize the genius in others, empower them to make decisions, challenge them to go beyond their perceived limits, and hold them to incredibly high standards. They also invest in helping their team develop their gifts. Tony was very generous in offering coaching to many members of his executive team because he knew that gifts are not static; they must be cultivated and developed.

Thinking about the gifts of people you work with:

- Who has a special gift they may not be aware of that you might be able to call out for them?
- If you can't think of anyone, what blindset might be keeping you from noticing the gifts in others? Is there something that you're not valuing?
- What could you do to help make space for more people to express their gifts?
- Conversely, what are you doing that may be keeping people from fully exercising their gifts?

What Makes Us Forget Our Gifts

This is a special chapter for us because it really begins to bring the whole book together. If you don't have your needs met, or only have your most basic needs met, you aren't going to have the resources or inspiration to bring your gifts to life. Similarly, we tend to shy away from expressing our gifts when we are overwhelmed with fear. Nor do we focus much on "giving away our gifts" when we are distracted by an unhealthy desire. Our client Ariane Goldman, CEO of maternity fashion brand Hatch, knows this all too well.

Ariane is one of the most brilliant branding and fashion minds of her generation. She doesn't just "get" expecting mothers because she is a mother of two herself. No, she has a true gift for seeing exactly what they want, what quality they expect, and how they want to feel about themselves during their pregnancy. According to one of her customers, "Wearing Hatch products made me actually forget for a little while the discomfort of being pregnant."

But when we met Ariane, she was losing touch with her gift. She was mired in fear about potential competitors, and she didn't have the support she needed in the office to rise above the dramas and distractions of the day-to-day. The conditions for her to live fully in her gift were not being met. She was spending all of her time putting out the flames of fears and tending to the organization's low-level needs.

In a coaching session, Edward asked her the simple question, "What is one thing you alone can do at this company?"

Her answer was straightforward: "Strategic and creative direction."

"And how are you spending your time?"

Silence.

Ariane was spending 90 percent of her time on the "small stuff" that zapped her energy. She wasn't giving herself the space to feel creative. She was also getting consumed by fears of failure that would paralyze her and take her even further away from being the creative leader she alone could be for the company.

After a series of coaching sessions in which she and Edward had some very real conversations, Ariane began to regain the ability to quell her fears and advocate for getting her needs met. She worked to trust her direct reports with more of the day-to-day and made time in her calendar for the creative and strategic work she loved. As a result, the company began to rebound. She did a massive deal with a major retailer, and investors started circling to infuse Hatch with the cash to scale the business even more.

When you step back and look at Ariane's insights, you begin to see that the Leading with Heart conversations do not live in isolation from each other but are instead an integrated system. Getting our needs met and quelling our fears and unhealthy desires gives us space to express our gifts. The more we get the flywheel of expressing our gifts spinning, the more our needs are met, and so on. It's a system that builds upon itself.

In the next chapter, we dive into the question that is the culmination of our journey together: What is our purpose? And if we don't know, how do we find it?

CHAPTER 4 TAKEAWAYS

- Everyone has a special gift, but we tend to undervalue our natural talents and strengths because we didn't have to work for them like all of our learned skills.
- Using our gifts to solve hard problems is one of the ways we get "in flow" and feel deeper satisfaction overall. Leaders need to challenge their teams with hard problems that keep them at the sweet spot between boredom and being overwhelmed.
- For many people, our greatest gifts come from painful or dark periods in our lives. Embracing those gifts and putting them to good use helps us make meaning of and heal from difficult experiences.
- Leaders' gifts and strengths can be overdone, often to the detriment of their teams. When morale is lagging or performance is off, it is smart for leaders to get curious and have conversations about the role they are playing in creating that dynamic.
- Through conversations about what we value in each other, teams begin to identify and unlock their natural gifts and, as a result, build trust.
- Our gifts can flourish most when they are compounded by the gifts of others. When we work in a constellation of gifts, teams maximize their highest potential.

CONVERSATION STARTERS

1. What have you been told is your greatest gift as a leader? Where do you think that gift came from? Was it a surprise to hear that at first? Why? How can you leverage your gifts more as a leader?
2. What are the gifts of members of your team? Who has a gift they probably aren't fully aware of? What's keeping you from having a conversation with them about it?
3. What, if anything, is keeping you from expressing your own gifts in more impactful ways? What unmet need or fear might be holding you back?
4. How are you using your gifts to stay in flow on challenging tasks?

5. What apparent flaws of your own or your team's could be actual gifts that are simply misapplied right now?

6. Who are the most gifted people you work with right now? Are they working together to solve the most important problems at the company? If not, why not?

5

WHAT IS YOUR PURPOSE?

The two most important days in your life are the day you are
born and the day you find out why.

—MARK TWAIN

When you first meet Valerie Ashby, dean of the Trinity College of Arts and Sciences at Duke University, you can't help but notice: this woman is on a mission.

Valerie has risen through the ranks to become not just one of the top Black women in academia, or women in academia, but as a dean of one of the top institutions in the country, she is one of the top *humans* in academia.

John was introduced to Valerie a few years ago when he was coaching Joe Desimone, founder of venture-backed Carbon, a start-up dedicated to reinventing how polymer products are designed, engineered, manufactured, and delivered, toward a digital and sustainable future (you will learn Joe's story later in this chapter).

Joe is one of Valerie's trusted mentors and doctoral thesis advisor from their days at the University of North Carolina at Chapel Hill, and he thought John would be a good coach for Valerie and her team as she began her leadership journey at Duke University. When John spoke to her recently for this book to talk about purpose and leading with heart, she stated without hesitation what her purpose and mission is today: *to educate, encourage, support, and develop the next generation of leaders.*

Valerie lights up when she talks about the students who come to Duke, and how she believes it is her job personally to help them find their place in the world. She takes her role as shepherd for her students and faculty seriously. Her sense of purpose is clear, steadfast, and unwavering.

Having so much clarity about her purpose gives Valerie another characteristic that has been a secret to her success: authenticity. She is just so genuine that you can't help but relax in her presence. Valerie is honest, engaging, and empathetic. You always feel *seen* when you are with her.

To carry out her purpose, Valerie uses her authenticity and her story as tools to help others learn. She has spoken extensively about her own struggles with impostor syndrome, and the challenges she has faced as a result in academia. But it is exactly that openness and vulnerability, that courage, that makes her the perfect person to fulfill her purpose: educating and developing the next generation of leaders.

She wakes up excited to break down barriers and create opportunities for others. Knowing there are thousands of young people out there struggling against a system that is stacked against them and dealing with their own negative self-talk inspires her to go to work.

Valerie credits her parents for her sense of purpose and authentic style. She gets her clarity and directness from her father and her deep sense of empathy from her mother. She also has a natural sense of humor that allows her to navigate tough issues effectively. Valerie's clear sense of purpose has enabled her to inspire the faculty to improve the student experience.

How do you feel when you wake up in the morning? Is it with excitement to do work that's filled with purpose and meaning? Or can no amount of coffee help you start your day with vigor and enthusiasm? Have you asked yourself why you're doing what you're doing? Do you have a clear answer like Valerie when asked about your mission and purpose in life?

If those questions just made you feel reflective or even bad about yourself, please don't despair. Very few people are as clear about their purpose as Valerie Ashby. In fact, as we work with clients and companies throughout Silicon Valley and around the world, we've met dozens of leaders for whom these questions are really hard to answer.

If you're not clear on what your purpose is, you're in good company. Most of us just start doing something for work because we are interested, because someone recruited us, or because we simply needed to pay the rent. But that doesn't mean that having conversations that help you see your own purpose clearly isn't important. In fact, we've left this topic for the end of the book because it's the *most* important.

So far, we have talked a lot about how to lead with heart by having conversations about your needs, your fears, your desires, and your gifts, as well as those of your teams. But without a clear sense of purpose, we don't have a place to put all that clarity and energy. Without a clear sense of purpose, it's hard to feel inspired personally, let alone to mobilize and inspire our teams and organizations.

This chapter will help you understand why purpose is so important to leadership effectiveness. What is our purpose, and how can we use it to have conversations that are both life- and organization-defining?

John's Personal Journey to Renewed Purpose

We haven't discussed John's story much so far. He is a bit more reserved with details of his personal life. But since we encourage our clients to be vulnerable, we thought we should both "walk the talk."

This is the story about how John lost his sense of purpose and meaning in his work and then found it again.

Let's hear it right from John:

It all happened over six years ago. I woke up one morning feeling down, with little energy to tackle my scheduled coaching sessions. I didn't feel like eating or doing anything. I just wanted to cancel everything on my calendar. This was unusual behavior for me, as I am a very positive person, and it takes a lot for things to get me down. I said to myself, "I am sure this will go away."

Three weeks later, the feeling was still there, and I kept asking myself, "What is going on? Why am I still feeling this way?" It was hard for me to understand, because after fifteen years my business partner and I had built one of the most successful coaching firms in Silicon Valley.

Our firm was established on early work at Apple and Nike, and we were now coaching leaders at some of Silicon Valley's most iconic companies. The company was doing great financially, the work was meaningful, and I couldn't have asked for a better partner. But something was different. I was not finding the joy I once experienced in my work.

I continued to plow forward, hoping that things would just get better. But instead, I became more irritable and began to take out my unhappiness on my wife by constantly talking about how frustrated I was. Finally, after hearing enough about it, she said, "Why don't you talk to your partner?" She always has such sensible ideas.

I called my partner the next day, and I talked to her openly about our company and how I was feeling. In hindsight, I wasn't totally transparent; I didn't tell her just how down on things I was at the time. Instead, I suggested that we might want to find a consultant to help us look at our clients and reset the direction of the company.

Even though I was still unsure about what was really going on with me, she immediately supported me and liked the idea of hiring a consultant to help us figure this out.

One month later, my partner and I flew out to Denver to meet with a husband-and-wife team we had hired to help us with our company focus and vision. Little did I know that each of us would separately be videoed as we responded to a series of questions about the things that brought joy to our life and work.

The questions were powerful and probed the things that brought us happiness and joy and the things that were missing in our lives. I was totally transparent and found the experience cathartic. Sitting there with a stranger, I found it easy to share my feelings about myself and the company. As more questions were asked and they probed deeper, I got totally honest about how I felt that I had lost any real sense of purpose to my work.

Indeed, this was an important moment, but the consultants were not done with us. Once our videoed interviews were completed, they brought us together to show us our interviews. They asked me if they could start with my video. I agreed but wondered if it was really best for me to go first. I had disclosed some things in my interview that I had never expressed to my business partner. I had a sinking feeling in my stomach as the consultants continued with their process.

Before they turned on the videos, the consultants introduced us to "lights-on/lights-off," a concept that we use with our clients to this day.

Lights-on *moments are when you express ideas or talk about topics with excitement, passion, and positive language. Your voice is louder, and your body language is animated, with lots of hand* gestures. Your face lights up with joy, and you feel like you could ramble on and on about the topic.

Lights-off moments, in contrast, come when you are talking about things with less animation and excitement. Your voice is lower and softer, and you tend to look down at the table or floor. In these moments, you might smile less or have fewer hand gestures and negative body language. Overall, there is noticeably less energy. When expressing lights-off ideas, you also typically use fewer words.

Once the consultants explained the lights-on/lights-off concept, they asked us to watch our interviews and note which ideas were lights-on and which were lights-off. The experience of watching my video interview was transformative for me. I saw my passion and excitement come alive when I talked about working with start-ups. The consultants pointed out how different my communication language was when I talked about the innovation happening in the start-up world.

As I talked about the chaos of the start-up culture, I became very animated and passionate about the joy I felt in bringing the right amount of order and process to early-stage companies. In contrast, I was more lights-off as I talked about how my continued work with larger companies was not bringing me the joy that it once did.

As we continued to watch my video, the consultants stopped the tape at one point. "We feel this next segment is the most significant moment in your video," they said. I started to feel a bit anxious. My adrenaline was pumping, and I was curious what part of my interview they had selected.

My partner leaned forward with anticipation and wonder as the consultants pressed the play button. As the video appeared on the screen, the consultants said, "John, this was your biggest lights-on moment." The video began playing, and I watched myself as I answered the question "John, what is missing in your *life?" My response was filled with passion and an energy that was different from the other segments of my video. I was animated, and my words had a clarity of conviction that is still memorable to this day.*

It went something like this:

"I am missing a real sense of purpose. I am not sure why I am doing what I am doing. I know I add value to the executives I work with in large companies, but I feel that I am making a bigger difference in the coaching work that I am doing with start-up founders and leaders at the top of companies, CEOs. I love the innovation and the chaos of the start-up world. Most of the CEOs and founders I work with in these new ventures are young and inexperienced and lack a lot of the fundamental leadership skills needed to scale their companies. I feel like I can really help them."

At this point the consultants stopped the video again, and one of them eagerly said, "It sounds like you are finding a lot of joy in working with CEOs and young entrepreneurs in the start-up world."

I responded quickly and clearly: "Yes, if I can get these leaders early in their careers, I can help them develop the practices of good leadership that can help them build strong teams and cultures. Besides, I love innovation and the ideas being generated from these cutting-edge companies. I find a lot of joy and satisfaction in thinking that my early-intervention work with these young leaders will help them build leadership practices that will sustain them on their leadership journeys. I wish I had more clients like this."

As a result of this process, I realized that it was time for me to make a change. This was a lights-on moment for me! I had found a new sense of purpose working with start-ups, and I couldn't waste any more time doing work that didn't feel satisfying.

Once we were back in the Bay Area, I began to pursue my

dream of starting a new company, one that would focus on start-ups. It was shortly after this that one of my former clients introduced me to the person who would help me start up Velocity. As Velocity got early traction, Edward joined as CEO, lending his energy and vision to help Velocity scale into what it is now.

Today, I look back at my experience in Denver as one that really took the blinders off and helped me see what was missing in my life. Since that time, I feel like I've been doing the most fulfilling work of my career.

We all have lights-on and lights-off moments in our lives, but most of them go by without us noticing their importance. If you can't experience something like John's intervention, it might take a friend, coach, or family member to help you reflect on your lights-on possibilities. Who in your life can give you feedback about what things light you up? If you don't have that person in your life, what would it take to find someone? Sometimes you just need the courage to ask.

What Is Purpose?

Purpose is a funny thing. For many of us it's an amorphous concept that we have a hard time defining, although we recognize it when we see it. You can also tell when people have no clear purpose: they are just doing a job, or they are out for themselves. They may just be lost or they may be so activated by fear or scarcity thinking that they can't even begin to identify the gifts that they could put to use for some higher purpose.

These next stories will give us a clearer look into what purpose is, and what it isn't.

MISSION MATTERS, BUT PURPOSE PERSISTS

The Nike World Headquarters building in Beaverton, Oregon, is the Taj Mahal of sports. Set on its own manmade lake just west of Portland, the 250-acre campus is dotted with buildings named after many of the greatest athletes of our time: Michael Jordan, Nolan Ryan, Bo Jackson, Serena Williams, LeBron James.

Early in his coaching career, John developed and facilitated a leadership program for forty of Nike's high-potential leaders. Walking into Nike HQ for the first time was an emotional experience. John grew up a competitive swimmer, and at the time he was participating in triathlons throughout California. Being at Nike felt like walking on hallowed ground.

Over a number of days, John worked with these emerging leaders to help them develop the skills to carry out their mission: to crush Adidas. Since the 1970s, Adidas had been the dominant athletic shoe company worldwide, across every category. But one by one, first in running shoes, then in basketball, and now in tennis, Nike was taking market share.

One day while John was coaching at Nike, Phil Knight, Nike founder and CEO, stopped by to share a clear and simple message: he wanted to crush Adidas and knock them off their pedestal, especially in Europe. Cheers erupted from the small audience. People high-fived and pumped their fists. This mission was a rallying cry that clearly resonated.

However, as energized as that made them, it was Phil Knight's personal story of why he founded Nike that was even more inspiring to this group. Nike, according to Knight, existed for the individual athletes. For the lonely runners hitting the road at 5:00 a.m. every day. For the little girl practicing her jump shot day in and day out.

It was then John learned that people might get infatuated with mission, but they fall in love with purpose. The plan to crush

Adidas gave everyone a short-term high, but Nike's overall purpose, as conveyed through Knight's compelling personal narrative, gave them the energy to carry on.

Phil's story is well documented in his best-selling book *Shoe Dog*. He was a decent but not record-setting runner for the University of Oregon track team. This is where he met track coach Bill Bowerman. Watching Bowerman tinker with shoes, he realized that his real purpose was to build a company that would manufacture products that would *enhance human performance*. Knight's purpose was to help kids all around the world live their dreams. To run with heart. To do their best.

While their mission may have been to crush Adidas, the participants in John's leadership program were even more inspired by Knight's story and sense of purpose. If the only thing they were trying to do was beat Adidas, Knight's throngs of employees would have run out of gas a long time ago. They needed to fall in love with the purpose of serving aspiring athletes to stay focused long enough to build Nike into what it is today.

PURPOSE IS ABOUT SERVICE

As we interviewed leaders for our book, we were struck by how many of them started their companies not out of a desire to make a lot of money but out of a *calling to make a difference in the lives of others.*

When we first met Matt Oppenheimer, CEO of Remitly, a leading digital financial services provider that helps immigrants send money back home to their families, we were immediately struck by how lights-on he was when he shared his passion for the millions of immigrant families Remitly was serving. He lived a life of service, and it was difficult to get him to talk about himself.

The inspiration for Remitly came after Matt finished his MBA at the Harvard Business School and had the opportunity to move to Kenya to work on mobile and internet-banking initiatives for Barclays Bank Kenya. It was there that he realized how challenging it was for families to send and receive money overseas. As someone living abroad, he faced similar challenges himself. He was being paid in British pounds, living on Kenyan shillings, and ultimately needed to get his money back to US dollars. In his interview with John, Matt got very emotional:

> *If this was so hard and frustrating for me, just imagine how challenging this must be for the Kenyan people. Or for other people around the world. More importantly, I became familiar with the world of remittances through many of my Kenyan friends and quickly learned how critical these funds are for those who receive them. Most often, remittances are used to pay for basic living expenses.*

Matt gets very passionate when he talks about the millions of immigrants who lose billions of dollars on high remittance fees that they may not even be aware of.

Matt and his cofounders, Josh Hug and Shivaas Gulati, became obsessed with the desire to better serve these families by disrupting the traditional financial service industry. Remitly was born out of a desire to serve others.

On one of John's early visits to Remitly's offices in Seattle, he was impressed with the big, colorful photographs of immigrant families and children hanging on the walls. It was like these families were in the room. The joy and happiness coming from their faces created a memorable image. As he walked through the corridors of the company, he was struck that all of these photographs were clustered around the company's core values. It was clear who Remitly served and why.

John had a conversation with a relatively new hire on the finance team. She had received many job offers, but she chose

Remitly because she wanted to work for a company that was making a difference for historically underserved people.

More and more people, particularly those entering the workforce now, want to work for companies that are making a difference in the world. The power of Remitly's purpose, rooted in a focus on serving others in marginalized communities, is a real motivator for attracting and retaining talent. Stories about the difference Remitly is making in the lives of their customers are a constant part of their all-company meetings as they remind employees how and why they are making a difference.

This strong sense of service and purpose has propelled Remitly to exponential growth and financial success with a valuation of approximately $7.8 billion.

In his best-selling book *Start with Why*, Simon Sinek says, "People don't buy what you do; they buy WHY you do it." Our experience in coaching purpose-driven leaders is that when we ask them about their purpose, they almost always begin with a story about *why* they are doing what they are doing and *who* they are serving— not *what* they are doing. It's the clients who are overly pleased with themselves and their innovation, rather than being focused on the communities they serve, who seem to fail in the marketplace.

In John's early days of working with the leaders at Apple, as the iPhone was getting ready to launch into the market, the *why* was never in doubt. It wasn't written on any wall, but it was known by all who worked with Steve Jobs. The *why* was always about the customer. Apple's purpose was to create products that customers loved and didn't even know they needed.

"We are out to change the world," Jobs often said in his speeches. It was a rallying cry that connected with his various constituencies. It motivated Apple employees to show up every day and give their best, and it inspired consumers to line up for hours to buy the first iPhone.

As big as Apple is today, we are amazed at how Steve's original purpose is still part of the Apple culture as its employees continue to disrupt the market by introducing innovative products and service solutions. Steve's *why* is alive and well at Apple.

PURPOSE CONNECTS WITH AND REINFORCES VALUES

We first met Dave Heath, CEO of Bombas, at our annual founder retreat in upstate New York. As we introduced ourselves on the first day, it was clear that Dave was more than just a founder, and Bombas was more than just a sock company.

As Dave talked about his story, it became apparent that he was building Bombas on a foundation of values central to his own overall purpose. Dave talked about an early experience in which he'd learned that socks—more than coats, more than shoes, more than shirts—were the number-one most requested article of clothing at homeless shelters. He reflected upon the deep empathy he developed as he took time away from the office to understand the struggles of people living without homes. These experiences caused him to confront his own values and realize that his real motivation was not to make money but to help others. Selling socks to people with homes and giving them away to people without homes seemed to Dave a rather elegant way to make a living acting on his values.

Dave is proud of the fact that for every pair of socks, underwear, or T-shirt he sells, one item is donated to people in need. As the population of homeless people increases, the need is even greater. We have become avid Bombas customers, and we love that our dollars are going to help others.

These values are an integral part of the Bombas culture. Within the first two weeks of their employment, new employees are asked to hand out socks to homeless people they meet on the streets of New York and to listen to their stories. This brings them to build a visceral and personal connection with the company's purpose and values.

As Bombas has grown to become one of the top companies in its category, there has been a continual need to reinforce its focus on purpose and values. During Covid, Bombas made sure that employees and consumers knew about the company's extensive network of partners across the country, and helped those partners distribute cleaning supplies, linens, and other needed items. Bombas lives and acts upon their values every day.

PURPOSE DRIVES PERFORMANCE

As you read all of these examples of the importance of purpose to effective leadership, you may be asking, "Does any of this correlate with building high-performing teams and organizations? Do purpose-driven leaders actually build successful companies?"

And the answer is unequivocally, YES!

A litany of studies has found that leaders who put purpose first create higher performing teams and organizations than their profit-first counterparts. According to research done at PwC, 79 percent of business leaders believe that purpose is central to their success. The "Insights 2020" study sponsored by the Advertising Research Foundation found that a majority of companies that outperform their peers tie back everything they do to purpose. In his book *Grow*, Jim Stengel revealed a ten-year study he and his colleagues performed that showed an investment in a collection of the top 50 purpose-driven companies would beat the S&P 500 by an impressive 400 percent.

And according to Kevin Murray in his book *People with Purpose: How Great Leaders Use Purpose to Build Thriving Organizations*, "Leaders who make purpose the beating heart of their organizations create more engaged employees, more committed customers, and more supportive stakeholders."

One leader we work with who has made purpose the beating heart of his organization is Jonathan Neman, CEO and cofounder of the fast casual salad chain sweetgreen. Speaking with Jonathan, you feel his sense of purpose and integrity in every word. And eating at sweetgreen, you see and taste their purpose in everything—from the fresh organic produce sourced from local farmers, to their passionate team members who are inspired by their mission to build healthier communities by connecting people to real food.

To hear it from Jonathan, he says the secret to sweetgreen's success has always been purpose and people: "Know your 'why' and 'who'! We are proud of the culture we have built at sweetgreen, and we have always put our people at the center of our organization. The 'why' and 'who' are the product. Both are very important, but the 'why' comes first, then the 'who.'"

Sweetgreen's commitment to purpose has converted into profits, as well, since their 2021 listing on the New York Stock Exchange can attest.

The research and our experience support the notion that when leaders lead with purpose, they see a very real boost in overall performance. But leading with purpose is not always easy. Leading with purpose first requires having clarity around what your purpose actually is.

How to Gain Insight Around Your Purpose

Despite the findings supporting the importance of leadership purpose to individual, team, and organizational success, engagement survey data indicates that fewer than half of employees know what their company stands for and why. Some percentage of that lack of understanding is likely due to poor communication about the purpose. But just as much or more of it is due to the fact that many leaders have not taken the time to get clear about their own *why*.

Let's check in with a number of leaders we've worked with and learn how they connect with and stay inspired by their sense of purpose.

INSPIRED BY LEGACY

When John met Betsy Nabel, president of Brigham Health in Boston, he was immediately taken by her tenacity and versatility. Her career had taken her from professor positions at the University of Michigan and Harvard to consulting at the NFL. And now after eleven years running at Brigham, she was entering the home stretch of her career.

As they sat in her office overlooking the hospital courtyard, Betsy stared out the window and reflected upon all the challenges that she had faced over the past year. It was a year like no other, with multiple crises: the Boston Marathon bombing, two on-campus shootings, and nurse contract negotiations. She was calm and collected as she described how her team had come together through all the turmoil and emerged stronger.

Betsy was determined to have the last few years of her leadership be ones that made an impact—a lasting impact. As John listened to her talk about her challenges, he gently asked, "So, Betsy, let's say it's three years from now. If you were to look back, what would you want people to say about your leadership and the legacy you're leaving at Brigham?"

She didn't waste any time responding. "I want to leave a legacy for patient care that will go on forever."

This was the first time John had coached a client whose stated purpose was to "leave a legacy." There are books written about legacy leadership, but this was an unexpected response. The more that Betsy and John explored this through their coaching, the more he came to understand that her legacy and purpose were in service of patients, partners, board members, donors, physicians, and all hospital staff.

As they developed her plan for leaving a legacy, it became clear that this was going to involve a cultural transformation at Brigham, driven by the values of integrity, purpose, family, and community. While Brigham had a history of strong patient care, Betsy was determined to take the overall patient experience to a new level. This patient-centered model became the core pillar of her transformation.

Brigham's values were at the core of this transformation:

- We care (period).
- We're stronger together (we all play a role).
- We create breakthroughs (it's in our DNA).
- We pursue excellence (because our patients deserve the best).

Betsy's transformation and legacy were embedded in a very clear strategic plan that involved leadership work at many different levels. She spent dedicated time as a leader to get the Brigham family to buy into the plan. She used the multiple crisis events as a way to rally the organization around her ideas. She invested in her team, giving her leaders training through the Sperling Executive Leadership Course, created in collaboration with the Harvard Business School.

She was also a master at fundraising, developing a president's advisory board that was critical in the success of one of the largest hospital campaigns in Boston's history, raising $1.75 billion. She grew the development team to over 150 people and expanded fundraising to social media and crowdsourcing. She spearheaded the creation of the Brigham Research Institute, paving the way for the Innovation Hub to invest in new medical science breakthroughs, a core value. Finally, Betsy established seventy-six new endowed Brigham and Harvard professorships as a part of her legacy.

As we reflect on Betsy's amazing transformational leadership success, it is easy to see why she chose "legacy" as her guiding mantra and purpose. She was interested in creating systemic changes that would last beyond her leadership tenure. Creating structures for innovation, endowing professorships, establishing a president's advisory board—these are all changes that will ensure that her legacy of patient-centered care will live on.

INSPIRED BY INNOVATION

John met Joe DeSimone through a former Apple executive who was now a member of Joe's management team. Joe is a former University of North Carolina chemistry professor turned entrepreneur. After spending twenty-five years teaching and doing research, he received funding for a number of promising research projects before starting Carbon in 2013.

Joe took a big risk leaving a successful academic career for Silicon Valley—but the risk paid off. He established one of the world's leading digital manufacturing companies, raising $680 million and getting the company valued at $2.5 billion. His groundbreaking Digital Light Synthesis technology has disrupted the 3D-printing market.

As Joe and John began their work together, Joe made it clear that he wanted to build a team with a purpose inspired by innovation. Joe was lights-on when he talked about innovation and the possibilities for his new technology in improving human health and well-being, as well as transforming the manufacturing world in big ways. The passion in his voice was contagious, as described by his new hires. He wanted to be sure that his new team was set up to successfully keep the purpose of innovation at the forefront.

Joe was a natural leader with an ability to teach, support, and engage his team in the process of establishing their working principles. With a desire to clearly define the behaviors and practices that would embed innovation into the culture, we began a series of team sessions. Joe had clear ideas on some of the rules and practices that were needed, but he was savvy enough to know that he needed to get buy-in from his team to implement them.

One of the early exercises that we engaged in was around the question "What are the dos and don'ts in fostering a culture of innovation?" Out of this discussion came a set of principles and practices that to this day are part of the Carbon culture.

One tool that has been embedded into the culture is the use of the "left-hand column," John's simple tool that encourages team members to say what they are thinking but not saying. The idea is that the right-hand column contains all the things that are easy to say—all the ideas and comments that don't rock the boat. The left-hand column is where potential conflict lives. It's the pushback, the probing question, the nagging doubt that often goes unsaid. In the meetings of many of our clients now, an executive will say "I have a left-hand comment," and everyone in the room snaps to attention, knowing the exec is about to say something that is hard to say but worth putting out there.

Joe wanted to encourage open debate and transparency, to push people to challenge each other without fear of reprisal and with the assurance that their differences of opinion would be respected. In Joe's mind, innovation requires intentional disruption. This can only occur within a climate of respect, transparent dialogue, and debate.

From the beginning, Joe was convinced that his purpose as a leader was to be sure that innovation became the company's core purpose. In team meetings, he strove to create a climate in which innovative ideas were encouraged. He intentionally fostered an environment of trust and safety, where people could challenge and be challenged. Today Carbon enables companies like Adidas, Riddell, Ford, and Johnson & Johnson to create state-of-the-art products to improve the lives of their customers.

INSPIRED BY TRAVEL

When John was a professor at San Jose State University, he spent almost a year as a visiting professor at the University of Bath in the UK. The year was full of travel and gave him time to reflect upon his life and career. He was happy in his teaching role at the university but longed to start something new. At the time, he was doing exciting research on the role and efficacy of coaching for developing leaders in companies. As he interviewed managers and executives at various corporations around the world for his research, he realized that there was a significant need to coach and develop these ambitious leaders, who were all domain experts in their fields, but basically unprepared for the challenges of managing their companies.

Shortly after he returned home, John left his university position and started his first coaching company, ExecutivEdge of Silicon Valley. John considers his travel abroad and his Denver lights-on experience to be significant factors in his decision to start his new company. Having had time to think, research, and write, he came home with a clear sense of purpose and direction on what he wanted to do next.

Travel doesn't have to involve a long stay in faraway places. It can be a week or long weekend—anything that can break the routine and allow you to step back, reflect, and gain new insights. John is coaching a CEO who takes a three-day weekend once a month. These getaways are planned and structured on the calendar. Employees know that they are not to bother the CEO during these long weekends. "These long weekends help me think through the big strategic decisions that I need to make and have little time for day-to-day during the week," the CEO says. "I come back refreshed and am much more able to deal with the stresses of my job. My time away helps me pause and step back to get a clearer perspective on the problems in front of me."

How has travel impacted your life? Can you recall a time

when travel resulted in a significant change or insight in your life? What about traveling helps you find clarity around your purpose?

INSPIRED BY HARDSHIP

Jeff Huber, the founder of Grail, an early cancer detection company, found his sense of purpose through the pain of loss.

Jeff spent most of his career at Google, where he led development and scaling for Google Ads, Google Apps, Google Maps, and Google X. When all was said and done, he was responsible for many aspects of building and scaling consumer products used by over a billion users around the world.

If those accomplishments weren't enough, he started fiddling with the field of biology and the untapped applications of the transition from analog to digital.

Jeff talks about this period of his life with emotion. He loved his time developing Google Apps and Google Maps. But he was at a crossroads in his career. He was fascinated with the big changes in the field of biology as it transitioned from analog to digital, making huge amounts of data available to advance our understanding of complex biological systems such as the DNA chain. He was already on the board at Illumina, a leading genetic sequencing firm, and was enjoying his transition into the biological sciences space and the possibilities that brought in terms of rethinking his own career.

Then everything changed. Out of the blue, his fit and active wife was diagnosed with a two-centimeter colorectal tumor. At first the prognosis seemed good, and it looked as if chemotherapy would do the job, but after months of further tests they discovered that the cancer had spread to other organs in her body. By then, it was too late for any surgery. Within a year she was gone, and Jeff was left as a single parent to two young children.

Stricken with grief, Jeff did what many of us would do: he dove into the one place he could find solace—his work. He put all of his energy into learning everything he could about the DNA sequencing machines Illumina was developing. He decided there and then that he would build an early cancer detection technology so that fewer people would have to die, and fewer families would have to lose their loved ones.

It was out of this clear sense of purpose that Jeff's company Grail was born. Jeff considers the company to be a living memorial to his late wife. Every patient who benefits from the early detection tests developed by Grail gives at least *some* meaning to her untimely passing.

Today, Grail is a highly successful company backed by high-profile investors like Jeff Bezos and Bill Gates with a market valuation of over $5 billion. But for Jeff it was never about the money.

When John did coaching work with Jeff, many of the employees he spoke with in the feedback process told him that Jeff's personal story and sense of purpose were the reasons they joined the company. To a person, everyone from his investors to his employees was moved and inspired by his story and experience—by his crystal-clear sense of purpose. In their coaching work, John encouraged Jeff to continue to tell his personal story in all-hands meetings and when onboarding new employees to inspire them with the true purpose of the company.

Even years later, Jeff says he continually thinks about his wife. It gives him great satisfaction that he was able to channel his grief surrounding her loss into the development of a technology that will save lives. While we are not therapists, helping our clients reflect on some of their biggest life-changing events can be a great way to help them gain perspective and new insights into what gives them a sense of purpose.

What struggles have you endured? What have you learned about yourself through painful experiences? How have your lowest moments made you who you are today? How have they shaped your sense of purpose?

INSPIRED BY PERSONAL NEED

They say necessity is the mother of invention, and in 2011, as a student at Harvard Business School, Justin McLeod needed to get over a breakup. He and his college sweetheart had split after graduation, so he did as any business school student who wants to heal an ailing heart would do—he started a dating app.

According to start-up guru and Y Combinator founder Paul Graham, "The way to get start-up ideas is not to try to think of start-up ideas. It's to look for problems, preferably problems you have yourself." Many of the best businesses in the world were founded to solve a problem that pained their own founders. Facebook, Uber, Spanx, Netflix, Rent the Runway—all were started by people with a personal need that existing solutions in the market were not solving.

Justin looked at the existing online dating services and felt uninspired. They were either antiquated Web 1.0 companies designed to help people find relationships or modern mobile-first companies designed for casual hookups. Justin wanted to help people find their Mr. or Ms. Right, not just their Mr. or Ms. Right Now, and to do it with a beautiful mobile-first experience.

But after gaining some early traction with a meet-friends-of-friends model, Justin realized he had accomplished neither, and that the app was frankly not that good. Many founders would have stuck with it. "Let's not make perfect the enemy of the good," they'd say. "Maybe our customers are telling us through their behavior what they want, and that's to hook up. Maybe having a beautiful mobile experience is secondary to having traction."

But it all just didn't sit right with Justin. He was clear about his core purpose: to help people find fulfilling, long-term relationships—the same thing he wanted for himself but found all too elusive in today's dating world. So he did the unthinkable: he blew up the company and started over.

And so, in November 2015, Justin sat down with a reorganized team to ask one simple question: "What app would we build if our sole purpose was to help people find love quickly and delete the app?"

Justin and his team decided they wanted to put purpose first and build an app that helps people find their person, regardless of their engagement numbers. They set out to slow the whole online dating process down—no more swiping, no more demographic screening—all in the hope that users would find love and delete the app. They even made their tagline "Designed to be deleted."

Justin's strategy of putting his purpose first seems to be working. Today, Hinge is the fastest-growing dating platform within the Match Group family of relationship apps. And to this day the only metric they measure to see if they are succeeding is whether their users actually go on dates and fall in love. Justin credits his clear sense of purpose and commitment to enduring values with helping him weather the darkest days of his entrepreneurial journey.

INSPIRED BY FRIENDS

Julia Oberottman is a petite firebrand who advises companies all over the world on innovation, opening new markets, and generally putting a dent in the universe. She is quick, insightful, and connects well with others. Edward met Julia years ago when they were MBA students together at the Wharton School. Wharton has a San Francisco campus for mid-career MBAs, and Edward and Julia had no fewer than half their classes together.

One day at lunch, Edward was regaling his table with war stories from his political consulting days—like the time he was whisked away from a car wreck in Kyiv by former KGB agents (don't worry, he was not the driver and was not injured—they just didn't want him talking to corrupt local police), or the time he was confronted by the president of Honduras in a bar in Tegucigalpa after Edward and his team leading the opposition campaign made an especially damaging ad about him, along with a number of less exciting stories that had to do with helping his clients develop better leadership skills.

After hearing these stories and seeing how Edward interacted with his fellow students and professors, Julia had an insight. She saw Edward in a new way. And without thinking, she reached across the table with a simple request: "Edward, if you've helped get leaders elected to office around the world, you can probably help me get a promotion. Would you be my executive coach? Just think about it. Most of your clients today just want to talk to you about leadership anyway. They don't want fancy decks or strategy advice. They want to learn how to be better leaders. That's your secret sauce!"

Julia was right. Edward was running a business strategy firm at the time, and most of his clients really did just want to talk about leadership. Her words stirred something in him, some awareness that perhaps he wasn't fully in touch with his purpose, but he needed time to think about it. He had his own coach in those days and discussed the matter with him. Without blinking, his coach said, "You know, sometimes when people call you to do something, that's the definition of your calling. Frankly, it's about time you started living in service of your gift."

As you might have guessed, Edward agreed to coach Julia. When she insisted on paying him, he was a bit uncomfortable, but he accepted that she wanted to feel she had skin in the game. Soon she told other classmates that she was working with Edward, and they asked him to start coaching them too. After a few months, he was coaching five executives at various well-known companies around the Bay Area, and the rest is history.

We include this little vignette because sometimes other people see our purpose better than we do. Edward found his true purpose as a coach through Julia, and he will forever be grateful to her for that. Sometimes the key is to stay open to the idea that other people can see things in us that we might not be able to see for ourselves.

What Keeps Us from Finding Our Purpose

While we consider ourselves executive coaches who help leaders build and scale businesses that make an impact in the world, every so often we encounter a client who simply wants help finding their personal purpose. We've detailed above a few ways that leaders we've worked with have found their purpose, but all their best efforts to do so will be for naught if they are engaging in some form of self-sabotage. Given that this chapter on purpose comes after the chapters on needs, fears, desires, and gifts, you may not be surprised to learn that we believe one needs to be living in full awareness of the answers to those first four questions to be able to answer the fifth.

NEEDS

Someone who is living without their critical needs being met is often not able to make space in their life for service to others, which is what finding your purpose is all about. When someone doesn't feel fully resourced, it is hard to feel that they have anything left to give. Sometimes people try to do what Edward calls a "needs bypass" and start working on their "life's purpose" when they can't even pay the bills, and this is when you end up with well-meaning but highly ineffective coaches, gurus, healers, and so on. Not that you need to be rich to be an effective coach or healer, but you definitely need to be fully resourced in terms of physical, emotional, and environmental needs.

FEARS

When we are living with fear, we are most often in a reactive mindset. When we perceive threats in the world, we are less likely to have the emotional capacity to focus on opportunities that would help us find our purpose. We can falsely begin to believe that our purpose is to control others or our environment so that we feel safe. We see this at play in our current political dynamic, in which individuals driven mostly by fear have made it their "mission" to muzzle, belittle, or demean their adversaries.

DESIRES

Just as our desires can derail us into unscrupulous behavior, they can also sell us a false narrative as to what our purpose is. Many people who desire power and prestige out of ego tell themselves that their purpose is to become an elected official. Others who want to feel successful make amassing wealth their purpose, often at the cost of their values and personal relationship. When we let our desires for power, wealth, or fame derail us, we can sell ourselves the story that quenching that desire *is* our purpose.

Additionally, our desire to make a big impact in the world can delude us into thinking that if our purpose isn't to eradicate poverty or reverse climate change, we aren't thinking big enough. The old adage "Think globally, act locally" comes to mind here. A right-sized sense of purpose starts with looking around ourselves at the places where we can make a difference.

GIFTS

As we outlined in chapter 4, "What Are Your Greatest Gifts?," the greatest expression of our gifts is using them for a higher purpose. Similarly, our truest purpose is often the application of our greatest gift. We've found that very often the people who feel most lost in life are those with the least awareness of their gifts. Not knowing what they are uniquely gifted at, they go through life dabbling here and there. A focused effort on uncovering that special gift would be a better use of energy than years of aimless trial and error.

We've also all known the person who has exquisite clarity about their purpose to be an actor, author, singer, performer, or what have you but, sadly, are not aware that they just don't have a gift in that area. When we live with the blindset of fantasy about what our gifts are, we can waste years pursuing a purpose that was never meant to be. Getting clear on what our gifts are is a crucial part of uncovering our true purpose.

The last of the five Leading with Heart conversations is about purpose because that's really where it all comes together. To find your purpose, you have to have full awareness of your gifts. And as we've discussed, to see your own gifts, you must achieve the necessary insights into your needs, fears, and desires. Being able to see your purpose clearly is the result of having clarity on all the other Leading with Heart questions.

We've learned in this chapter that purpose is more about giving than receiving. When clients talk about purpose, they use action words that are pointed outward toward people or places. To them, purpose can mean:

- guiding young people on their career journey;
- building a way for immigrants to send money back to their families;
- protecting the rain forest or fighting against climate change; or
- helping others find their gifts and how to use them for a higher purpose.

There are myriad ways you and your teams might tap into your purpose. Perhaps you might think about the legacy you want to leave, the people you want to serve, or the adversity you've faced in your own life, adversity you want to protect others from. Often we are able to see our purpose clearly for the first time when we step out of our normal routines, through travel, talking with mentors, or even a call from a friend.

As you begin to see your own purpose more clearly, we hope you will be kind to yourself and not let ego (or your parents) tell you that you should be doing something else. Turning our backs on our purpose is a costly mistake. We may achieve greater financial outcomes in the short run doing something we aren't called to do, but money cannot buy self-worth and fulfillment in the long run. Only living your purpose can.

- When we are feeling stuck, it may be time to take a good hard look at whether we are living our purpose.
- It is hard for an organization to have a sense of purpose if the leader does not have one.
- We are not born with purpose; it's gained from life experiences.
- We have to reset or renew our sense of purpose at regular intervals throughout our lives.
- Organizations and teams with a clear sense of purpose outperform those lacking purpose.
- Changing up your routine through travel, or even walking, can help you find moments in which to gain clarity of purpose.
- If you are not having conversations that help you gain awareness of your needs, fears, desires, and gifts, tapping into your sense of purpose may be elusive.

CONVERSATION STARTERS

1. On average, how much time a month do you spend connected to your higher sense of purpose?
2. Can you describe a "lights-on" moment for you that resulted in a renewed sense of purpose?
3. Describe an experience in your life, good, bad, or otherwise, that has shaped your sense of purpose.
4. In what ways does your sense of purpose drive you to accomplish your goals, both personal and professional?
5. Looking across your company, how good of a job are you doing at connecting the organization at large to a higher sense of purpose? What else could you be doing to make your team even more connected?

6

HELPING YOUR COMPANY
LEAD WITH HEART

Culture makes people understand each other better. And if
they understand each other better, it is easier to overcome
barriers.

—PAOLO COELHO

Close your eyes and imagine a mythical company. This company is one that leads with heart. It considers all of the questions posed so far in this book and converts what it learns from the ensuing powerful conversations into cultural norms.

This company takes into account people's needs and creates an environment in which employees feel safe to be creative, resourceful, and bold. Instead of playing on people's fears and stoking their anxieties, this company gives people a sense of security and safety by investing in them as they grow, including offering them opportunities to work with a coach to expand their leadership potential.

What if this same company gave people a jolt of healthy competitiveness and made them feel like they belonged and were learning, but avoided unethical or corner-cutting behavior? And how about if this company did its best to build upon their natural gifts and encouraged them to leverage them in every aspect of their work, from the most mundane to the most impactful? And finally, what would you say if this company united everyone around a commonly held sense of purpose, whether it be serving a social good, bringing some new technology to the world, or helping others realize their full potential?

Is this your company? Could this be your company? How does your company do in terms of having the five conversations explored in this book? In short, does your company lead with heart?

Harvard Business School professor John Kotter defines corporate culture as the shared attitudes, behavioral patterns, and values among employees that persist over time.

Some companies have high-performance cultures in which people feel creative and committed for the long haul. Others have low-performance cultures in which people feel uninspired and noncommittal. We believe that the difference between these two kinds of companies comes down to how willing they are to make the Leading with Heart conversations part of the fabric of how they work together—part of their culture.

Culture Is the Conversation

Culture is not created by posting a list of values on the wall. It's not your kombucha on tap or your summer camp–themed off-sites. Culture is the conversations that are *actually* happening between the people employed by your company. It's the manifestation of how you as an organization help each other see and understand your needs, fears, desires, gifts, and purpose. It's ingrained in how people treat each other. How they make each other feel. How they *see* each other. How they support each other and collaborate.

Impacting a company's culture starts with getting clear on the specific conversations and behaviors you want to promote and reward. Since culture is the outcome of literally dozens or hundreds of conversational and behavioral habits bundled together, our best chance at shaping culture is to influence those habits through guiding principles and values.

If we take the five Leading with Heart conversations and turn them into statements, we begin to see a set of core principles take shape that can guide behavior at companies that aspire to lead with heart.

Leading with Heart companies are those that:

1. Are inclusive and account for a diversity of **needs**.
2. Are safe and trusting and acknowledges people's **fears**.
3. Leverage people's core **desires** without letting them get derailed.
4. Ensure that people express their **gifts** and do not languish in mediocrity.
5. Prioritize values and **purpose** above everything else, including profit.

For this last chapter, we'll explore the stories of several clients who have shaped behaviors and values at the team and company levels around each of these Leading with Heart principles. We'll also outline in detail a number of simple exercises you can do with your company to help people have richer conversations about their needs, fears, desires, gifts, and purpose to give you practical tools to develop the cultural habit of leading with heart.

Be Inclusive and Account for a Diversity of Needs

Companies that are inclusive and account for a diversity of needs create a rich environment in which creative people and their ideas can flourish. This stands in stark contrast to the antiquated idea of trying to create uniformity in the workplace that many companies still seem to aspire to. Let's explore a couple of companies that are purposeful and proactive about creating inclusive culture.

CULTURAL PERKS ARE THE ONLY ONES THAT MATTER

Café-quality coffee in the morning. Healthy lunches prepared by an in-house chef. Yoga classes in the afternoon led by a team member. Free shuttles so you don't have to drive yourself.

Sounds like a great place to work, right?

If you said yes, you likely have a healthy lifestyle, but might be focusing on the wrong things in terms of office perks. Many companies that have amazing perks actually have horrible cultures. The posh benefits are often a weak attempt to make up for the fact that people no longer see their families, live in fear of their managers, or receive no encouragement or praise. It's sad, but true.

The best perks are cultural. They help you get your full spectrum of needs met, not just your culinary ones. They are found in the ways in which people treat each other, support each other, and push each other to grow. One company that has built an effective system of cultural perks to help meet the diversity of needs of its team is Noom, the behavioral change and digital health company based in New York.

Like many people, we first heard about Noom on NPR. Their ubiquitous ads (maybe they are technically called "sponsorships") on *Morning Edition* or *All Things Considered* paint a picture of a modest company that helps people lose weight. But when Noom CEO Saeju Jeong reached out to talk about coaching, we learned that his seemingly low-profile company was actually quite the heavyweight. With over $650 million raised and a few thousand employees, Noom is a blockbuster weight-loss and behavior-change start-up. Millions of users trust Noom's behavioral psychology principles to help them lose weight and lead healthier lives.

After the 2020 Christmas holiday, Noom revenues ballooned to more than $200 million, up fourfold from the previous year. Even though most New Year resolutions to lose weight are forgotten by February, Noom adds new users at a remarkable clip throughout the entire year. There have been dozens of weight-loss start-ups over the years, but Noom seems to be leading the field these days.

John learned in his first meeting with Saeju that the CEO views the incredible success the company has had in acquiring users as outcomes of the thoughtful and supportive culture he's painstakingly built over the years. Among the many reasons Noom customers say they use the app, the fact that they can "start where they are" and "don't feel judged" are two of the most important. Noom employees say exactly the same thing. As a product and a company culture, Noom is inclusive.

Saeju embedded these principles in the company culture through values that aren't merely parroted but actually drive behavior. As a company, its mission is to help people live healthier lives through behavior change. They use that same principle to guide their thinking about corporate culture. Each value we outline below contributes to making Noom an inclusive place that accommodates a diversity of individual needs.

VALUE #1: BE TRANSPARENT, BUT BE KIND

The Noom app will not lie to you or coddle you. It will let you know when you are hitting your goals and when you are not. Yet it is also kind and not shaming in sharing that information. That same principle holds true for employees, as well. Noom prides itself on being a place where divergent thoughts are welcome.

Saeju values open and honest conversations and works to hear all voices. While making decisions may take longer, the inclusive process creates more buy-in with employees who have to implement solutions. With a focus on getting people to *disagree and commit*, Noom leaders make decisions that drive action while not running over people.

VALUE #2: CLEARLY IDENTIFY THE GOAL, DO THE MATH, AND PRIORITIZE RUTHLESSLY

For Noom's customers, behavior modification is about having clear goals and creating change through repetition and validation, and progress is tracked through data in the app. The approach to employees is similar: Saeju asks every employee to establish, revise, and track success metrics related to their own performance. Key performance indicators are monitored and adjusted to changing roles and the particular needs of employees.

At Noom, everyone has measurable goals. Without measurement, there is no accountability, which is critical to helping Noom's employees make progress toward their goals, just as it helps its users meet their own. But when a Noom employee misses a goal—just like when a user fails to meet a goal in the app—the first question is not "Why didn't you meet your goal?" but "What do you need to do better?"

The difference in wording may seem semantic, but the difference in outcome is monumental. Making it a cultural norm to *ask employees what they need to succeed* should be mandatory for all managers in every company. But sadly, most managers resort to language that shames and belittles employees. "Why didn't you . . ." has a finger-pointing tone. It implies that the problem is with the person, and not with the emotional or environmental context in which they are working. Staying curious longer creates more psychological safety.

VALUE #3: INVEST IN YOUR GROWTH AND LET NOOM INVEST IN YOU

People use the Noom app to improve their lives. It is an investment they make in a better and healthier future for themselves. Working at Noom, you are expected to invest in your own growth too. Every employee is encouraged to focus on learning new skills and growing as a person. But the company leaves it up to employees to figure out what their growth needs are. Some people want to learn about public speaking, while others want to take a class in cooking.

By not forcing employees into a cookie-cutter learning and development program, Noom's leadership has created an inclusive environment in which a diverse array of needs can be met all at once. Just as Noom's customers are encouraged to start where they are and take on the challenges and new behaviors that suit them, Noom employees are similarly given the freedom to grow in a way that works for them as individuals.

VALUE #4: CARE FOR EACH OTHER

Saeju prides himself on having created a very family-oriented culture in which people can feel accepted. Believing that people need to experience a sense of belonging to do their best work, he has made "Care for Each Other" one of his four corporate values. Few things make us feel safer than knowing that the people genuinely care for us.

Noom's company gatherings and outings are designed to bring people together and create a sense of unity. Saeju is known for bringing audiences to tears with his emotional personal stories, whether they are drawn from his own experience growing up in Korea or from customers' tales. We often tell ourselves that only positive emotions are permitted in the office, but in reality, trying to "put on a happy face" when we are feeling off only makes things that much worse. At Noom, all emotions are welcome. By modeling a healthy connection to his own emotions and needs, Saeju encourages his team to embrace their own. It makes everyone feel safer and connected to themselves and to each other.

Through this championing of transparency, kindness, personal growth, and empathy on top of a foundation of close measurement and accountability, Noom has developed a high-performing culture where people feel that their unique needs are met on a daily basis. Users of the Noom app would be impressed to know that the same behavioral principles being applied to their health goals are also implemented by Noom's employees internally.

TAKE DECISIVE ACTION WHEN NEEDS ARE NOT BEING MET

Robert's voice trembled as he described what his last couple of months had been like. Unreasonable deadlines. Late nights—even all-nighters. Skipped meals. No time to exercise. Not enough time with his family.

As a product manager at any start-up, Robert would expect to have stressful moments. Weeks, or even a month or two, of especially high-intensity work are typical in Silicon Valley. Nearly every household-name technology product we take for granted today, from hardware like the iPhone and Tesla Model X to software platforms like DoorDash and MasterClass, was built through the extreme commitment and periodic unhealthy work hours of their core teams.

But those periods of intensity are not meant to last forever. Many companies ask their teams to pull late nights and work all weekend from time to time around product launches or to meet specific deadlines. At Robert's company, however, it seemed like the unsustainable work culture had become the new norm.

This was surprising to both of us, since through our coaching work with the firm's top executives, we believed that as a company it put values like work-life balance at the center of its culture. Senior team members were all required to take vacation to signal to the rest of the org that taking vacation was okay. They offered some of the best benefits money could buy around mental health and career development. They had even recently hired a "Head of Culture," who reported directly to the CEO.

Yet, as part of an assessment we were doing on a top executive, Robert described an unhealthy organization that was driving its team to burnout. When we informed the CEO about this, he seemed legitimately surprised. Yes, they had a hard-charging, performance-based culture, but he didn't want to be running a company that kept its employees from spending time with their children. That was not in keeping with his own personal values.

Unfortunately, we see this all the time. Depending on your boss in the organization, you might feel a healthy relationship to work or a completely unhealthy one. Those burned-out employees who are not getting any of their basic needs met are often working for poorly trained senior managers who push their teams too hard in pursuit of their own advancement in the firm. What those relentless managers don't realize is that even if they get better results in the near term, they are likely to get worse and worse performance over time.

What's most surprising is how often the CEO is completely unaware of this dynamic. Although well-intentioned CEOs may have policies in place to create a healthy culture, they are often unknowingly incentivizing bad behavior by rewarding only bottom-line results, and not tracking indicators of organizational health like employee retention, morale, and engagement. Senior managers who observe that delivering results is the only way to get ahead often end up driving their people much too hard and for too long in an effort to get ahead.

Heart-led CEOs avoid this situation by spending more time down in the organization, getting the pulse of their teams. They engage deeply with their employee survey data. And they take very seriously any complaints of unnecessarily aggressive dead-lines or abusive management tactics. Where there is one complaint, there are often many more burned-out employees who are too afraid to speak up.

After becoming aware of these problems, Robert's CEO made employee health a topic on the next executive team agenda. Unreasonable deadlines and driving employees to the brink of burnout were not going to be tolerated. They decided to make the overall satisfaction and mental health of subordinates two of the key metrics managers would be judged on during performance reviews. The executive team also allocated resources to support training and mental health benefits across the entire org.

In situations like this, executive leadership is often what's required to right the ship. When a company's culture starts to list, leaders need to move quickly and take decisive action. Leaders build cultures that meet a diversity of needs by having conversations across the organization, checking in with their employees, monitoring engagement survey data, and making sure they are optimizing for long-term organizational health and not just short-term business outcomes.

TEAM EXERCISE: STAND UP FOR YOUR NEEDS

A simple exercise we do with teams to make it safe for people to name their needs is called Stand Up for Your Needs. It is so simple it's almost silly, but it works.

First, we ask everyone to take three Post-its of three different colors, for a total of nine Post-its. Next, we designate one color for each category of need: physical, emotional, and environmental. We give them a few examples in each category if they aren't familiar with the concept. We then ask everyone to write *one* important or quirky need they have from each category on each Post-it.

The facilitator then collects the Post-its and posts them by category on a whiteboard or wall. They attempt to categorize them as best they can, but there are almost always some fun and wacky outliers.

Next, the group sits in a circle, and the facilitator goes through each of the needs in every category, saying, "Stand up if you need _____ to feel creative, productive, or safe." It might be nine hours of sleep. Four meals a day. Lots of emotional support. Direct sunlight on your face. Whatever the need, you communicate to your team that you need it by simply standing up. And what invariably happens is that people start standing up for needs they didn't even write down. Soon, what someone once worried seemed quirky or weird now has a small band of supporters. Once these themes are identified, the facilitator encourages each individual to choose a goal or goals to work on in the various categories. Leadership is encouraged to pay attention if certain popular needs are not being addressed company-wide. In future team meetings, people can report on their progress getting their needs met, and leadership can report on efforts to meet people's needs.

What this exercise does is create a sense of safety and community around our shared needs. We see that we are not alone or wrong for having needs, and just by doing the exercise, we learn that this is a safe place to have a conversation about them.

Make People Feel Safe by Acknowledging Their Fears

CHANNELING FEAR INTO OUTCOMES

Fear is a little like steam. If you try to contain it, it might blow your lid off. It stands to reason, then, that companies that do not have healthy norms around talking about fears end up with an inordinate number of blowups.

One CEO of a company that had a toxic culture that was only getting worse called us to see if we could help diagnose what was going on. They had amazing IP and very loyal customers, but the company had missed its sales numbers and was having trouble raising its Series B. As a result, everyone was freaking out. They were caught in a cultural death spiral, and the CEO knew that they were only a few months away from being in an irreversible free fall. If they could only get their sh*t together and focus their energy on one common goal, they could reverse the trend, raise a round, and live to fight another day.

In our experience, when things are *really* bad at a company, fear is most often the culprit. Fear of the unknown. Fear of failure. Fear of being let go. Fear of not getting a bonus.

The problem is that fear compounds in organizations. We get more fearful when we sense the fear in others. It's even worse if the boss is fearful. Yet, for some reason, no one talks about it. Everyone tries to hide their fear and instead engages in their own unhealthy fear response, as we discussed in chapter 2. Some pick fights. Some withdraw. Others flee and go find other jobs. This CEO had the bad luck of having an office full of fighters. Marketing was fighting with sales. Product was fighting with engineering. And nearly everyone was fighting with HR.

When we sat down and named the fact that his team was riddled with fear due to uncertainty about the company's future, he nodded. "I wish I could tell them something that would quell the situation, but I can't lie to them. We will run out of money in six weeks. They have every reason to be fearful."

As leaders dealing with fear, we often make the mistake of thinking that our job is to make the fear go away, to make people feel safe. While that might be true when the fear is imaginary, like that child who is afraid of the monster under her bed, when the fear is justified, our job as leaders is to help people deal with it—or, even better, to channel that fear into action.

As you might recall from chapter 2, a little bit of fear in a system is helpful. It creates energy and urgency. It can spawn spirited debate. But too much fear can trigger negative fear responses, like those on display in spades at this company.

Chip Conley, formerly the founder of Joie de Vivre Hotels and head of hospitality at AirBNB who now runs the Modern Elder Academy, says, "Especially during difficult times, it's essential that leaders are transparent and almost over-communicate. They have to help their people know what is within their sphere of influence." In accordance with Chip's advice, Edward and the CEO devised a plan to call a town hall meeting with every employee so the CEO could address the situation and try to unify the team around the one thing they had in common at that moment: fear. It was time to involve the organization in a conversation that named the fear transparently and engaged everyone in a coordinated effort to solve the company's problems.

First, the CEO would have to build a "container" with his own authentic vulnerability. A container is a unifying sensation that comes from acknowledging our shared experience and responsibility. The container leaves people with a feeling that, "Yes, we are up sh*t's creek, but we are up here together." Fear that is hidden divides us; fear that is shared openly unites us.

At the meeting the CEO began by sharing a little bit about his personal journey at the company, from founding it in the Brooklyn apartment he shared with three friends in his twenties through landing their first customer and raising their Series A. Sharing his story helped everyone connect with the time, energy, and commitment he had shown through various periods of deep uncertainty to get them all this far.

He then shared how scared he was that all of that would be for nothing. That his mom and girlfriend would be disappointed. That his dad would say, "I told you not to quit that job at the bank." That everyone he'd ever known would see him fail publicly. But most of all, that he would fail this incredible team, the people who had entrusted him with their faith and their futures.

He then fell quiet and looked around the room. Every set of eyes was on him, many of them welling with tears. He'd put it all out there, and they could feel how boldly vulnerable he was. The container had been built.

Then, instead of launching into some galvanizing speech, as everyone expected, he instead moved into the second part of the plan, which involved asking everyone to go around the room and name what they were most fearful of. The meeting lasted well over two hours, and nearly everyone in the room told their own story of commitment and fear. Once they had put all their fears on the table, the fears no longer divided them. Now, it was actually their fear that most united them. Their fear of not being able to afford grad school. Their fear of telling their kids they couldn't go to Disneyworld. Their fear of missing a payment to their mother's retirement home. Every person in that room had a reason to feel afraid—which meant they also had a reason to *fight*.

It was at that point that the CEO did one of the things he was most fearful of: he asked for help. "I didn't call you all here to tell you I have a magic bullet—that I've solved all of our problems. I called you here expressly to tell you I don't have all the answers, and I need your help. Because I believe there is an answer, and that the answer is in this room. If we are going to get through this, we will get through it together."

In Hollywood, courage often looks like a soldier charging into battle against all odds. In real life, it sometimes looks like a skinny founder in a hoodie telling his team of eighty people that he has no idea what to do.

Although cultural interventions like this can sometimes fall flat if done poorly, the impact of this intervention was nothing short of miraculous. Reunited by a common fear, and thus a common enemy, the team got to work solving the sales problem that the CEO had been previously hell-bent on solving himself. While we can't say they blew the doors off their numbers and raised a heroic Series B in a matter of weeks, the team was able to show enough progress over the next month to raise a bridge round that bought them enough time to resolve the issue for good.

Fear is a sneaky one. It knows that if you get vulnerable and talk about it, it dissipates. So it convinces us to fight, shut down, or leave. It kills communication and breeds distrust. Companies that build naming and discussing fear into their ways of working from the outset don't require dramatic interventions like the one described above.

TEAM EXERCISE: NAMING YOUR FEARS

We use various exercises with teams when fear is impacting the functioning of the team and the organization. We usually begin by framing the fear and the resulting behaviors that are playing out in the organization. Sometimes the coach or facilitator can identify the dysfunctional behaviors through confidential interviews. Such framing identifies the problem that needs to be solved and the resulting behaviors. Post-its are used to ask people to identify the fears they are experiencing that are causing dysfunctional team dynamics. Once team members have named their fears, the fear Post-its are collected and categorized into themes using the fight, flight, and freeze categories presented in chapter 2. After the Post-its have been sorted into categories, team members begin to see their common fears and can initiate conversations with the people who share their fears.

After openly naming and acknowledging the fears that they have in common, the group can move to problem-solving. We then group people around the fear response categories (fight, flight, freeze) and ask them to generate possible solutions. These solutions are then presented back to the larger team with discussion on possible next steps or changes that need to occur in team interactions.

While some of these fears are personal to individuals, many of them result from actions or inaction of the leadership. Often a new set of team norms or rules of engagement is generated to hold the team accountable for their new behaviors. This is a powerful exercise that can result in a major turnaround for the team. Naming fears becomes a cathartic process, encouraging people to channel those fears into a positive energy that can increase team effectiveness.

WE DON'T EVEN TRY ANYMORE

Creating a trusting culture that accounts for a diversity of fears is the foundation of building a Leading with Heart culture. Every leadership team we have coached has had to deal with trust and fear issues. We know that teams characterized by high levels of trust, and in which fears are openly expressed, are more likely to perform well.

Getting team members to open up in front of their colleagues can be difficult, though, especially when there isn't much assurance of psychological safety. *What if they judge me? What if no one else opens up? What if I'm the only one feeling this way?* We try to create a safe space for these conversations by setting the emotional barometer with our own stories of vulnerability, and by sharing anonymous feedback submitted by the group ahead of time, but still, it's hard.

In John's work with Maria, the CEO of a security software company, he experienced this vulnerability in action. He had conducted interviews that brought to the surface problems with the team and the performance of the company. During a meeting in which he was discussing his summary of the interviews with the executive team, Jenna, the vice president of marketing, dropped a truth bomb: "My team doesn't even try anymore because we know you guys are going to tear whatever we propose apart anyway."

What she said came as a jolt, but bolder and truer words had not been spoken with this group all day. Others soon piled on. "Yep!" "Plus one." "Us too . . ." Jenna had been worried that she would be all alone in her assertion, but she actually named the important thing others were thinking but no one had the guts to say. It seemed this company had fallen into what we call "the culture of nitpicking." This can often lead to the feeling of helplessness Jenna was expressing.

Studies on what is known as learned helplessness have shown that animals subjected at random to small electric shocks will try to figure out how to avoid the shocks at first, but eventually will give up and just accept their fate. (For the record, we find studies like this unethical and disturbing, and do not support any forms of animal abuse to further our understanding of how the brain works.) In some ways, our constant nitpicking of employees is similar to those random electric shocks. At first, the lack of positive feedback and nitpicking will drive higher performance and more effort. "I will prove that I can do this!" is the prevailing reaction. But when even after great effort no praise is forthcoming, employees eventually give up. Their fear of failure degrades into apathy, and performance plummets.

How many smart, dedicated middle managers have gotten caught in this cycle? As we learned in chapter 2, when employees only receive negative feedback, it can trigger their fear/fight response. At first they will fight harder to prove themselves, only to get more and more nitpicking negative feedback. Eventually they will give up, and executives will look at each other and say, "You see? This is why we have to do everything. We can't trust our VPs and directors to do high quality work."

And that's it right there. The culture of fear that creates poor performance in companies often begins at the top. Leaders who are afraid of failing become perfectionistic, which then leads them to nitpick their reports. This constant nitpicking triggers fear in the reports, which at first causes a fight-for-survival response but eventually degrades into giving up.

The fear of failure is one of the most prominent fears we see in start-ups. It feels like everything is on the line every day. Founders think that one wrong move can tank the company, so they spend all their time putting out fires.

What if, instead of spending all their time looking for what's wrong, these leaders spent more time looking for what's right? What if they noticed small areas in the business worth holding up as examples of excellence and success? What if they celebrated failure as a learning opportunity?

Jenna's bold share with her colleagues set off a cascade of changes. The founders have since committed to asking more questions and giving less direction. The entire C-suite has agreed to celebrate small wins and provide more positive feedback across the board. And Jenna's team has agreed to stop calling it in, and to start trying to do their best again.

Shifting the culture away from one of fear to one of celebrating success and getting curious about failures often requires every person in the entire organization to have some open and tough conversations and make new commitments to change course. These changes can be painstaking, but they are so, so worth it.

TEAM EXERCISE: THE TEMPERATURE READING
A lighter and less threatening way of checking on the fears of people on your team is the Temperature Reading exercise. Teams that make a habit out of naming their fears rarely find themselves

paralyzed or divided by fear. One of the simplest ways to develop the fear-naming habit is to embed it into other exercises—the same way pet owners bury their pet's medicine in the pet food.

The Temperature Reading exercise was stolen fair and square from a men's retreat Edward attended in Gavilan, New Mexico, over twenty years ago. We do an adapted version.

At the beginning of any meeting, the meeting host asks participants three simple questions:

- What or whom are you grateful for today?
- What are you worried or concerned about?
- What are your hopes and wishes for this meeting?

Question 1 primes attendees to feel full and abundant. Question 2 asks them to name their fears or preoccupations. And question 3 asks them to set an intention. It is so simple, and yet so effective. It only takes five to ten minutes, and many of our clients use this format religiously, with great results.

Leverage People's Core Desires Without Getting Them Derailed

SURFING AND SOLVING HARD MATH PROBLEMS

On a breezy day at Rincon Beach, a legendary surf spot south of Santa Barbara, John gazes out at the ocean and catches a glimpse of his client Pete Muller, who is paddling into a particularly gorgeous wave. Pete admits he's no Kelly Slater, but for a mid-fifties financial executive, he really rips.

Pete catches one more wave all the way to the beach and meets John at his bungalow on the point. As part of his coaching, John often hosts clients at his beach house in Santa Cruz or visits them at their homes. Spending a few days together walking along the beach and having a few gin and tonics on the balcony allows the conversations to go a few layers deeper. This weekend-long visit with Pete was no different.

"Wow, Pete, that was amazing. I didn't realize you could surf so well! You're the CEO of a successful company, a singer, a song-writer, a husband and father of two, and now apparently a decent surfer! How do you have the energy to do it all?"

Pete is the CEO and founder of PDT, a top quantitative hedge fund. Although PDT is not a household name like Bridgewater, Pete prefers it that way. It gets results and has the respect of those in the know, and that's all that matters to Pete.

Pete smiles as he contemplates John's question. "Having the freedom to do it all is exactly what gives me the energy to do it all," he eventually says. John nods, knowing exactly what he means.

When you close your eyes and think of a typical hedge fund, you might envision something akin to the television show *Billions.* High stress. Long hours. Backstabbing. Questionable ethics. But walk into PDT's headquarters, a few blocks south of Columbus Circle in Manhattan, and it feels oddly relaxed. Quiet. Collaborative. Contemplative. Sterling ethics.

Working at PDT is a dream come true for someone with a PhD in math or physics. Employees get to work on tough problems that are fun to solve in an environment that rewards their curiosity. It's no wonder the firm gets a thousand applications for every one hire they make. Pete is an avid learner who is relentlessly focused on self-improvement, and one can see that attitude imbued in the firm's culture.

In describing what makes PDT different from other firms, Pete replies without hesitation, "It's the culture, John. At PDT, we let the smartest people in the world work on problems that interest them in an environment that makes them feel safe taking risks."

As we explored at "the Lab" in chapter 3, curiosity and learning are huge motivators for many people. If you want to leverage the intellectual horsepower of brilliant people, keep them challenged with more and more interesting problems to solve.

Pete figured this out early on through his own experience. He's happiest when he is learning something new about his passions, whether it be surfing, songwriting, or investing. He founded PDT Partners in 1993 as part of Morgan Stanley's trading division, and the company became independent in 2013. He has since scaled PDT by hiring bright and curious people with academic backgrounds in quantitative science.

When you talk to Pete, it's clear that he wants to be sure people are in roles where they can be motivated by the things that they are naturally good at and where they find satisfaction. Pete walks the talk. His most creative moments happen when he juggles all the things that he loves to do—solving problems, writing and singing music, surfing, and being a father and a husband.

You can see the PDT culture in action as Pete talks about what motivates people in the organization: "They love solving hard problems, and they all have a curiosity for learning. Oh, and they make decent money in the process." Pete is in his zone when he is connecting to the desires and needs of his employees.

Pete lights up when he talks about the importance of supporting growth, learning, and development for his team. One of the things he looks for in people is a desire to solve problems differently. He says, "I learn a lot about people by the questions they ask and the assumptions they challenge."

As time goes on, and people have been in their roles for a while, Pete revisits the question "What is motivating this person *now*?" He believes that you can't assume that motivations and core desires are static; people and circumstances change.

When employees show noticeable changes in behavior and performance wanes, Pete puts on his coaching hat and has a conversation that gets at the underlying motivational issue. For Pete, these conversations are an opportunity to reset expectations and to figure out where people are now, not assuming that what motivated people before is still primary for them.

PDT has built a culture of performance that mirrors the motivational desires of its CEO. Pete is at his best when he is doing the things he loves to do. He applies this to his employees and manages performance based on the assumption that if people are doing what they love, the organization will thrive.

And thrive it does.

TEAM EXERCISE: WHAT DO YOU *REALLY* WANT?

Self-help guru Tony Robbins is known for encouraging people to answer the question "What do you *really* want?" It's rather provocative, when you think about it, because we don't often give ourselves permission to think big or explore our desires. And we certainly don't allow ourselves to express those desires in a public setting. Building a culture in which people feel comfortable talking about what they really want takes courage and patience.

Our exercise to get people thinking and talking about their deepest desires is surprisingly simple: What were your childhood dreams? As kids, our dreams and desires knew no bounds and had very little ego. They were at the same time outlandish and innocent.

At team off-sites, when we sit executives in a circle and ask them to talk about their childhood dreams, they share a bright and optimistic part of themselves that the rationality of adulthood may have dimmed.

- Did you want to be well known or famous? For what?
- Did you want to help people? Whom?
- Did you want to win awards or competitions? Which ones?
- Did you want to be "in the club"? Whose?

- Did you want to learn or travel? What and where to?
- Did you want to learn more? About what?

Getting to know each other at this level unlocks a unique understanding of what really drives us, what makes us do what we do, and what we've already given up on.

Make Sure Others Express Their Gifts and Do Not Languish

WORKING IN OUR ZONE OF GENIUS

As we talked about in chapter 4, we all have special gifts. We all have a natural ability that was born out of some early interest or experience, whether it be a positive or negative one. And when we are doing that thing, it feels effortless to us while seeming extraordinary to others. This is what people call your "zone of genius." In our experience, the companies that achieve outsized results have designed their cultures around helping as many people as possible operate in their zone of genius. Yet it is often an elusive goal because so few people are aware of their gifts, or if they are aware, they do not express them.

One company we have a long-standing coaching relationship with came to us recently, asking us to help their team unlock more of their people's gifts. Their purpose as a company is to help everyone around the world unlock their true potential, so it only stands to reason that they would want everyone in their company working in their "zone of genius," as well.

The problem is, this is very hard to do at scale. There are personal assessments that help people uncover their strengths by answering a battery of questions, but those can feel a little bit like "What job should you get after high school?" assessments. (Edward was told he should be a firefighter.)

We prefer exercises that help people see themselves through the eyes and experiences of their colleagues, friends, and peers. At this company and at many of the companies we work with, this looks like formal 360s for all executives. In this process we collect feedback from six to eight colleagues on each executive and compare the aggregate feedback to their own self-assessment. We often find that execs judge themselves harshly on key areas in which the feedback says they are actually strong. We call these unsung strengths, and often point leaders in the direction of what their gifts really are.

It's one thing to gain awareness of your gifts—it's another altogether to feel that those gifts are valued. Much of our work at this company has been helping to facilitate conversations between the executive team and their direct reports, vice presidents, and directors. As we've discussed extensively throughout the book, this is a critical interface that breaks down at many companies. Executive teams that do not recognize and honor the gifts in the next layer of leaders create a culture in which those leaders don't honor the gifts in their own direct reports, and it cascades down through the ranks.

Very often, the 360 process is a private one. People get their feedback and work on their development areas with a coach or in concert with their supervisor. With this company, we decided to ask them to get a little vulnerable and share their 360 feedback in a group setting with all execs and VPs present. But instead of focusing on sharing all the constructive feedback, they were instructed to share only the *positive* feedback. Standing in front of a room of colleagues sharing a strategy you've developed can be terrifying enough. But standing in front of them talking about how great you are is something else altogether.

The good news is that it really works. After spending an afternoon listening to the feedback each team member received about their gifts and strengths, the team started seeing each other in a new light. They had a better idea of whom they could go to with certain kinds of requests. They began to see each other as *resources* and not just coworkers.

Everyone in the room was then instructed to carry out the same exercise with their teams, and the program began to scale. Within a few months, nearly everyone in the company had the chance to "claim their gifts" in front of their teams. We received reports that the experience was energizing and deeply bonding. A few people even changed roles when it became clear that they had gifts that were going underutilized.

TEAM EXERCISE: THE ACKNOWLEDGMENT CIRCLE

The exercise we described above is quite involved and takes a lot of time to execute well. You need to perform 360s, consolidate the feedback, and so on. A much simpler exercise we've performed dozens of times is called the Acknowledgment Circle. Essentially, you take one person from the team and put them in the middle of a circle of colleagues, and for about two minutes, everyone in the circle shares some acknowledgment or praise of that person. "You are brave. You are resilient. You are funny. You are insightful."

The person in the middle looks to whoever is speaking and acknowledges them with eye contact. If you have more time, people can share short vignettes of specific times when that person did something spectacular. It's important to remember that this is not about flattery or roasting. The acknowledgments we share must be core insights about the person, not just that they dress well. And it's not a competition for telling the funniest story.

If you want to raise the bar, after acknowledging them, give each person in the middle a standing ovation for thirty seconds, as well. There is nothing quite like being recognized and praised in such a spectacular way.

Prioritize Values and Purpose above Everything

WE DRIFTED TOO FAR FROM THE SOCKS

A fundamental characteristic of Leading with Heart cultures is that they place purpose and values above everything else, including profit and internal politics. This is a hard one for leaders to sustain, as too often they feel pressure to compromise enduring values to improve short term profits, only to regret it later.

In our work with Dave Heath, CEO of Bombas—remember the "gardener" you met in the intro?—conversations often come back to this balance of purpose and profit. You might recall that Bombas is the apparel company that, for every pair of socks, underwear, or T-shirt purchased, donates a similar item to homeless shelters. Many Bombas employees carry extra socks and Ts in their backpacks to give to homeless people they might encounter on the streets of New York.

On a coaching walk with Edward around New York's Union Square, Dave shared how Bombas had experienced tremendous growth, with hundreds of millions in annual revenue. "Things have really been going great, as you know, but for us to continue to grow, we need to diversify our product offerings. We'll always have the core sock business, but where we go next is the million-dollar question . . . literally. And we're having a really hard time making this decision."

Edward listened intently, as he had never seen Dave this distraught before. Dave proceeded to discuss how he had engaged the product design team over the previous six months to design a bevy of new products. Introducing new products that customers could purchase in addition to their core lineup of socks has been a long-term strategic goal for Bombas.

Dave had just come from a meeting in which his product team had shown him for the first time the designs for some new product categories, and he was visibly excited. "These new products are fantastic—the colors are killer. The team has done such a great job up to this point. I'm so proud of them," he said, with that infectious Dave Heath enthusiasm. But then he trailed off, looking up at the budding trees. After a few seconds lost in thought, he rubbed his face a little as he does and sighed. "But should we be introducing these new products? I'm not sure this is the right thing for the company."

Dave knew that long-term growth would only come with the introduction of new products. This is Business School 101 for how you build and scale a company. But Dave then proceeded to tell the story of a conversation he'd had with some of his employees, who reflected back to him that developing all these new products wasn't in line with the values and fundamental purpose of Bombas. His employees had pointed out that certain garments were not what homeless people need or request. "Introducing some of these new products would take us away from our basic values and the reason we started Bombas in the first place," they said.

This feedback from his employees had a real impact on him. He was torn because they had already invested over $1 million developing this new product line. They'd hired new designers to bring more experience to the table. How could he let these designers down? A million dollars was a lot of money to throw away.

The stress he felt grappling with this issue was making him lose sleep. As CEO of a company, you always have competing priorities and obligations. There are various parties who are deserving of your loyalty and dedication: your team, your investors, your cofounders, your customers, and—in the case of a social-good corporation like Bombas (they are a certified B Corp)—the community you serve.

The obvious solutions often make us feel we are being forced to choose between those various constituencies. "Sometimes we have to make hard trade-offs," we say. And while trade-offs are part of life, the less obvious solutions can often be win-win solutions. There is almost always a path forward that is good for profits *and* for purpose.

Dave's instincts told him that this was true, and that moving forward with the new product plan as it was currently conceived was putting profits above purpose. He was taking the bait of a false trade-off. He also had a gut feeling that focusing on winning in fewer product categories was also just good business.

As they continued to walk among the spring shoots in Union Square, Dave reminisced on why he started the company in the first place and reminded himself of the importance of giving back to the homeless. As a reminder, socks are the number-one requested article of clothing in homeless shelters. Underwear and T-shirts are numbers two and three, respectively. The other products under consideration weren't even in the top ten.

Reminding himself of these facts, Dave saw clearly that socks, underwear, and T-shirts fit the mission and purpose of the organization and would also help them have greater operational focus. It was a clear win-win.

Edward continued to coach Dave on the messaging that was needed to communicate the change in strategy. With all the time and effort put in by the design and marketing teams, this decision was going to be a tough to communicate. While the designers were upset and initially pushed back on the decision, Dave stood firm, and after he explained the *why* behind his decision, people began to come around.

Building a company with a purpose-driven culture is difficult.

As Dave realized, getting caught up in fear of losing market share or being derailed by our desire to win at all costs can make it difficult to keep purpose at the center. When we succumb to those fears and desires, we may have short-term wins, but we lose sight of the long-term consequences.

While this decision was a hard one for Dave to make, in the long run, both customers and employees respected it. The decision caused Dave and the leadership team to rethink their product innovation process to ensure they developed products that fit their fundamental values as the organization and served their community of beneficiaries.

When companies deviate from their core principles, it can impact both customer and employee loyalty. We, your coauthors, both buy Bombas socks and give them out to all our coaches and clients not just because they are great socks but because Bombas is a company that puts purpose first and gives back to those in need.

We love this Bombas example because Dave and his executives made decisions that felt risky at the time around keeping their purpose and values at the center of their work. We are happy to report that eighteen months later, they are now reaping the rewards both on their bottom-line and in their culture.

TEAM EXERCISE: WRITE YOUR OBITUARY

Building a purpose-led organization requires everyone in the company to be in touch with their own sense of purpose. As we discussed in chapter 5, there are various ways we can dig in deep to bring out the unexpressed sense of purpose in us. One simple way you may have seen before is to ask everyone to write their own obituary and share it at a company meeting.

This simple exercise accomplishes two things at the same time:

1. It helps people get in touch with their priorities. What values do they have? What relationships are most important? What communities do they want to serve?
2. It helps teams learn things about each other that they otherwise might not have the opportunity to explore. When we hear how a colleague wants to be remembered, we see them through the lens of purpose and service, and not just as the annoying guy who never responds to our Slacks on time.

If your company is too large or it is simply impractical for everyone to read their obit to everyone else, break the company into teams of ten to twelve. The entire exercise only takes about an hour and is incredibly illuminating.

CHAPTER 6 TAKEAWAYS

- Companies with a Leading with Heart culture make intentional decisions to integrate the needs, fears, desires, gifts, and sense of purpose of their employees into how they work.

- Leaders model positive and negative behaviors every day that trickle down into the organization and create cultural norms.

- Fear of change can poison culture and keep companies from embracing the exact kinds of gifts they need to transform and thrive again.

- Companies that forget their purpose or fail to see how their purpose has evolved run the risk of being out of step with their employees and customers.

CONVERSATION STARTERS

1. What purposeful steps are you taking in your company to weave curiosity and the Leading with Heart conversations into the fabric of your culture?

2. What would be different about your culture if everyone in the company was constantly monitoring how well their colleagues' needs were being met, how triggered by fear they were, or how potentially derailed they were by desires?

3. In what ways is fear affecting how your company embraces the gifts of new people who can help the company thrive?

4. What would be different for us as a company if everyone was using their gifts and operating out of their zone of genius? How do we help people get there?

5. How would you know if your company was confused about its purpose? Who is the holder of purpose for your firm? Is everyone, including your customers, in agreement?

CONCLUSION:
THE LEADING WITH
HEART CHALLENGE

Over the course of this book, we hope you've learned what it takes to lead with heart. We began with the controversial notion that exceptional leadership is less about cheap formulas, lists of hacks, and antiquated ideas of presence than it is about having powerful conversations that build resilient relationships with the people we lead.

We tried to help you see that learning to lead with heart begins with developing your own understanding of yourself: *your* needs, *your* fears, *your* desires, and so on. Leaders who do not have an exquisite understanding of and relationship with themselves can never hope to have conversations that unlock creativity, purpose, and results with their teams. Empathy begins with self-awareness. So, if you skirted around the discussion questions in every chapter, now is the time to go back and answer them. We challenge you to do so right now. After all, leading with heart is a process, not a formula.

Once you have answered the Leading with Heart questions for yourself, we challenge you to take the next step and engage your teams in conversations around these questions. We included team exercises throughout the last chapter, but you will likely invent even better ways to spark these conversations yourself. The important thing is not getting the exercises precisely right—it's having the conversations at all.

The leader who builds a great company is constantly adapting to changes internally and externally. The pandemic presented leadership challenges most of us had never seen before. How do we effectively work remotely? How do we build high engagement among employees when we are not together? How will office space be used in the future? How do we deal with political differences that are now more out in the open?

The Leading with Heart conversations provide leaders with a framework to examine themselves, their teams, and their cultures on an ongoing basis as they learn to adapt to new realities, new contexts, and new competitive landscapes. Each of these conversations can provide the necessary springboard for rich insights, reflection, and change. Dave Heath learned to incorporate each of the conversations into his daily process of managing and leading. The attentive gardener is always paying attention. Remember: this damask rose might need more water, that Juliet rose more light, and the batch of Black Beauties a touch more fertilizer.

Thriving organizations continually challenge themselves to be better. The Leading with Heart framework suggests a constant interplay between a leader's self-inquiry and her ability to stay open and curious about her teams. This enduring curiosity and willingness to learn leads to discoveries that improve teams and organizational cultures.

Our challenge to you is to dive into the questions and begin your journey of self-discovery. You may be surprised how having your own deep insights about yourself opens your heart and your eyes to the inherent goodness, gifts, and potential within others.

ACKNOWLEDGMENTS

This book would not have been possible without the infinite patience, loving encouragement, penetrating insights, and brutal honesty of a number of individuals.

Before we'd even nailed down the concept, Tom Chavez generously introduced us to Jim Levine, the best business book agent in the business, who bafflingly signed us on as clients. Soon after, the dynamic mother-son duo of Sam and Andrew Horn helped us hew an unruly pile of ideas into a cogent concept and book proposal.

Getting into the research and drafting phase of the project, a number of generous individuals coached us on how to approach writing the book, provided valuable insights on the framework, and introduced us to some other very smart people: Safi Bahcall, Erik Dane, Adam Grant, Esther Perel, and Thomas Wedell-Wedellsborg.

A legion of clients and friends took the time to sit down with us to talk about their companies and provide their perspectives on leadership: Valerie Ashby, Michele Bolton, Tom Chavez, Chip Conley, Erik Dane, Sumbul Desai, Joe Desimone, Didier Elzinga, Jessica Encell Coleman, David Goldberg, Ariane Goldman, Dave Heath, Lee Hnetinka, Jeff Huber, Saeju Jeong, John Kotter, Mike Maples, Trevor Martin, Justin McLeod, Fazal

Merchant, Pete Muller, Betsy Nabel, Jonathan Neman, Matt Oppenheimer, David Rogier, Jon Rubinstein, Tomi Ryba, John Whitmore, Melody Wilding, Mark Williamson, and Tony Xu.

Various friends, family members, and colleagues have helped us with edits, ideation, inspiration, moral support, coffee runs, and wine curation over the years: Priscilla Babb, Stephanie Bagley, Andy Ellwood, Phil Eichenauer, Keith Ferrazzi, Daniele Ferreira da Silva, Jonathan Gass, Susan Hwang, Colleen Jansen, Amy Jin, Elizabeth Kurfess, Sharon Loeschen, Ryan Mullins, Jorge and Yolanda Rueda, Ginger Sledge, Peter Smith, and D. Ann Williams. John would like to thank in particular his wife, Susan, and his children, Ryann, Josh, and Julie, for their continued love and support.

We'd like to give a special shout-out to our team at Velocity Group—Maggie Adams, Kremi Arabadjieva, and Lana Le Joe—for helping us make time to actually sit down and write this book while also running an explosively growing coaching business. And to Sherry Spangler for her project management, coordination, and meticulous attention to detail in the editing and completion of the final manuscript.

And finally, we'd like to thank two people without whose bold and insightful coaching and editing this book would never have seen the light of day: the world's best editor, Trish Hall, who helped us find our voice, and our publisher, Hollis Heimbouch, who basically taught us how to write a book and pushed us to strive for excellence and write with heart every step of the way.

NOTES

Introduction

6   According to Gallup: Jim Harter, "U.S. Employee Engagement Holds Steady in First Half of 2021," Gallup Workplace, July 29, 2021, https://www.gallup.com/workplace/352949/employee-engagement-holds-steady-first-half-2021.aspx.

6   "dread going to work": "Survey: 84 Percent of U.S. Workers Blame Bad Managers for Creating Unnecessary Stress," Society for Human Resource Management, August 12, 2020, https://www.shrm.org/about-shrm/press-room/press-releases/pages/survey-84-percent-of-us-workers-blame-bad-managers-for-creating-unnecessary-stress-.aspx.

6   Gallup estimates: Harter, "U.S. Employee Engagement Holds Steady."

8   "*more* elusive than ever": Phil Rosenzweig, *The Halo Effect* (New York: Simon & Schuster, 2007).

1: What Do You Need to Be at Your Best?

25   recent research supports this theory: Douglas T. Kenrick et al., "Renovating the Pyramid of Needs: Contemporary Extensions Built on Ancient Foundations," *Perspectives on Psychological Science* 5, no. 3 (May 2010): 292–314, https://www.ncbi.nlm.nih.gov/pmc/articles/PMC3161123/.

29   National Institutes of Health report: Kenrick et al., "Renovating the Pyramid of Needs."

30   Duke study: Michael Babyak et al., "Exercise Treatment for Major Depression: Maintenance of Therapeutic Benefit at 10 Months," *Psychosomatic Medicine* 62 (2000): 633–38, https://www.madinamerica.com/wp-content/uploads/2011/12/Exercise%20treatment%20for%20major%20depression.pdf.

32   one of the first studies: Jon Kabat-Zinn et al., "Effectiveness of a Meditation-based Stress Reduction Program in the Treatment of Anxiety Disorders," *American Journal of Psychiatry* 149, no. 7 (July 1992): 936–43, https://pubmed.ncbi.nlm.nih.gov/1609875/.

32   makes you a happier person: Britta K. Hölzel et al., "How Does Mindfulness Meditation Work? Proposing Mechanisms of Action From a Conceptual and Neural Perspective," *Perspectives on Psychological Science* 6, no. 6 (2011): 537–59, https://uihc.org/sites/default/files/documents/how_does_mindful

ness_meditation_work_-_proposing_mechanisms_of_action_from_a_con
ceptual_and_neural_perspective.pdf.

32   study funded by the US Army: Melissa Myers, "Improving Military Resilience through Mindfulness Training," USAMRMC Public Affairs, June 1,
2015, https://hypnosishealthinfo.com/wp-content/uploads/2016/08/U.S.
-Army-Medical-Research-and-Materiel-Command-June-2015.pdf.

32   A 2015 study: Michael A. Freeman et al., "Are Entrepreneurs 'Touched with
Fire'?," April 17, 2015, https://michaelafreemanmd.com/Research_files/Are
%20Entrepreneurs%20Touched%20with%20Fire%20(pre-pub%20n)
%204-17-15.pdf.

34   the book *Immunity to Change*: Robert Kegan and Lisa Laskow Lahey, *Immunity to Change: How to Overcome It and Unlock the Potential in Yourself and
Your Organization* (Boston: Harvard Business Review Press, 2009).

42   "Leaders often think about": Safi Bahcall, interviewed by Edward Sullivan,
October 7, 2020.

43   "The bottom line is": Safi Bahcall, interviewed by Edward Sullivan, October
7, 2020.

44   A recent report by McKinsey: Aaron De Smet et al., "Psychological Safety
and the Critical Role of Leadership Development," McKinsey & Company,
February 11, 2021, https://www.mckinsey.com/business-functions/organiza
tion/our-insights/psychological-safety-and-the-critical-role-of-leadership
-development.

44   psychological safety: Amy C. Edmondson, *The Fearless Organization* (New
York: John Wiley & Sons, 2018).

44   According to Edmondson: Amy C. Edmondson, "The Competitive Imperative of Learning," *Harvard Business Review* 86, nos. 7/8 (July–August 2008):
60–67, https://hbr.org/2008/07/the-competitive-imperative-of-learning.

45   "Psychological safety is not about": Edmondson, "Competitive Imperative
of Learning."

48   40 percent less burnout: Paul J. Zak, "The Neuroscience of Trust," *Harvard Business Review*, January–February 2017, https://hbr.org/2017/01/the
-neuroscience-of-trust.

49   people they like: Robert Cialdini, *Influence: The Psychology of Persuasion*
(New York: HarperCollins, 2007).

50   "Vague or impossible goals": Edmondson, "The Competitive Imperative of
Learning."

55   A 2017 study: Amna Riaz, Umar Shoaib, and Muhammad Shahzad Sarfraz,
"Workplace Design and Employee's Performance and Health in Software Industry of Pakistan," *International Journal of Advanced Computer Science and
Applications* 8, no. 5 (2017), 542–48, https://thesai.org/Downloads/Volume
8No5/Paper_67-Workplace_Design_and_Employee's_Performance.pdf.

55   improve self-control: Kathryn E. Schertz and Marc G. Berman, "Understanding Nature and Its Cognitive Benefits," *Current Directions in Psychological Science* 28, no. 5 (October 2019): 496–502, https://journals.sagepub
.com/doi/full/10.1177/0963721419854100.

55   students who glanced out: Kate E. Lee et al., "40-Second Green Roof Views
Sustain Attention: The Role of Micro-breaks in Attention Restoration,"

Journal of Environmental Psychology 42 (June 2015): 182–89, https://www
.sciencedirect.com/science/article/abs/pii/S0272494415000328.

55   college students who watched a short nature video: John M. Zelenski, Rae-
lyne L. Dopko, and Colin A. Capaldi, "Cooperation Is in Our Nature:
Nature Exposure May Promote Cooperative and Environmentally Sustainable Behavior," *Journal of Environmental Psychology* 42 (June 2015): 24–31,
https://www.sciencedirect.com/science/article/pii/S0272494415000195.

55   A 2018 survey: Jeanne C. Meister, "The #1 Office Perk? Natural Light,"
Harvard Business Review, September 3, 2018, https://hbr.org/2018/09/the
-1-office-perk-natural-light.

55   A similar study from 2019: Jeanne C. Meister, "Survey: What Employees Want
Most from Their Workspaces," *Harvard Business Review*, August 26, 2019,
https://hbr.org/2019/08/survey-what-employees-want-most-from-their
-workspaces.

56   proximity of the engineers' desks: Thomas Allen and Gunter Henn, *The
Organization and Architecture of Innovation* (New York: Routledge, 2007).
Ben Waber, Jennifer Magnolfi, and Greg Lindsay, "Workspaces That Move
People," *Harvard Business Review*, October 2014, https://hbr.org/2014/10
/workspaces-that-move-people.

56   two-and-a-half-minute walk: "First Look: Google's New HQ Is Engineered
for Creative Collisions," *Building Design & Construction*, February 25, 2013,
https://www.bdcnetwork.com/first-look-googles-new-hq-engineered
-creative-collisions.

58   a busy café: Stephen C. Van Hedger et al., "Of Cricket Chirps and Car Horns:
The Effect of Nature Sounds on Cognitive Performance," *Psychonomic Bulle-
tin & Review*, 26 (October 2018): 522–30, https://link.springer.com/article
/10.3758/s13423-018-1539-1.

60   2018 survey: Megan Cerullo, "Most Americans Check In at Work Even
While on Vacation, LinkedIn Survey Shows," July 10, 2019, https://www
.cbsnews.com/news/most-americans-check-work-email-while-on-vacation
-linkedin-survey.

60   vacation days on the table: Shawn Achor, "Are the People Who Take Vacations the Ones Who Get Promoted?," *Harvard Business Review*, June 12,
2015, https://hbr.org/2015/06/are-the-people-who-take-vacations-the-ones
-who-get-promoted.

61   Cornell study from 1999: Susan S. Lang, "When Workers Heed Computer's Reminder to Take a Break, Their Productivity Jumps, Cornell Study
Finds," *Cornell Chronicle*, September 23, 1999, https://news.cornell.edu
/stories/1999/09/onscreen-break-reminder-boosts-productivity.

61   and actually triple revenue: Jeffrey Borenstein, "The Importance of Taking
Vacation Time to De-stress and Recharge," Brain & Behavior Research Foundation, July 27, 2019, https://www.bbrfoundation.org/blog/importance
-taking-vacation-time-de-stress-and-recharge.

63   Campbell and his team: Angus Campbell, *The Sense of Well-Being in America*
(New York: McGraw-Hill, 1981).

64   2014 Citigroup and LinkedIn survey: Rachel Feintzeig, "Flexibility at Work:
Worth Skipping a Raise?," *Wall Street Journal*, October 31, 2014, https://
www.wsj.com/articles/BL-ATWORKB-2141.

2: What Fears Are Holding You Back?

72   article on the positive benefits of fear: Andrew Colin Beck, "EuFear: Embracing Our Fears' Positivity," Issuu, August 11, 2013, https://issuu.com/andrewcolinbeck/docs/eufear.

72   the concept of *eustress:* Hans Selye, *Stress without Distress* (New York: New American Library, 1974).

74   in 2012: Amy Shipley, "Michael Phelps has mastered the psychology of speed," *Washington Post,* June 14, 2012

77   mistakes CEOs make: John Kotter, interview with Edward Sullivan, October 26, 2021.

78   have been discussed: Patrick Lencioni, *The Five Dysfunctions of a Team: A Leadership Fable* (Chicago: Jossey-Bass, 2002).

79   zone of constructive conflict: Robert M. Yerkes and John D. Dodson, "The Relation of Strength of Stimulus to Rapidity of Habit-Formation," *Journal of Comparative Neurology and Psychology* 18, no. 5 (1908): 459–82, doi:10.1002/cne.920180503.

79   "While few executives": Roger Jones, "What CEOs Are Afraid Of," *Harvard Business Review*, February 24, 2015, https://hbr.org/2015/02/what-ceos-are-afraid-of.

92   A 2019 review: D. M. Bravata et al., "Prevalence, Predictors, and Treatment of Impostor Syndrome: a Systematic Review," *Journal of Internal Medicine* 35, no. 4 (April 2020): 1252–75, doi: 10.1007/s11606-019-053 64-1.

95   research on leaders: Tonya Jackman Hampton, "Know Fear: How Leaders Respond and Relate to Their Fears," PhD diss., University of St. Thomas, Minnesota, 2013, https://ir.stthomas.edu/caps_ed_orgdev_docdiss/21/.

106   A 2015 study: Alison Wood Brooks, Francesca Gino, and Maurice E. Schweitzer, "Smart People Ask for (My) Advice: Seeking Advice Boost Perceptions of Competence," *Management Science* 61, no. 6 (June 2015): 1197–1471, https://pubsonline.informs.org/doi/10.1287/mnsc.2014.2054.

3: What Desires Drive You, and Which Might Derail You?

116   an extensive study: Steven Reiss, "Multifaceted Nature of Intrinsic Motivation: The Theory of 16 Basic Desires," *Review of General Psychology* 8, no. 3 (September 2004): 179–93, https://www.researchgate.net/publication/232454071_Multifaceted_Nature_of_Intrinsic_Motivation_The_Theory_of_16_Basic_Desires.

126   According to Deloitte: Josh Bersin, "Why Diversity and Inclusion Has Become a Business Priority," Josh Bersin Company, March 16, 2019, https://joshbersin.com/2015/12/why-diversity-and-inclusion-will-be-a-top-priority-for-2016/.

126   A Gartner study: John Kostoulas, Melanie Lougee, and Jason Cerrato, "How HCM Technologies Can Scale Inclusion in the Workplace," Gartner Research, January 22, 2020, https://www.gartner.com/en/documents/3979855/how-hcm-technologies-can-scale-inclusion-in-the-work place.

126   And a BCG study: Rocfo Lorenczo et al., "How Diverse Leadership Teams

Boost Innovation," Boston Consulting Group, January 23, 2018, https://www.bcg.com/en-us/publications/2018/how-diverse-leadership-teams-boost-innovation.

126   Esther Perel: Esther Perel, interview with Edward Sullivan, November 29, 2021.

127   According to *Harvard Business Review*: Gary Hamel and Michele Zanini, "The End of Bureaucracy," *Harvard Business Review*, November–December 2018, https://hbr.org/2018/11/the-end-of-bureaucracy.

128   Esther Perel advocates: Esther Perel, interview with Edward Sullivan, November 29, 2021.

130   engage in unscrupulous behavior: Gavin J. Kilduff et al., "Whatever It Takes to Win: Rivalry Increases Unethical Behavior," *Academy of Management Journal*, http://people.stern.nyu.edu/sworthen/kilduffpublications/amjwhateverittakes.pdf.

132   Simon Sinek: Simon Sinek, *The Infinite Game* (New York: Portfolio, 2019).

132   Carse's ideas: James P. Carse, *Finite and Infinite Games* (New York: Free Press, 1986).

138   cut corners or sabotage colleagues: Anna Steinhage, Dan Cable, and Ducan Wardley, "The Pros and Cons of Competition among Employees," *Harvard Business Review*, March 20, 2017, https://hbr.org/2017/03/the-pros-and-cons-of-competition-among-employees.

139   randomly selected employees: Kari Bruursema, Stacey R. Kessler, and Paul E. Spector, "Bored Employees Misbehaving: The Relationship Between Boredom and Counterproductive Work Behaviour," *Work & Stress* 25, no. 2 (April 2011): 93–107, doi: 10.1080/02678373.2011.596670.

145   Other studies: Ian H. Robertson, "How Power Affects the Brain," *Psychologist* (British Psychological Society) 26 (March 2013): 186–89, https://thepsychologist.bps.org.uk/volume-26/edition-3/how-power-affects brain; Christopher Shea, "Why Power Corrupts," Smithsonian, October 2012, https://www.smithsonianmag.com/science-nature/why-power-corrupts-37165345/.

145   Another more recent study: Christopher Shea, "Why Power Corrupts," *Smithsonian*, October 2012, https://www.smithsonianmag.com/science-nature/why-power-corrupts-37165345/. Katherine A. Decelles, D. Scott LaRue, Joshua D. Margolis, and Tara L. Ceranic, "Does Power Corrupt or Enable? When and Why Power Facilitates Self-Interested Behavior," *Journal of Applied Psychology* 97, no. 3 (January 2012): 681–89.

147   in the early days: David A. Garvin, "How Google Sold Its Engineers on Management," *Harvard Business Review*, December 2013, https://hbr.org/2013/12/how-google-sold-its-engineers-on-management.

150   "to give formal or legal authority to": *Merriam-Webster's Collegiate Dictionary*, "Empower," https://www.merriam-webster.com/dictionary/empower.

153   global pandemic: Mike Maples, interview with Edward Sullivan, September 15, 2020.

154   quest to change the world: Kyle McCarthy, "67% of Techies Think They Are Changing the World," *Blind Blog—Workplace Insights*, October 23, 2018, https://www.teamblind.com/blog/index.php/2018/10/23/67-of-techies-think-they-are-changing-the-world/.

4: What Are Your Greatest Gifts?

160   price is a signal for quality: Hilke Plassmann et al., "Marketing Actions Can Modulate Neural Representations of Experienced Pleasantness," *Proceedings of the National Academy of Sciences of the United States of America*, January 22, 2008, https://www.pnas.org/content/105/3/1050.abstract.

160   free, and therefore not of any value: Jonah Lehrer, "Should We Buy Expensive Wine?," *Wired*, April 26, 2011, https://www.wired.com/2011/04/should-we-buy-expensive-wine/.

177   their "interpersonal attractiveness" increases: Elliot Aronson, Ben Willerman, and Joanne Floyd, "The Effect of a Pratfall on Increasing Interpersonal Attractiveness," *Psyconomic Science* 4 (June 1966): 227–28, https://doi.org/10.3758/BF03342263.

177   credible to supervisors: Alison Wood Brooks, Francesca Gino, and Maurice E. Schweitzer, "Smart People Ask for (My) Advice: Seeking Advice Boosts Perceptions of Competence," *Management Science* 61, no. 6 (June 2015): 1421–35, http://citeseerx.ist.psu.edu/viewdoc/download?doi=10.1.1.721.7786&rep=rep1&type=pdf.

178   groundbreaking book *Multipliers*: Liz Wiseman, *Multipliers: How the Best Leaders Make Everyone Smart* (New York: HarperBusiness, 2010).

183   "the factory didn't run us": Kathy Holub, "Losing Battle at Age 32, Deborah Coleman Proved She Could Manage a Fortune 200 Company. But Managing Her Weight Was Almost Too Much For Her," *Buffalo News*, November 19, 1989, https://buffalonews.com/news/losing-battle-at-age-32-deborah-coleman-proved-she-could-manage-a-fortune-200-company/article_4fe9e548-4ccd-5a69-923d-08ff95646b3d.html.

183   "to run this kind of operation": Chelsea Ritschel, "The Non-Negotiable Quality Steve Jobs Looked for When Hiring Top Employees," *Independent*, December 12, 2017, https://www.independent.co.uk/life-style/jobs-what-look-steve-jobs-hiring-top-employees-a8106641.html.

184   "how to do anything": Ritschel, "Non-Negotiable Quality."

184   "I've built a lot of my success": Jordan Etem, "Steve Jobs on Hiring Truly Gifted People," https://www.youtube.com/watch?v=a7mS9ZdU6k4.

185   "ever have in their life," reflected Jobs: Etem, "Steve Jobs on Hiring."

189   confirmed they had indeed washed their hands: Tali Sharot, "What Motivates Employees More: Rewards or Punishments?," *Harvard Business Review*, September 26, 2017, https://hbr.org/2017/09/what-motivates-employees-more-rewards-or-punishments.

190   "can help you do better": "Peter Thiel on the Right Way to Think About Talent, Optimism, and Luck," *Inc.*, October 17, 2014, https://www.inc.com/250-words/peter-thiel-on-the-right-way-to-think-about-talent-optimism-and-luck.html.

5: What Is Your Purpose?

208   *Start with Why*: Simon Sinek, *Start With Why How Great Leaders Inspire Everyone to Take Action* (New York: Penguin, 2011).

210   research done at PwC: Shannon Schuyler, "Putting Purpose to Work: A Study of Purpose in the Workplace," PwC, November 6, 2017, https://www.pwc.com/us/en/purpose-workplace-study.html.

210   "Insights 2020" study: "Insights 2020 Survey," Advertising Research Foundation, https://thearf.org/insights-2020/.

210   In his book *Grow*: Jim Stengel, *Grow: How Ideals Power Growth and Profit at the World's Greatest Companies* (New York: Crown Business, 2011).

210   "more supportive stakeholders": Kevin Murray, *People with Purpose: How Great Leaders Use Purpose to Build Thriving Organizations* (New York: Kogan Page, 2017).

219   "problems you have yourself": "How to Get Startup Ideas," Paul Graham website, November 2012, http://paulgraham.com/startupideas.html.

6: Helping Your Company Culture Lead with Heart

228   defines corporate culture: John P. Kotter and James L. Heskett, *Corporate Culture and Performance* (New York: Free Press, 2011).

ABOUT THE AUTHORS

JOHN BAIRD is one of the premier executive coaches in Silicon Valley, and over the past twenty-five years he has worked with top leaders at start-up organizations as well as at Fortune 500 firms like Apple, Nike, and Twitter. He founded several companies, including ExecutivEdge, Edgeman Coaching, and the Velocity Group, where he is currently chairman, and serves as a fellow at Sapphire Ventures and on various nonprofit local and national boards. Baird holds a PhD in organizational communication and leadership from Purdue University.

EDWARD SULLIVAN is the CEO and managing partner at Velocity Group. His twenty-five-year career as an executive coach and political consultant has taken him around the globe coaching and advising start-up founders, Fortune 500 executives, and heads of state of foreign nations. His work has been featured in the *New York Times*, the *Washington Post*, *Forbes*, *Fast Company*, *USA Today*, and *Nasdaq*, among others. He holds an MBA from the Wharton School and an MPA from the Harvard Kennedy School.

Through their company, Velocity Group, a leading global executive coaching firm, Baird and Sullivan work with top executives at such companies as Apple, DoorDash, Geico, and MasterClass.